THE CONSCIOUSNESS OF CHRIST

REV. WILLIAM G. MOST

CHRISTENDOM PUBLICATIONS
Christendom College Press
Route 3, Box 87
Front Royal, Virginia 22630

ISBN: 0-931888-03-4
LC Cat. Card. No.: 80-68761

NIHIL OBSTAT:
  Rev. Cornelius O'Brien, *Censor Deputatus*
  November 12, 1980

IMPRIMATUR:
 ✠ Most Rev. Thomas J. Welsh
  Bishop of Arlington
  November 12, 1980

CONTENTS

ABBREVIATIONS

CBQ *The Catholic Biblical Quarterly*

DS H. Denzinger, *Enchiridion Symbolorum*. Ed by A. Schonmetzer

DTC *Dictionnaire de Theologie Catholique*

HSB James M. Robinson, "Hermeneutic since Barth" in *New Frontiers in Theology*. Vol. 2. Ed. by James M. Robinson and John B. Cobb, Jr. New York, Harper & Row. 1963.

HST Rudolf Bultmann, *The History of the Synoptic Tradition*, tr. John Marsh. New York. Harper & Row. 1963.

JBC *Jerome Biblical Commentary*. Ed. by R. Brown, J. Fitzmyer, R. Murphy Englewood Cliffs, N.J. Prentice-Hall. 1968.

JBL *Journal of Biblical Literature*

JCM Rudolf Bultmann, *Jesus Christ and Mythology*. New York. Charles Scribner's Sons. 1958.

JSNT *Journal for the Study of the New Testament*

KM Rudolf Bultmann, in *Kerygma and Myth*. ed. by H.W. Bartsch. tr. Reginald H. Fuller. New York. Harper & Row Torchbooks. 1961 2nd ed. I.

NTS *New Testament Studies*

PG *Patrologia Graeca*. Ed. by J.P. Migne. Paris 1857-66.

PL *Patrologia Latina*. Ed. by J.P. Migne. Paris 1878-90.

RSV *The Holy Bible. Revised Standard Version*.

SSG Rudolf Bultmann, "The Study of the Synoptic Gospels." in *Form Criticism*. Tr. F.C. Grant. New York. Harper & Row Torchbooks. 1962.

TDNT *Theological Dictionary of the New Testament*, Ed. by G. Kittel. tr. G.W. Bromiley. Grand Rapids. Eerdmans. 1964-76.

WGH Gerhard Ebeling, "Word of God and Hermeneutic." in *New Frontiers in Theology*. Vol. 2. Ed. by James M. Robinson and John B. Cobb, Jr. New York. Harper & Row. 1964. 78-110.

Z Th K *Zeitschrift fur Theologie und Kirche*

Preface

"Can you show me now that I would not be killed in vain? Show me just a little of your omnipresent brain. Show me there's a reason for your wanting me to die. You were far too keen on where and how, and not so hot on why."

So speaks Jesus Christ Superstar, the day before the great Passover. Obviously He is presented as being quite ignorant not only of who He is—there is no trace of awareness that He is divine, if indeed the author of *Superstar* thought Jesus was divine; and Jesus does not even know the fundamental reason for His dying, to redeem and save mankind by atoning for sin.

Nor only popular rock musicals express such egregious error. Many scripture scholars today do much the same, e.g., "The New Testament gives us no reason to think that Jesus and Paul were not deadly serious about the demonic world.... I do not believe the demons inhabit desert places or the upper air, as Jesus and Paul thought... I see no way to get around the difficulty except by saying that Jesus and Paul were wrong on this point. They accepted the beliefs of their times about demons, but those beliefs were superstitious."(1)

The writer, Father Raymond Brown, thinks Jesus was so ignorant as to preach error based on superstitions. He also wonders if Jesus knew much about the future life: "Perhaps he had nothing new to say about the afterlife other than emphasizing what was already known, that God would reward the good and

5

punish the wicked."(2) As to whether Jesus knew who He was, we find Fr. Brown inclined to prefer the opinion that Jesus had "some sort of intuition or immediate awareness of what he was, but...that the ability to express this in a communicable way had to be acquired gradually."(3) To put it simply: Jesus knew in some vague way who He was but somehow could not manage to say it!

This view is basically the same as that of Karl Rahner, who holds that the self knowledge of Jesus paralleled that of ordinary humans. We do not know our own soul directly; we get to know it indirectly by observing its actions. To express that information is, of course, something additional.(4)

In ancient times similar ideas were expressed in the aftermath of Nestorianism, a heresy propounding the presence of two *persons* in Jesus. That is the same as saying there were two *he's* in Him, a divine person and a human person. The divine person, Nestorians often said, took the human person and lived in him as in a temple. Another sect, the Agnoites, followed logically with the conclusion: the human in Jesus might not know he was bound up with a divine person, and might lack various other kinds of knowledge also. Their error was condemned, with an anathema, by Pope Vigilius in 553 A.D.(5)

The current storm about the consciousness of Jesus was sparked by a book written by P. Galtier in 1939.(6) Without holding for two persons in the Nestorian sense, Galtier sought to distinguish a psychological self apart from the ontological self. So, he asserted, there can be a "real psychological autonomy" in the human soul of Jesus.

The heart of our modern problem, then, is this: without claiming two persons in the Nestorian sense, we can still ask, 'Did a given fact (e.g., the day and hour of the last judgment) *register on the human mind of Jesus'?* Unfortunately, even theologians are often very loose in their language. They say: *He* did not know that. Such a statement is heresy, for the *He* is a divine *He*. But it is not heresy to ask: Did that point register on His human mind?

To examine the question adequately, we must consider data from four different sources: Scripture, patrology, the magisterium, and speculative theology.

Before considering the Scriptural evidence, we must face the fact that in our day there are numerous challenges to the reliability of the Gospels. So before we can appeal to the Gospels, we must examine whether or not we can believe the Gospels. The introduction is devoted to this problem.

NOTES

1 In *St. Anthony's Messenger*, May 1971, 47-48.
2 R.E. Brown, *Jesus, God and Man*, Macmillan, N.Y. 1967. 101.
3 *Ibid.*, 100.
4 K. Rahner, "Dogmatic Reflections on the Knowledge and Self-Consciousness of Christ" in *Theological Investigations*, tr. K.H. Kruger, Helicon, Baltimore, 1966, 5, 193-215.
5 DS 419.
6 P. Galtier, *L'Unite du Christ—Etre, Personne, Conscience*, 3rd ed. Beauchesne, Paris, 1939.

Introduction:
Can We Trust the Gospels?

There are three chief challenges today to the reliability of Gospel evidence, upon which our knowledge of Christ's consciousness heavily depends. It is said: (1) even the Catholic Church, long one of the strongest champions of the inerrancy of Sacred Scripture, has now made significant concessions; (2) if we examine the literary form or genre of the Gospels, we find they were not really meant to be factual; (3) form criticism of the Gospels has undermined their credibility. This introduction will treat the first two problems by way of establishing a basis for the use of Scripture in the central argument of this work. Form criticism is a more cumbersome and technical problem which, if treated by way of introduction, would delay the reader too long in approaching the fundamental question of the consciousness of Christ. I have therefore included a straight forward and concise analysis of form criticism in the Appendix, for those who have been unable in today's confusion to complete an analysis of this exegetical method.

In the encyclical letter *Divino afflante Spiritu* of Septmeber 30, 1943, Pope Pius XII firmly insisted on the inerrancy of Scripture and cited the teaching of Vatican Council I that the books of Scripture, "being written under the inspiration of the Holy Spirit, have God as their author." Therefore, adds Pius XII, Holy Scripture "enjoys immunity from any error whatsoever."(1) He complains that "certain Catholic writers dare to limit the truth of

Sacred Scripture to matters only of faith and morals (and to say) that other things, of a physical or historical nature, or things said in passing (*obiter dicta*)" are not protected by inspiration.(2)

These positions of Pius XII and his predecessors are far from fundamentalism; they contain no inkling that the Scriptures are, as it were, to be understood as if written by twentieth-century men. Pius XII, following Leo XIII,(3) insists that, "there is no error when the sacred writer, speaking of physical things, 'follows what appears to the senses,' as St. Thomas says."(4) Thereby he implies that one need not take a simplistic view of Genesis 1-3. And among other points the encyclical reminds us that the ancient Semites used "approximations" and "hyperbole".(5)

However, what most sets Pius XII apart from fundamentalism is his insistence that we not only may, but must take into account the literary genre or form of each passage before trying to work out its meaning in other ways. An illustration would be an historical novel in English, one on the Civil War. Since we are native to American culture, we automatically adjust to such a novel. We expect the main line of the story to be factual history. We expect the background descriptions to fit the period; there can be telegraphs and steam trains, but no airplanes or television. But when we read word-for-word accounts of discussions held by Lincoln with various officials, we do not assume these to be verbatim truth. We know that novel writers may fill in to make the story more interesting, while keeping their fill-ins in character or in accord with known facts. And if we read of a romance carried on by some minor characters, we do not feel obliged to regard it as historical. It may or may not be so. Thus an historical novel is a blend of fact and fiction. We do not for that reason charge error or falsification; we know how it was intended, and we take it that way.

All peoples and cultures have many and varied literary patterns, forms, or genres. Natives adjust to them automatically; non-natives must make a conscious adjustment. Scripture belongs to a different cultural stream than ours; hence we must take pains to learn how people in that culture understood each of their many genres.

Failure to do so can lead to many errors. For example, Clement of Alexandria seems to take the worldly-wise advice of Sirach 32:7-8 as a religious precept, not understanding the underlying genre.(6) Sirach urged old men to speak at a banquet, but directed young men not to open their mouths unless asked a second time, and then to speak briefly. Again, a person in our own times was relieved when he learned of the existence of ocean currents. He felt that Ps. 8:8, which tells of fishes that go through the "paths of the sea", required him to believe in such things.

In any case, many difficult problems about the inerrancy of Scripture are easily resolved with a knowledge of genres. Thus the genre of Genesis 1-3 can easily leave room for human bodily evolution.(7) And it is possible to think of much of the Pentateuch as in a genre resembling Greek Epic, which, as Schliemann showed, did enshrine basic facts.(8) Similarly, difficulties associated with the book of Jonas(9) readily disappear if we suppose—a matter not really proved at present—that the book is in a genre similar to an extended parable, intended as a means of teaching that since God loves even the Assyrians (the worst of men, to Jewish eyes) He must love everyone.

It is singularly odd that today, when we have so many resources not known to past ages by which vexing difficulties may be solved, scholars remain prone to accept the idea of errors in Scripture. Many a problem that baffled previous generations— who had to take it mostly on faith that Scripture could not be in error—yields easily to the application of literary genre principles and other approaches now common.

While modern new techniques are most helpful, however, they do expose us to the possibility of rampant subjectivity, especially if someone, without adequate evidence, tries to classify various parts of Scripture as examples of very loose genres. For this and other reasons Pius XII insisted on the need of heeding the Church—not private judgment—in interpreting Scripture:(10) "However let exegetes, mindful of the fact that there is here question of a divinely inspired word whose care and interpretation is entrusted by God Himself to the Church—let them not less carefully take into account the explanations and declarations of the magisterium of the Church, and likewise of the explanations given by the Holy Fathers, and also of the 'analogy of faith', as Leo XIII...wisely noted."(11)

At first sight, Pius XII seems to weaken his statement greatly when he adds: "...there are few [passages] whose sense has been declared by the authority of the Church, nor are there more on which there exists an unanimous teaching of the Holy Fathers."(12) It is true, there are not many texts of the magisterium that explicitly point to a line of Scripture and declare its meaning. Yet the Pope also mentioned the analogy of faith. That is, whatever meaning one selects must harmonize with, and not contradict, the entire structure of Catholic belief. Thus, even though the magisterium and the Fathers do not *explicitly* settle many passages, yet *implicitly* they often do narrow the range of possible interpretations.

Many claim that Vatican Council II changed the teaching of Pius XII and his predecessors on inerrancy. The critical text is in the *Constitution on Divine Revelation:* "Since all that the inspired authors, or sacred writers, affirm should be regarded as affirmed by the Holy Spirit, we must acknowledge that the books of Scripture, firmly, faithfully, and without error teach *that truth which God, for the sake of our salvation wished to see confided to the sacred Scriptures.*"(13) So, it is said, Vatican II teaches that Scripture is inerrant only on matters needed for salvation. One might even claim that certain matters of faith could be in error, namely, points not necessary for salvation.

But we need to note that the italicized words can be taken readily in two ways: as *restrictive*, or as *descriptive*. If taken in a restrictive way, they mean *only* that which is set down for the sake of salvation is inerrant. If taken in a descriptive way, the words merely describe what Scripture does, without making any comment on things not pertaining to salvation.

Now what judgment did Vatican II put into these words? There are two methods of resolving the question. First, when something in a later text is capable of being understood in several ways, it is to be assumed that what is meant coincides with the earlier teaching. After all, to change a teaching, especially one of such great moment as the inerrancy of Sacred Scripture, is no small matter. Nor is the Church accustomed to change officially proclaimed doctrine. If the Council really meant to abandon biblical inerrancy, we would find it stated in a clear and unambiguous manner. (The Council could have easily made it clear it meant a restrictive sense by using the Latin *qui quidem* with the subjunctive—a structure which is always restrictive.)

Secondly, the Council did not leave us without the needed help. It gave a footnote on this very sentence, in which it refers to the very passages cited above from Vatican I, Leo XIII, and Pius XII. Surely, it would be more than slightly strange if a Council undertook to make a momentous change in teaching, did it in ambiguous language, and, to clarify the ambiguous language, referred us to numerous earlier documents all teaching the opposite of the supposed change!

In addition, Vatican II reminded scholars:

> But, since Sacred Scripture must be read and interpreted with its divine authorship in mind, no less attention must be devoted to the content and unity of the whole of Scripture, taking into account the Tradition of the entire Church and the analogy of faith, if we are to derive their true meaning from the sacred texts. It is the task of exegetes to work according to these rules, toward a better understanding and explanation of the meaning of Sacred Scripture in order that their research may help the Church to form a firmer judgment. For, of course, all that has been said about the manner of interpreting Scripture is ultimately subject to the judgment of the Church.(14)

Nonetheless, Father Raymond Brown insists that even Pius XII sharply reversed the position of the Church:

> The pontificate of Pius XII marked a complete about-face in attitude.... His encyclical *Divino Afflante Spiritu* (1943) instructed Catholic scholars to use the methods of scientific biblical criticism that had hitherto been forbidden them...the critical method had led (by mid-1950s) to Catholic exegetes abandoning almost all the biblical positions taken by Rome at the beginning of the century.... Now it was permissible to think that the early stories of Genesis were not historical; that Isaiah was not one book; that Matthew was not the first Gospel...that the

Gospels...were sometimes inaccurate in detail.(15)

As already shown, Pius XII vigorously reaffirmed previous teaching on the Bible's absolute inerrancy. Yet Fr. Brown says that the changes made by Pius XII led scholars to abandon almost all "biblical positions taken by Rome" early in the 1900s. While he is right in saying that scholars no longer took Genesis 1-3 in a fundamentalistic sense, neither had Rome ever taken it in a fundamentalistic sense, for, as we learn from encyclicals of Leo XIII and Pius XII, cited above, the intent of the sacred writers was not to teach science; rather, they often wrote according to the way things appear to human observation.

The use of literary genre, called for by Pius XII, did open the way to the solution of many problems, including many in Genesis 1-3. Was that approach ever "forbidden" as Fr. Brown says? Not really. On June 23, 1905, the Pontifical Biblical Commission formulated the question whether it was permissible to hold that some "books...that are considered historical (completely or partly) at times do not retell history strictly...but [instead] have only the appearance of history, so as to convey something other?"(16) Their answer was guarded, yet it allowed a certain latitude:

> No, except in the case—not easily or rashly to be admitted—in which, when the sense of the Church does not oppose it, and subject to the judgment of the Church, it is proved by solid arguments that the Sacred Writer did not intend to hand down history properly and truly so called, but, under the appearance and form of history, he gave a parable, an allegory, or a sense differing from the properly literal or historical sense of the words.

Rome was telling scholars that not all which seems to be history in Scripture is such. One must use great care in deciding when different forms are possible. Yet it can be done, under the precautions listed. Pius XII did offer greater encouragement, but it is not at all correct to say flatly that the literary genre approach was "forbidden" previously.

On June 27, 1906, the same commission gave four responses on the Pentateuch, and admitted that we could say that Moses used other persons as writers, that Moses made use of oral and written sources, that if we credit Moses with "substantial" authorship we can hold that over many centuries there were modifications and additions by other inspired authors.(17) Have scholars today repudiated this absolutely? Fr. Eugene Maly, a first rank exegete, has this to say in the *Jerome Biblical Commentary*: "Moses, therefore, is at the heart of the Pentateuch, and can, in accord with the common acceptance of the ancient period, correctly be called its author."(18)

Moreover, even in the age of the Fathers, the Church never did officially teach fundamentalism. It is one thing, after all, to recount the creation story of Genesis in the same or similar words—quite another to officially interpret that same story. The Church has always done the former, never the latter. We state again the principle of St. Thomas Aquinas, cited with favor by Popes Leo XIII and Pius XII, that, "there is no error when the sacred writer, speaking of physical things, 'follows what appears to the senses', as St. Thomas says."(19)

Centuries earlier, St. Augustine warned against fundamentalism, when he wrote in his commentary on Genesis: "That God made man with bodily hands from the clay is an excessively childish thought, so that if Scripture had said this, we should rather believe that the one who wrote it used a metaphorical term than to suppose God is bounded by such lines of limbs as we see in our bodies."(20) Augustine, as quoted by Leo XIII, also warned that "the Spirit of God, who spoke through them [the biblical authors] did not want to teach these things (the inner make-up of things) which would have no profit for salvation."(21)

Still further, we must recall that many of the Fathers quite often were *not* intending to give a literal interpretation; they followed an *allegorical* interpretation. Therefore, they simply could not teach fundamentalism.

There are, we grant, some positions taken by the Pontifical Biblical Commission which are widely rejected today, such as the statement that Matthew was the first Gospel. Two observations are appropriate here: first, these positions were more disciplinary and prudential than a matter of exegesis (the question of date or authorship is purely historical, and not a point of doctrine at all);

second, there is still no proof that Matthew did not write the first Gospel. The ancient sources, external evidence, do say he did. We do not have the Hebrew text of Matthew. It could easily be that our Greek Matthew is later than Mark, while the Hebrew Matthew was earlier. Really, as we shall see, the evidence adduced by the critics to prove the priority of Mark, and other things too, is quite unsubstantial, and certainly never conclusive. Hence, to speak of an about-face by the Church is hardly the fruit of careful scholarship.

Our task is not, however, so easily finished. Before we can even consider whether the Gospels belong to a genre having anything in common with history we meet with a vigorous challenge from Norman Perrin of the University of Chicago, an ardent admirer of Rudolph Bultmann, the pioneer form critic: "We must strenuously avoid the assumption that the ancient world thought as the modern western world thinks.... No ancient texts reflect the attitudes characteristic of the modern western world."(22)

As we shall see later, Perrin violates his own principle, for he, following Bultmann, tries to make the Semitic-authored Gospels mean the same as an influential modern existentialist, Martin Heidegger.(23) But to return to Perrin's claim that there is nothing in ancient patterns like ours, we must note that while there are indeed differences, Perrin leaps beyond all bounds. We are concerned here with historical thought, for which a reading of the ancient Greek and Roman historians is very revealing. We do not pretend, of course, that they had our technical resources. Yet, they did intend to convey facts, even when they added something to those facts, namely, an interpretation. Modern students of the ancient pagan authors find it quite possible to distinguish the facts from the interpretations.

Let us survey the expressed intentions of some of these ancient historians. The earliest among the Greeks, Herodotus, though not possessing modern critical skill, still wrote: "I ought to report all that is said, but I am not obliged to believe it all—let this statement apply to my whole history."(24) Thucydides, in the judgment of classical scholars,(25) is much like a modern historian though he lacked some of our skills and liked to include speeches of which he says: "It was hard for me...and for others who reported them to me, to recollect the exact words. Things are expressed according as it seemed to me each person would say the things needing to be said on each occasion. I held as close as possible to the thought of what was actually said."(26) Such speeches, then, are comparable to similar passages in modern historical novels.

This presents no problem; they are in character, and are easily distinguished from the factual recital outside the speeches. Thycydides reports: "As for the things that were *done* in the war, I judged I should not write on the basis of just any informant, nor as I thought [things should be] but with the greatest possible accuracy about things I took part in, and things reported by others. [The facts] were found out with great labor."(27) Polybius tells us how he consulted the actual texts of treaties preserved on bronze tablets.(28) Diodorus Siculus reports that he spent thirty years going about gathering his data, and gives examples: "I have learned exactly all the deeds of this [Roman] empire, from records kept by them over a long period."(29) He knows enough not to trust things too poorly supported: "Of the periods covered in this work, I do not attempt to define definitely those before the Trojans, because no dependable annals have come before me."(30)

Flavius Josephus, the Jewish historian, undoubtedly exaggerates the merits of the writers among his own people, yet he is not entirely wrong in saying: "For words and cleverness in them we must yield to the Greeks, but not for true history of ancient [things or peoples]."(31) And: "I made a true written account of the entire war and the individual happenings in it, having been present myself at all events."(32) The Roman historian Tacitus comes in for some criticism today, yet we can and do get priceless facts from him so much so that "even his severest critics concede the general accuracy of the facts that he records."(33) The criticism bears really on the *interpretations* Tacitus makes, rather than on the facts he gives. It is not really difficult to distinguish one from the other.

It would be easy to fill pages with similar statements of the attitudes of ancient historians to their work, but the above should suffice to make our point, namely: The ancient writers of Greece and Rome did intend to convey facts.(34) They differed from us chiefly in two things: (1) in lesser technical skill, (2) in their habit of composing speeches that were in character. They did, in addition, add interpretations; but so do modern writers. In any event, it is quite possible to distinguish interpretation from fact.

While making their interpretations, the ancient writers hoped that the facts would teach lessons. Polybius wrote: "There is no more ready corrective for men than the knowledge of past events."(35) Obviously, we can separate the lesson-teaching interpretations from the facts.(36)

Not only Greek and Roman writers could and did record facts: other ethnics were no less gifted. Mircea Eliade takes an almost extreme position when he writes (but yet expresses an important point): "The Hebrews were the first to discover the meaning of history as the epiphany of God, and this concept, as we should expect, was taken up and amplified by Christianity."(37) And again: "For Christianity, time is real because it has a meaning—the Redemption.... The development of history is thus governed and oriented by a unique fact, a fact that stands entirely alone."(38) We called his position almost extreme in that he thinks all other peoples held beliefs of eternal cyclical repetition, in a mythical framework. But he is certainly right in saying that Hebrew and Christian thought is non-cyclical: "The destiny of all mankind, together with the individual destiny of each one of us, are both likewise played out once, once for all, in a concrete and irreplaceable time which is that of history and life."(39) Even if one thinks cyclical beliefs were absent from people other than the Hebrews,(40) it remains true that the Hebrews were indeed very special in their insistence on a strictly *factual* basis for their beliefs.

Christianity, as Eliade says, shared the Hebrew concern for facts. This is to be expected, for the first Christians were all Hebrews. And the Christians, even more clearly than the Hebrews, knew their eternal destiny depended on the factuality of the reports about Jesus. Many of them died wretchedly rather than deny that factuality. And there was a host of witnesses to the events on which Christianity is based. Many of these witnesses certainly survived to a date later than the latest dates proposed for the Synoptic Gospels.

Quadratus, the earliest of the Greek apologists, writing around 123 A.D., observed:

> The things done by the Savior remained present always, for they were true. Those cured, those who rose from the dead were not only seen when they were being cured and raised, but were constantly present, not only while the Savior was living, but also for some time after He had gone, so that certain of them came down even to our own time.(41)

Quadratus does not say whether they were still around in the year 123, when he wrote, but it would suffice for our purpose that they were on hand in the earlier part of his lifetime, which is later than the latest proposed dates for the compositon of the Synoptic Gospels. And of course, most history is not written by eyewitnesses. It is considered very good if the writer consulted eyewitnesses. That does not prevent acceptance of the history. In the decade 80-90 A.D. many would be alive who had spoken to eyewitnesses, e.g., Pope Clement I (92-101 A.D.) who says he was of the same generation in Rome as Peter and Paul, and Polycarp, who knew St. John.

This insistence on facts emerges with great clarity in St. Paul, whose writings antedate the Gospels. In 1 Cor. 15:1-18 he stresses how he is handing on facts that he had received, facts that were predicted long in advance by the prophets, i.e., that Jesus died for our sins and rose. See verses 14 and 19, "If Christ has not been raised, then our preaching is in vain and your faith is in vain...if for this life only we have hope in Christ, we are of all men most to be pitied."

St. Ignatius of Antioch, on his way to Rome to be devoured by the wild beasts in 107 A.D., wrote to the Trallians: "But if, as some atheists, that is, unbelievers say, His [Christ's] suffering was only make-believe—when actually they themselves are make-believes—then why am I in bonds? Why do I pray to fight with the beasts? Then I die in vain. Then I give false testimony against the Lord.''(42) The point is Pauline and clear: a man is saved and made holy if, and to the extent that, he is a member of Christ and like to Him. But Christ went through two phases: first, suffering and death; then, glorification. So too will we be glorified if and to the extent that we imitate His suffering and death.

The Docetists denied the reality of the flesh of Christ, and hence, the reality of His death and resurrection. If Christ did not really die and rise, it would do Ignatius no good to die. In dying, Ignatius would be giving false witness, witness to what did not happen. No fancies suffice for a man on the point of being eaten alive by lions. Yet Ignatius, in the absolute conviction of factuality, could even be glad to face the beasts. So he wrote to the church of Rome: "I fear your love, that it may wrong me."(43) He means he is afraid that some influential Christian might be able to get his martyrdom cancelled. Igantius says that would be harmful to him, for it would deprive Him of the chance of following Christ. So he continued:

> May I enjoy the beasts prepared for me, and I pray they may be prompt. I will even entice them to eat me promptly, so they will not refrain from touching me, as they have for some, out of fear.... Understand me, brothers, do not hinder me from living [eternally by being eaten]. Do not wish me to die [by having to stay in this life].

There are two further proofs for the factuality of the Synoptics. First, the spread of the Gospel message was confirmed by so many miracles. If someone wishes to deny that fact we ask: how then account for the fact that sophisticated Greeks and Romans would accept a set of difficult beliefs and strict morals (and the danger of a miserable death) from uneducated men from a backwoods part (Galilee) of a remote province (Judea) if these men had no better support for their claims than their own bare word? It is true, St. Paul had a good rabbinic education, but that sort of training did not impress pagans. A. Oepke is right in pointing out: "We can see from the Gospel of Thomas and the apocryphal Acts what shape miracles take when they owe their origin to literary imagination. If there had been nothing outstanding in the story of Jesus, the rise of the community would itself be inexplicable."(44)

Second, such unanimity on the basic facts as found in the four Gospels could not have been reached so early—before 100 A.D.—in communities so widely scattered all over the Mediterranean world, if there had been no control by apostles and other eyewitnesses deeply concerned about facts. Fancy and lies—as any husband knows who tries to fabricate a tale for his wife—do not yield a harvest of delectable fruit.

We may conclude that the Synoptics were intended as an expression of faith and as a basis for faith. But it was a faith founded on historical facts. Hence *the Synoptic genre is one that presents facts within a theological framework.* We mean, of course, the overall basic genre of a Synoptic Gospel, for we admit that there are sections within a Gospel using apocalyptic, sapiential and other genres. The existence of the theological framework and Gospel interpretation does not change the factual character of its data any more than do the interpretations added by the ancient Greek and Roman historians. Further, just as it is quite possible to distinguish the facts from the interpretation in the pagan writers, so also it is possible with our evangelists.

An important case in point is the Gospel of St. Luke. In the opening lines to his Gospel the evangelist provides a preface which reminds us of the prefaces of the Greek historians; this is not really surprising, for Luke was a well-educated Greek, a physician. In that preface he claims to have carefully investigated the facts and to have checked with eye witnesses and earlier accounts. Since he used earlier written sources, it would not be strange if he consulted documents in each of the three languages then current in Palestine: Aramaic, Hebrew, and Greek. For it is now well established that all three languages were in use as native tongues in various parts of the land of Israel at that period.(45)

Since Luke was an educated Greek, we should expect he would follow the pattern of the Greek historians, and his preface says he investigated everything from the start precisely *(akribos)* so that the reader might have the firm truth *(asphaleia)*. Just as the historians added interpretations, so did Luke, namely the theological setting. The historians also added speeches, for which they would use the exact text if available, otherwise the substance.

Lacking that, they would compose a speech suited for the occasion. From what follows, we see that Luke did have the substance, and probably wording that is at least close, for his speeches in the Gospel.

It is generally recognized that Luke's Gospel shows more Semitic traits than do the other Gospels. The most common explanation is that Luke was consciously imitating the language of the Septuagint, the current Greek translation of the Old Testament, to give a sort of "churchy" flavor.(46) To evaluate that claim, let us list some concrete features.

First, as Sparks observes, Luke's Gospel is notable for a "continual rephrasing of St. Mark: in order to add Semitisms."(47) Thus in the parable of the wicked husbandmen, Mark (12:1-12) is content to say that the master "sent another slave" and later, "he sent another." But Luke (20:9-19) reads: "And he *added* to send another servant;" and later, "he *added to send* a third." This is pure Hebrew idiom; the root *ysf* is not used that way in Scriptural Aramaic.(48) On the other hand, in a few places, Mark has pure Hebraisms (6:39 and 8:12) which Luke does *not* copy, though he has an otherwise parallel account—another indication that Luke did not always copy from Mark.

The most interesting and impressive evidence, however, is Luke's use of apodotic *kai*—a feature largely overlooked by scholars in studying Luke. For example, in Lk 2:21, a literal translation would read: "And when eight days were fulfilled for circumcizing Him, *and* they called His name Jesus." Hebrew idiom has an apodotic *wau* (*and*), which is used very extensively to connect sentences to sentences. The Septuagint nearly always reproduces this Hebrew *wau* by an apodotic *kai*. Johannessohn found that some Old Testament books in the Septuagint use the apodotic *kai* absolutely every time the Hebrew has it (Numbers, Ruth, Deuteronomy, 2 Samuel). Even those books that sometimes omit it, retain it most of the time, e.g., Exodus uses it 69.23% of the time; Josue 63.63%; 1 Samuel, over 83.33%. The most frequent omissions occur in Genesis, which nevertheless retains it 45.83% of the time. In fact, Johannessohn notes that there are eight passages in which the Septuagint *adds* the apodotic *kai* even where the Hebrew lacks the *wau*.(49)

There is an additional feature often found in these passages with apodotic *kai*: the sentence frequently begins with the Greek words *kai egeneto* (Hebrew *wa yehi*—of this there is no parallel in Aramaic).(50) Further, after the *kai egeneto* there is usually a time expression, mostly a clause. An example of this is found in Lk 5:1, "And it happened, when the crowd pressed around Him and heard the word of God, *and* He was standing by the lake of Genesareth...."

Statistics on these three features—the opening *kai egeneto*, the time expression, and the apodotic *kai*—reveal something very significant. By my own count, Luke uses apodotic *kai* only 20 to 25% of the time; that is, he omits it in about 75 to 80% of the places in which classical Hebrew (which the Septuagint imitates most of the time) would have it.(51)

We must ask then: Is Luke really imitating the language of the Septuagint to give his composition a church flavor? If Luke intended to imitate the Septuagint, he was doing a strangely bad job of it. The Septuagint uses apodotic *kai* in nearly every instance where the Hebrew has the corresponding *wau*. But in similar structures, Luke uses the *kai* only 20 to 25% of the time. Suppose someone today wanted to give a church flavor by the use of *thee* and *thou*, but remembered to do so in only 20-25% of the cases. The critics would think him a strangely dull fellow. So we cannot really believe Luke was using apodotic *kai* to imitate the Septuagint.

The other alternative is fascinating: he must have meant it when he said in his preface that he made a careful investigation, checking with eyewitnesses and documents. Now a recourse to documents could easily have led to using sources in Hebrew, Aramaic, and Greek. If he was doing that, then we would have a plausible reason why he would employ apodotic *kai* only a small part of the time; for only at those points was he translating from a Hebrew document. The other sources would have been Aramaic or Greek, oral or written. We know he was using a Hebrew, not Aramaic document, because there was no normal equivalent to apodotic *kai* in Aramaic.(52) This conclusion is reinforced in the many instances in which a sentence opens with *kai egeneto*, since Aramaic has no equivalent for this expression. And, of course, neither the apodotic *kai* nor the *kai egeneto* is native Greek.

Further proof that Luke was not imitating the Septuagint may be derived from the second component of the pattern described, namely, the time expression that appears between the *kai egeneto* and the apodotic *kai*. In such combinations the Hebrew Old Testament uses mostly a preposition, such as *be*, followed by an infinitive with its subject. However, the Septuagint much prefers a more normal Greek construction, namely, a dependent clause with a finite verb introduced by *hos, kathos, henika* or *hote*. However, Luke has precisely the reverse preference, that is, he uses a dependent clause with a finite verb, like the Septuagint, only four times, while nineteen times he follows the Hebrew pattern, using a preposition with an articular infinitive, usually having a subject.(53)

So we find Luke using *apodotic kai* far less often than the Septuagint, and having the reverse preference to the Septuagint on the time expression that usually comes before the apodotic *kai*, in a sentence with *kai egeneto*. It is clear that he was not imitating the Septuagint: any dullard could have done much better. It is also clear that in these cases he was translating from Hebrew, not Aramaic, for the reasons given.

Why would Luke translate so closely, even slavishly? That is easily answered, for we meet the same phenomenon elsewhere, namely, in the early Latin translations of Scripture, made from the Septuagint and from the Greek New Testament, in which the early translators actually brought Greek structures into Latin. They did it out of zeal for fidelity and accuracy. Luke was clearly acting the same way; he was taking great pains to achieve accuracy and factuality. And that is simply what he himself stressed in his preface. Educated Greeks would be concerned about facts, following the pattern of the Greek historical writers as already noted. But Luke had an even greater reason for concern with facts than any ordinary historian: eternity for him and others depended on it.

Although this is a powerful confirmation of our conclusion that the Synoptics do intend to report facts, and to do so accurately, an objection could be raised to our observations that Luke was not just imitating the Septuagint. It is known that his Old Testament quotations usually follow not the Hebrew but the Septuagint. But consider these circumstances: (1) Luke (or his sources) may well have done his own Old Testament reading in the Septuagint; (2) we know today, thanks to the Qumran discoveries, that the Septuagint itself is likely to have been made from a Hebrew text differing from our Masoretic Hebrew text.(54) Luke or his sources, obviously, could have used that Hebrew text.

Further confirmation of the fact that Luke is often translating, with painful care, is found in the observation that in some passages he writes stylistically good and proper Greek, as is to be expected from an educated man; but in others his style is foreign and labored. For example, when he describes the baptism of Jesus, he uses language which cannot be reproduced in English, but we can try to convey the effect; thus Lk 3:21-22, "It happened, during all the people being baptized [the preposition *en* with the article *to*, with the accusative and infinitive], and Jesus having been baptized and praying, that [accusative and infinite] the heavens were opened and the Holy Spirit came down [infinitve] upon Him in bodily form as a dove, and that [accusative and infinitive] a voice from the sky came...." True, each one of these structures is known in the Greek of his day. Yet taken together the result is extremely clumsy; it is not what one would expect from an educated writer, or from someone bent on dramatizing fancies or even merely reporting so great an event. Of course, there are passages in which Luke is obviously not translating, but is writing in good Greek style. For these he must have used oral sources or Greek documents.

In passing we can also make some observations about the widely held Two Source Theory, according to which Luke (and Matthew) closely followed Mark much of the time, and for most of the rest of the time followed closely a hypothetical source called Q. (No copies exist: it is merely supposed there was such a thing.) That theory does not explain how it is that Luke so often adds Semitisms to Mark, yet sometimes omits Semitisms which Mark has. Nor does it explain why he uses the apodotic *kai* far more frequently than do Mark and Matthew. Nor does it explain why Luke employs that *kai* only 20% of the time, and not at other times. Nor does it explain why Luke very often uses an Aramaic type paraphrase with a form of *to be* plus a participle instead of an imperfect indicative: of all instances of this structure in the New Testament, Luke has 50%, of which there are 30 examples in his Gospel and 24 in Acts. Yet, where this structure occurs in Mark, Luke usually avoids it—though he does use it in places that he has parallel to Mark, but in which Mark does *not* use it.(55) It seems, then, that Luke did not really follow Mark so much, and that he had more than two sources, sources in three languages, both oral and written. This is, incidentally, the same conclusion Albright reached, for other reasons.(56)

Similarly, Luke 14:26 has: "If anyone comes to me and does not *hate* his own father and mother...he cannot be my disciple." *Hate* is a Semitism for *love less.* Matthew has instead (10:37): "He who *loves* father and mother more than me is not worthy of me."

Some less conclusive but still impressive evidence that Matthew did not depend on Mark appears in a recent study by John M. Rist, a Professor of Classics at the University of Toronto.(57) Classicists have learned from long experience that one cannot prove one author depended on another without very detailed agreements in extended passages. Rist examines many passages in which all three Synoptics present the same episode. He notes that there are strong similarities, yet such strong differences that one cannot say there is any *proof* that Matthew depended on Mark. For example, in the narrative of the raising of the daughter of Jairus, Matthew omits the name, and just calls the man an *archon*, an official; Mark and Luke give the name, and call him ruler of the synagogue. Mark and Luke say Jairus asked to come because his daughter was *dying*; Matthew has some messengers come to report she is *already dead*. One can, of course, show that these things need not involve contradiction, but it hardly looks as though Matthew is using Mark. Again, in the account of the blind Bartimaeus, there are strong similarities, yet Matthew and Mark say the cure took place when Jesus *was leaving*

Jericho; Luke puts it when He was *approaching* Jericho. Matthew has *two* blind men; Mark and Luke have just *one*. Semitic approximation could account for the differences, but again, we have no good reason to suppose Matthew or Luke depended on Mark, when such notable differences occur.

Rist concludes that all three Synoptics used several oral and written sources, which did not have identical wording, but the same substance.

If, then, there were several sources for the Gospels, their very agreement in a multitude of minute details testifies to the care for accuracy and to their authors' precise recollection. Memories then were better than now, for they were exercised more by people who lacked recording machines. Further, the things Jesus said were striking, and accordingly more easily remembered; as Jeremias rightly observes, they were often expressed in antithetic parallelism, a method which lends itself to being remembered precisely.(58)

In discussing the genre of the Gospels thus far we have treated only of the Synoptics; no mention has been made of John. We do not, of course, reject the testimony of that Gospel. But we think it obvious that it is in a quite different literary genre.

One of the more important differences between John and the Synoptics is that John seems to use retrojection while the Synoptics do not. That is, John seems to present Jesus saying things before His resurrection that He would more likely have said after His resurrection. So we must ask whether, and to what extent, retrojection can be found in the Synoptics, considering their genre of presenting facts as the basis for faith.

N. Perrin states his position bluntly. He asserts that the early community "absolutely identified the risen Lord of [its] experience with the historical Jesus and *vice versa*.... [Paul] claims, as the basis for his apostleship, to have 'seen the Lord' (1 Cor. 9:1), by which he certainly means the risen Lord....''(59) And then he adds, "Luke considers Paul an eyewitness!" Similarly, R. Bultmann points to Apocalypse 16:15 and 3:20 as evidence that things seen in a vision could be attributed to the pre-Easter Jesus.(60)

A preliminary comment is needed: Bultmann and Perrin reject *a priori* any possibility of any resurrection, without even trying to offer a proof of that position.(61) As a result, they must suppose that Paul, the apsotles, and others who claimed to have seen the risen Jesus were deluded visionaries. They would retroject sayings from their deluded visions.

Note too how some critics, astoundingly, seem to forget the question of genre. They seem to suppose, without examination, that the genre of the Synoptics is the same as that of the Apocalypse. No serious exegete would dare to say that. The Book of Apocalypse is obviously in apocalyptic genre. Within the freedom of a such a genre, things could easily be retrojected; it is likely that the genre of John is likewise free enough for retrojection. In contrast, the genre of the Synoptics is a factual genre, aimed at presenting the basis of faith. The use of this factual genre was called for by the very life situation (*Sitz im Leben*),(62) by the need to present that factual basis. Such a genre and need rules out fiction; it also rules out a mere collection of anecdotes ''in character'', such that one cannot tell if any given story is actually historical.

Since the genre of the Synoptics is such, we can determine what sort of retrojection is *possible* (it is a separate question what retrojection is *likely*):

1)a prophecy cannot be retrojected. For a prophecy not made in advance is not a prophecy at all. A prophecy has no point unless it was made beforehand. Even in a modern historical novel—a genre looser than that of our Synoptics—the rules would not permit the author to place the details of Lincoln's death on the president's lips by way of retrojection.

2)clarity cannot be added to a genuine prophecy if the added details would entail falsification. To use again our comparison with Lincoln in a historical novel, suppose it were historically true that Lincoln did express a vague premonition, and the novelist made that into a precise and detailed prediction: such would be beyond the limits even of a historical novel.

3)to retroject an actual saying of the risen Jesus to the period before Easter would not be a substantial falsification, for He would have really said it; chronological exactitude is not always intended by writers and speakers. Yet, though such a thing is *possible* in the Synoptics, it is not *likely*. The Synoptics paint Jesus, and the apostles too, as quite different in the two periods. Actually, the chief instances in which the critics suggest retrojection of this sort is on things they have decided, *a priori* that Jesus did not know before Easter.

4)to make a pre-Easter teaching clearer, or to express it in different language, adapted to the current audience, would not be falsification, provided that the substance of the clarified or reworded saying was really expressed by Jesus. We note that Lk 24:45 reports that Jesus did open their hearts to understand the Scriptures after His resurrection.

5)in a similar way, the Church after the resurrection could create a different title, e.g., Son of Man, to express some aspect of the earlier self-revelation of Jesus. Whether or not this is likely needs to be considered in detail for each title.

6)in the early Church, as today, there could have been false visionaries, even though the resurrection did take place But if such visionaries attempted to falsify in any substantial way the teaching of Jesus, there were many who could and would have objected.

What some critics envision is a gradual idealization leading to the Divinization of Jesus. But such an evolutionary process is incredible. First, the time between Christ's death and the earliest writings, the letters of Paul, and even the Gospels, is much too brief; much more than 20 years would be needed to idealize a person into a transcendent God (it would be different were Jesus made only into the type of "god" known to pagan Greece and Rome). But second and more importantly, in the *vagueness* of claims about idealization there is a factor that is often overlooked: at a certain point such an idealization would become pure and conscious fraud. For example, Jesus was reported to have cured a man born blind. He either did or did not work such a cure. There is no half-way stage that could be exaggerated.

Such fraud, however, is ruled out in the Gospels, by the concern of the witnesses for their own eternity and other factors mentioned above. Hence, the claim of idealization in the case of

Jesus can survive only if one caters to *vagueness* and refrains from analyzing concrete instances. The critical question is this: were there certain *steps* from one claim to another, steps so *gradual* that people could go from one to the other without dishonesty? Or, is there but one great leap, in which case, only conscious fraud could bridge the gap? For example, if people see a springboard diver do a difficult dive beautifully, someone might say: "He can do any dive." That would actually be a reasonable assumption. It could be made without dishonesty. But if someone claims to see Jesus give sight in an instant to a man born blind, there are no gradual steps. The claim must be either true or evidently false.

A further objection could be raised to the Gospels and to any and all history, even that given by eyewitness reports, on the basis of a recent scientific experiment reported in *Science News*.(63) Elizabeth Loftus of the University of Washington in Seattle reported at an American Psychological Society meeting on an experiment in which 100 students viewed a short film showing a multiple car accident. They then filled out a 22 item questionnaire. It was found that there was considerable disagreement on what they saw, and also that suggestion could play a part in what they thought they saw.

But this does not mean that we must scuttle all eyewitness reports, and, as a consequence, everything in history. For we need, as always, to make distinctions in dealing with problems. It is one thing to see a car accident and quite another to recall if one saw a broken headlight, how fast a certain car was going, whether a stop sign was there or not. Loftus admitted that "the wording of a presumption into a question asked immediately after a recently witnessed event can affect the answer to a question." Such method clearly amounts to deliberate suggestion. But we must be more specific. For example, what if a space ship landed in the middle of the street at a busy intersection in the downtown area of a city? While there might be disagreement on some details—due to the shock itself—it is not conceivable that anyone present could fail to report correctly the ship's landing, something of its appearance, and whether or not living beings came out of it. Similarly, the miracles of Jesus were so utterly striking that no one could fail to recall and to report the essential facts.(64) And His sayings, at least the major ones that carried with them the burden of life and death for His hearers—how could persons forget that message?

A final concern relates to our own understanding of ancient cultures, on which there are two faulty schools of thought. First, the fundamentalists believe in ignoring cultural differences and taking everything as though written by a twentieth century American for twentieth century Americans. The results are partly ludicrous, partly tragic, e.g., some think Jesus commanded children to really *hate* their parents! The other school believes little in the Gospels, yet concurs with the fundamentalists in imposing modern ideas on ancient texts—but in a different way: they force the Gospels to mean the same as what the modern German existentialist Heidegger thinks. We will see details of their proposals in the appendix.

Common sense rejects both these methods. Common sense neither believes in a simplistic fundamentalism nor twists the whole New Testament into a current philosophy. Chiefly, we refuse to impose modern ideas, existentialist or other, on the Gospels. We see the need of making distinctions, of taking up individual facets separately. At the end, we add up the results.

First, there are numerous details on which the differences of times and cultures have no bearing, e.g., when the Gospels report how a man called Jesus came to the town of Capharnaum. Time and culture do not change the reality. Next, suppose the account tells how Jesus cured a man blind from birth. Here not so much time and culture as the reader's presuppositions or prejudices can make difficulties. Thus the older rationalists, Bultmann, and many of his followers deny *a priori* the very possibility of any miracle. They have a naive confidence that science will eventually explain everything. They ignore well-attested, documented proof of miracles happening even today. But persons who are free from prejudice against the possibility of miracles can readily see if the man whom they have long known as blind from birth, is presently enabled to see. The absence of prejudice to the contrary is all that is needed. A man witnessing such a cure simply cannot deny that the person formerly blind is so no longer.

There are other things in an older culture, especially ideas and beliefs, which it may in fact be difficult for us to correctly understand, but hardly impossible. We begin by noting how a native learns the words and concepts of his language and culture. He does not take classes, he is unlikely to use a dictionary even if one is available. Rather, as a young child, he meets things in varied combinations. For example, suppose little Marcus is playing outside his house in Rome, on the street. Mother sees a horse coming, and shouts in Latin: "Equus venit." Marcus probably does not know whether the thing galloping along is an "equus" or a "venit"—but he gets the message. As time goes on, he meets these same words, and others, in many combinations. From the intersecting possibilities, as it were, he gathers that a certain four-legged animal is an "equus". The case is similar for him with less concrete things, or abstract ideas. He hears words like *amor, iustitia, pietas*. At first, he does not get much more than some vague notion, gathered from the setting of the word among other words that he does understand. But as time passes, from meeting the same word frequently and in different combinations, he discovers more and more clearly and precisely what it stands for. And if he learns to read, his understanding will be greatly sharpened, for then he will meet words as used by *educated writers* who are more careful in their use of language than boys on the street are. In this way he develops a good and accurate vocabularly.

Linguistic studies show that we can do the same across the centuries. For example, the ancient Hebrew concept of covenant was almost lost in the history of early Christianity. We need not go into the possible reasons, but a major one was the fact that the Greek word *diatheke* used to translate the Hebrew word *berith* carried multiple meanings. The Greek term could stand for either a covenant or a last will and testament. The latter meaning was the one that was favored; so still today we speak of an Old and a New Testament. Another part of the problem was the Hebrew word *hesed*, which highlighted the bond between parties to a covenant. Since in Greek there existed no equivalent for *hesed*, the

Septuagint translators usually used *eleos* (mercy). Now it is true that at the most fundamental level, all that God does for His people is an act of mercy, for they cannot, in a basic sense, generate any claim against Him. Yet, on a secondary level, He could and did allow them to acquire a claim by fulfilling covenant conditions. When God honored such claims, He was acting basically in mercy, but also, secondarily, in moral rightness, for He had pledged His word.

Latin could have chosen a better translation for *hesed* than Greek, with its *pietas*, but since the Latin versions were translated from Greek, which had lost the *hesed* concept by the *eleos* translation, Latin rendered *hesed-eleos* by *misericordia* (mercy). And so the covenant concept largely disappeared.

In spite of that, we today can recover, and actually have recovered, that lost idea.(65) For we can read the Old "Testament" in Hebrew; we can gather, especially with the help of a Hebrew concordance, all occurrences of *hesed* and related words. We can learn from the way the word was used in Hebrew parallelism, in which two halves of a poetic line each say the same thing in different words. We can find help in the choice of Greek words made by the ancient Hebrew translators of the Septuagint. That is, we find that at times (e.g., Exod. 15:13) the Septuagint uses Greek *dikaiosyne* (*moral rightness*) to reproduce Hebrew *hesed*—a clear indication that the ancient translators understood that for God to observe *hesed* was a matter of moral rightness.

By such means as this we can obtain a more precise knowledge of an ancient Hebrew concept than that had by many an ancient Hebrew who could not read. So instead of nebulously staring at the problem of whether modern readers can understand ancient texts, we need to examine concrete cases and see what can be done. The illustration just given shows that even where an ancient concept had been virtually lost, its rediscovery is not too difficult. Further, there was a real continuity of language and culture between the Greek Fathers of the first centuries and the New Testament authors who were coversant with two cultures, Hebrew and Greek. Paul, for instance, was well versed in both cultures, Hebraic and Hellenic; and we know from Galatians chapter 2 that he compared notes with the original Apostles, who lived in the company of Jesus. The evidence to the contrary is so compelling that it becomes ridiculous to maintain that twentieth century man is unable to understand documents from a bygone age.

Being endowed with reason, the ordinary man tends naturally toward objective evaluations in his thinking unless prejudice or bias distorts sound judgment. Some observations obviously should not be affected even if a person is prone to prejudice, such as the report that Jesus came to a town called Capharnaum. Further, prejudice can hardly prevent a man from seeing that Jesus cured a man born blind. Bias or prejudice can operate only if the person who *hears* the report has already made up his mind there can be no such phenomena as miracles.

The slowness of the disciples to understand and to believe is excellent evidence they were not biased in favor of Christ's claims. They were slow to realize who He was, slow to comprehend His teaching, slow to accept His resurrection even when confronted by witnesses from the empty tomb. In a way we might even say that they were prejudiced against accepting the miraculous. Could this report of their attitude be faked? No, for there were too many witnesses, witnesses whose life and death were at stake, witnesses who for their insistence on the facts had to risk opposition and often suffered persecution, ostracism, imprisonment, discrimination, martyrdom.(66) Further, the apostolic preaching was confirmed by many miracles, and the same honesty and concern for eternity precludes false reports of these.

Finally, how much do we need to strictly establish from the Gospels to reach a basis for faith? Rather little, and that little does not include difficult ideas, long lost, which must be recaptured through patient research, such as we described for the covenant idea. Nor does it include things on which presuppositions are apt to control a man's view, except of course if a man is committed in advance to denying divine intervention. The required facts would be merely these: that a man called Jesus claimed to be a messenger from God (we did not say yet that He was divine), that He proved this claim by working miracles in such a way that the miracle was expressly done to prove a claim (as when He cured the paralytic to prove He had power to forgive sins), that He gathered disciples, formed an inner circle of twelve, commissioned them to carry on His teaching, and promised them that the work in His name would be divinely protected.

In establishing these points we do not, of course, appeal to the Gospels as inspired or sacred, but only as ancient documents whose credibility is determined in much the same way we use in checking other ancient authors.

Anyone who can accept these few fundamental points has inescapable grounds for believing what the continuing, on-living teaching group, the Church, proclaims about God and about Jesus. In fact, we not only may believe it, we are *intellectually compelled* to do so once we work to the point described.

Incidentally, the most basic, recurring pattern in the speeches in Acts reflects precisely the sort of process we just sketched, except, of course, that the speakers could use their own testimony instead of that of a book. Thus Peter, after healing the cripple (Acts 3:12-26) said in substance: We did not do it—God is glorifying Jesus, whom you killed, the author of life. But God raised Him. Faith in Jesus has healed this man. This is really the same as saying: Jesus was a man approved by God. God manifested His approval by working miracles through Him; and finally God raised Him up gloriously from the tomb—all this to make us believe, to make us put our faith in Him.

NOTES

1 *Enchiridion Biblicum* 538, citing *ibid*. 77.
2 *Ibid.*
3 *Enchiridion Biblicum* 539.
4 *Summa Theol.* I.70, 1 ad 3.
5 *Enchiridion Biblicum* 559.
6 Clement of Alexandria, *Pedagogue* 2.7. PG 8.462.
7 *Cf.* Pius XII, *Humani generis*, DS 3896.
8 By his excavations at Troy and Mycenae, Schliemann showed that the Trojan War, described in Homer, was an historical event.

9 Chiefly the size of the city; it took Jonah three days to walk through it. But A. Parrot, *Nineveh and the Old Testament*, Philosophical Library, New York, 1955, 2nd ed., 85-6, suggests the term Ninevah might have referred to a twenty-six mile string of settlements in the Assyrian triangle. As to the great fish: D. Wallechinsky and I. Wallace, *People's Almanac*, Doubleday, N.Y., 1975, 1339 report that in February 1891, the ship Star of the East caught an eighty foot sperm whale. A seaman, James Bartley, had disappeared and was presumed drowned; but the next day, when the crew was cutting up the whale, he was found alive inside the fish.

10 *Enchiridion Biblicum* 551.

11 *Ibid.*, 109-10.

12 *Ibid.*, 565.

13 *On Divine Revelation*, ¶11.

14 *Ibid.*, ¶12.

15 R. Brown, *The Virginal Conception and Bodily Resurrection of Jesus*, Paulist Press, New York, 1973, 4-5.

16 *Enchiridion Biblicum* 161.

17 *Ibid.*, 181-84.

18 I.5.

19 Note 3 above.

20 *De Genesi ad Litteram* 6.12.20. PL 34:347.

21 *Enchiridion Biblicum* 121, citing Augustine, *op. cit.*, 2.9.20. PL 34:270.

22 Norman Perrin, *Rediscovering the Teaching of Jesus*, Harper and Row, N.Y., 1967, 26.

23 In Appendix, p. 180 below.

24 Herodotus, *History of the Persian Wars*. 7.152.

25 *Cf.* G.F. Abbott, *Thucydides, A Study in Historical Reality*, Routledge and Sons, London, 1925; A.W. Gomme, *A Historical Commentary on Thucydides*, 4 vols. Clarendon, Oxford, 1956-70.

26 Thucydides, *History of the Peloponnesian War* 1.22.

27 *Ibid.*

28 Polybius, *Histories* 3.26. *Cf.* F.W. Walbank, "Polybius" in *Sather Classical Lectures* 42, University of California Press, Berkeley, 1972.

29 Diodorus Siculus, *Historical Library* 1.4.

30 *Ibid.* 1.5.

31 Flavius Josephus, *Against Apion* 1.27.

32 *Ibid.* 1.47.

33 M.L.W. Laistner, *The Greater Roman Historians* in *Sather Classical Lectures* 21, University of California Press, Berkeley, 1947, 129.

34 For a convenient collection, see A. Toynbee, *Greek Historical Thought*, New American Library, N.Y.

35 *Op. cit.* 1.1.

36 *Cf.* also Thucydides 1.22.
37 Mircea Eliade, *The Myth of the Eternal Return*, tr. W.R. Trask, Bollingen Series XLVI, Princeton University Press, 1974, 104. *Cf.* James M. Robinson, *A New Quest of the Historical Jesus*, SCM, London, 1963, 81; and Eugene Kevane, *The Lord of History*, St. Paul Editions, Boston, 1980. 13.26.
38 Eliade 143.
39 *Ibid.*
40 *Cf.* J.J.M. Roberts, "Myth versus History" in CBQ 38 (1976) 1-13.
41 Cited in Eusebius, *Church History* 4.3.1-2.
42 St. Ignatius of Antioch, *Epist. to the Trallians* 10.
43 *Idem, Epist. to the Romans* 1.2.
44 A. Oepke, *s.v. Iaomai*, in TDNT III.206.
45 *Cf.* Joseph A. Fitzmyer, "The Languages of Palestine in the First Century A.D." in CBQ 32 (1970) 501-31; J.M. Grinta, "Hebrew as the Spoken and Written Language in the Last Days of the Second Temple" in JBL 79 (1960) 32-47. On the resemblance of Luke's preface to prefaces of other ancient historians, see W.G. Kurz, "Hellenistic Rhetoric in the Christological Proof of Luke—Acts" in CBQ 42 (1980) 171-95, esp. 185. On p. 187 Kurz notes that Luke "explicitly and continuously distinguishes this [eye] witness from mere hearsay."
46 *Cf.* H.F.S. Sparks, "The Semitisms of St. Luke's Gospel" in JTS 44 (1943) 129-38.
47 *Ibid.* 130.
48 *Cf.* E. Vogt, *Lexicon Linguae Aramaicae Veteris Testamenti*, Pontificium Institutum Biblicum, 1971, 76.
49 M. Johannessohn, "Das biblische *kai egeneto* und seine Geschichte" in *Zeitschrift fur Vergleichenden Sprachforschung*, 1926, 161-212, esp. 184-85, 190.
50 *Cf.* Klaus Beyer, *Semitische Syntax in Neuen Testament*, Vanderhoeck & Ruprecht, Gottingen, 1962. I. 29-30, 67-69.
51 The reason for the bracket 20 to 25% is this. Luke uses the apodotic *kai* in only 17 clear instances (there are two ambiguous ones, where the *kai* could mean "also"). He omits it 51 times, if we count only instances where by strict classical rules Hebrew would have had *wau* (equals Greek *kai*). However, we may be able to add 14 more instances, in which a substantive comes at the start of the main clause in Luke. Classical Hebrew generally omitted the *and* before such words, but that may not be the reason for Luke's omissions, for in 9 of the 17 clear examples where he does use the *kai*, a substantive, *autos* ("he") follows. So we suspect that the older fine distinction may have dropped, at least in part. If this is the case, we could reasonably add the 14 to the previous 51, for a grand total of 65. To use the *kai* 17

times out of a total possible range of 17 plus 65 gives the result that Luke used the apodotic *kai* only 20.73% of the time. Without the 14, the total would be 51 omissions, for the 25% use as above.

52 A fascinating further development appears: Luke uses *kai egeneto* in 20 instances in which he *omits* apodotic *kai*. At first sight there seems to be a contradiction: *kai egeneto* points to Hebrew—omission of apodotic *kai* seems to point away from Hebrew. The answer is that Luke must have used two kinds of Hebrew documents: new and older conservative. We know there was a revival of Hebrew, and that in general the apodotic *wau* (*kai*) was omitted, but *we yehi* (*kai egeneto*) could be used. There was also an older conservative Hebrew that had never died out, but was the native language in some "pockets of Hebrew" (*cf.* J. Fitzmyer, "The Languages of Palestine in the First Century A.D." in CBQ 32 (1970) 531). It would keep the apodotic *wau* (*kai*), while being apt to lose the finer distinctions mentioned above in note 51. On the newer Hebrew *cf.* Beyer, p. 67 and F.L. Horton, "Reflections on the Semitisms of Luke—Acts" in C.H. Talbert, ed. *Perspectives on Luke—Acts*, Danville: Association of Baptist Professors of Religion, 1978, pp. 4 and 6.

53 Johannessohn, *art. cit.*, 199, 201.

54 *Cf.* R.W. Klein, *Textual Criticism of the Old Testament*, Fortress, Philadelphia, 1974.

55 *Cf.* M. Zerwick, *Graecitas Biblica* ed. 4, Pontificium Institutum Biblicum, Romae, ¶361.

56 W.F. Albright and C.S. Mann, *Matthew*, in *Anchor Bible*, Doubleday, Garden City, N.Y., 1971, xli-xlviii. W.R. Farmer, *The Synoptic Problem*, Western North Carolina Press, Dillsboro, N.C., 1976, shows well how flimsy is the evidence for Marcan priority; equally revealing is the study, *Matthew Luke and Mark*, by Dom Bernard Orchard, Koinonia Press, Manchester, 1977. *Cf.* also E.P. Sanders, *The Tendencies of the Synoptic Tradition*, Cambridge University Press, 1969, and T.R. Rosche, "The Words of Jesus and the Future of the 'Q' Hypothesis" in JBL 79 (1960) 210-20, and Sanders, "The Argument from Order and Relationship between Matthew and Luke" in NTS 15 (1968-69) 249-61. Similarly, O.L. Cope in *Matthew, A Scribe Trained for the Kingdom of Heaven* in *CBQ Monograph Series* 5, 1976, 12, writes: "Matthew's use of Mark is hypothetical."

57 John M. Rist, *On the Independence of Matthew and Mark*, Cambridge U. Press, 1978.

58 J. Jeremias, *New Testament Theology*, tr. J. Bowden, Scribner's, New York, 1971, 20.

59 N. Perrin, *op. cit.* 26-28.

60 R. Bultmann, *The History of the Synoptic Tradition*, tr. John Marsh,

Harper and Row, N.Y., 1963. 127-28. (Hereafter cited as HST).

61   KM 39.

62   HST 4.

63   Robert J. Trotter, "The Truth, the Whole Truth and Nothing But..." in *Science News* 108 (1975) 269-70.

64   On the prejudice of form critics against miracles, see Appendix, pp 175-179 below. On miracles claimed in paganism, see pp 218-219 below.

65   *Cf.* W.G. Most, "A Biblical Theology of Redemption in a Covenant Framework" in CBQ 29 (1967) 1-19.

66   For the answer to other arguments against the historicity of their slowness, see Appendix, pp 205-06 below.

1. Charges of Ignorance

Experienced teachers know what will happen if they confront a class with a huge, complex problem. Most students will simply sit and gape, flabbergasted. They need what Socrates taught long ago in his persistent questioning of the Athenians: the teacher should break up his proposition, subdivide, make distinctions, and then ask the students to deal with each of the smaller pieces separately; thereupon many in the class will reach answers they would not have dreamed of.

In less complex matter all that may be needed is the ability to see more than one possibility, and, in that sense, to make distinctions.

Critics who charge Jesus with ignorance on the basis of Scriptural texts commonly fail in this regard. Bultmann especially seems strangely unable to see more than one possibility in many texts, with the result that he charges the New Testament with many contradictions. Take this passage, for example: "...some of its [the New Testament's] features are actually contradictory. For example, the death of Christ is sometimes a sacrifice and sometimes a cosmic event."(1) We wonder where the contradiction lies: a death to redeem all mankind is surely of cosmic significance! Or this: "Sometimes his person is interpreted as the Messiah and sometimes as the Second Adam." Why not admit both aspects in one person, i.e., the promised One of old, *and* the

new Head of the human race (second Adam)? Or this: "The
kenosis of the pre-existent Son (Phil. 2:6ff.) is incompatible with
the miracle narratives as proofs of his messianic claims." St. Paul
says the Divine Word "emptied Himself"; need this mean He
ceased to be divine? Could it not easily and reasonably mean that
He refused to use His divinity as a claim to exemption from normal
human discomforts? For example, He would not turn stones into
bread (Mt. 4:3-4), a thing He could have very reasonably done, for
He needed food, and He had the power. His policy, however, was
to use divine power for the good of others, not for Himself. "The
Virgin birth is inconsistent with the assertion of his pre-
existence." Why, Dr. Bultmann? Could not a divine, preexistent
Person in taking on human nature, decide to have a human mother
but not a human father? What contradiction is there in that? And
so on for the long, boring, wearisome list of charges by the
Bultmannians.

A similar strange inability to understand appears in the
charges based on Scripture that claim to show ignorance in Jesus.
In dealing with these we are not obliged, of course, to prove
positively what each text *must* mean. We need merely to show that
there is a fully *plausible* interpretation that does not imply
ignorance. It is usually difficult to prove a text has only one
meaning unless one can (as Catholics should) fall back on the
interpretation of a providentially guided tradition and Church.

1. Jesus' Knowledge of Ordinary Affairs

According to R. Brown, "The best example from the public
ministry" of a text indicating ignorance of ordinary affairs is Mk
5:30-33.(2) Jesus was walking through a crowd on the way to raise
the daughter of Jairus. A woman in the crowd who had suffered
twelve years from a flow of blood touched His garment, hoping for
a cure. Then (v.30), "Jesus, perceiving in himself that power had
gone forth from him, immediately turned about in the crowd, and
said, 'Who touched my garments?'" His disciples pointed out the
obvious: many had brushed Him in the crowd. But the woman
admitted she had done it. Brown comments, "The narrative seems
clearly to presuppose ignorance of Jesus' part." And he adds in

his note 13, "Obviously, the Marcan form is more original, and Mt. reflects an uneasiness about the ignorance that Mk. attributes to Jesus." (Matthew does not mention Jesus' question, he merely reports briefly that the woman touched His garment, that Jesus turned and said to her that her faith had saved her).

Brown has missed an easy distinction; for Jesus to turn and ask such a question need not imply ignorance at all. It was simply a ploy—familiar to all classroom teachers—of bringing out responses and reactions. Similarly, in Mt 15:21-28 Jesus acts as though He is refusing the Canaanite woman: "I was sent only to the lost sheep of the house of Israel." He merely wished to elicit from her a more earnest expression of faith, before granting her request. Again, in Mt 14:16 He told the disciples, when faced with a crowd of 5000, to give them something to eat—actually it was obvious that such was impossible. Even to His own Mother He seemed to refuse a request at Cana. Some think the language sounds like a rejection. Yet the outcome showed He really granted what she asked. Many of the Fathers of the first centuries, as we shall see in chapter six, observed, in speaking of Jesus' question as to where Lazarus was buried that that question implied no more ignorance than did God's questions, in Genesis: "Adam, where are you?" or to Cain: "Where is your brother Abel?"

A similar desire to draw answers out of His hearers can easily account for the fact that Jesus at the age of twelve (in the Temple) was found asking questions. Of course, we grant that Jesus could and did have two *channels* of knowledge, divine and human. Thus it would be possible to indicate a time in His life at which His bodily senses had not yet reported that roses are red. Yet even before that point of time, the divine *He* could not fail to know.

Already in the patristic age there were discussions on Lk 2:52 which, after describing the finding of Jesus in the Temple, continues: "And Jesus increased in wisdom and age and favor with God and man." There is no problem about growing in age and favor. As to growth in wisdom, the expression could mean one of three things: (1) actual growth in what the *Person* knew; (2) growth in knowledge acquired via the human channel; (3) growth in the manifestation of wisdom to men. The first is ruled out by the fact of

Jesus being a divine Person. The second and third are quite possible, so there is no need to draw a conclusion of ignorance. Brown adds the helpful observation that the formula is stereotyped: cf. 1 Sm 2:26 and Lk 1:80.(3)

Problems are raised because Jesus shows various emotions. Particularly, He is sometimes said to have marveled (actually, the word *ethaumasen* is used of Jesus only three times in the Synoptics, once in each Gospel). Translations vary. RSV for Mk 6:6 has: "He *marvelled*." The New American Bible has: "So much did their lack of faith *distress* Him." However, regardless of the translation, *ethaumasen* need not imply ignorance in Jesus. First, the word displays a broad spectrum of meanings in Scripture. In the Septuagint of Lv 19:15 the meaning is approximately "be influenced by"—"You shall not be influenced by the face of a powerful man." This usage is frequent in the Old Testament.

Of course, that sense would not fit Mk 6:6. Yet, since we know the word has a broad spectrum, we can rightly compare it to English "be surprised." I can say to someone: "I am surprised at you" and not mean I did not know about the matter before. It is just a way of expressing dismay. Still further, a man may "marvel" at a sunset, even though it is not new to him; he has seen many similar sunsets before. The marveling is simply a normal emotional reaction to something that calls for emotion. There need not be something strictly *new* to provoke the reaction, only something moving or remarkable.(4)

What of the fact that, according to one way of understanding Mk 14:33, Jesus experienced not just anguish in Gethsemani, but even fear? Here again, translations vary. RSV renders "greatly distressed and troubled." The New American Bible reads: "He began to be filled with fear and distress." The crucial Greek word is *ekthambeisthai*. The Arndt-Gingrich dictionary offers the following entries for the word: "be amazed, be alarmed, be distressed" and suggests "be distressed" for Mk 14:33.(5)

However, no matter which translation we adopt, there is no need to maintain that grave fear implies ignorance in Jesus. Here Bultmann provides another choice *non sequitur*: "If the Christ who died such a death was the preexistent Son of God, what could death mean for him? Obviously very little, if he knew that he would rise again in three days!''(6) But Jesus did have real humanity. The fact that He foreknew clearly what lay ahead would not mean that to die after being scourged, spat on, crowned with thorns, ridiculed, and nailed to a Cross would exact nothing from His human nature.

Further, modern psychology has shown that fear and other emotions can be generated biochemically in spite of a patient's knowledge. Ferris Pitts experimented in producing anxiety in patients. He found: ''A 20-minute infusion of lactate into a patient with anxiety neurosis realiably produced an anxiety attack that began within a minute or two after the infusion was started, decreased rapidly after the infusion, but was often followed by from one to three days of exhaustion and heightened anxiety symptoms.''(7) The results in patients who did not have an anxiety neurosis were less marked but still present: ''Nonpatient controls had fewer and less severe symptoms in response to lactate.'' Yet, ''...a high concentration of lactate ion can produce some anxiety symptoms in almost anyone.''

Interestingly, he also found it was possible to cancel out the effects of the lactate to a large extent: ''...calcium ion largely prevents the symptoms in both patients and controls.'' In addition, the experience of a personal acquaintance may be instructive. he was taking a prescription medication, but one day wanted to take aspirin also for a touch of flu. He consulted a pharmacist about the combination and was told it was all right. But it was not. Soon after taking the two, he found himself becoming frightened. He was not fearful of anything in particular—he succumbed to a state of generalized fear. His *mind* remained calm throughout, for he recognized himself as a victim of some unfortunate biochemistry. But in a bodily way, he was still very afraid for several hours.

The practical conclusion is this: knowledge of what is happening does not necessarily eliminate fear. Neither did the knowledge of Jesus have to rule out fear.

It is objected that if Jesus had the beatific vision He could not have feared or suffered. That problem we will consider in chapter eight.

A final example: a person goes to see Shakespeare's Hamlet; he has seen it several times before; as he watches, he experiences various emotions. All this happens even though there is nothing new in it for him, and even though he realizes that it is only a stage play.

2. Jesus' Knowledge of Scripture

Some(9) see a problem about Jesus' knowledge in Jn 7:37-38, "On the last day of the feast, the great day, Jesus stood up and proclaimed, 'If anyone thirsts, let him come to me and drink. He who believes in me, as the scripture said, 'Out of his heart shall flow rivers of living water.'''(8) Now research can find no Old Testament passage containing this wording or message. So, was Jesus in error in quoting Scripture? Two comments are in order. First, the literary genre of John is such that John is possibly theologizing, adding his own reflections in the light of what he learned after Easter, and putting them in the mouth of Jesus. Thus if there were any charge, it would fall on John, not on Jesus. However even so, we could say the evangelist was quoting loosely; few of the three hundred Old Testament quotations that are in the new Testament are given verbatim; many are recast creatively to suit the argument at hand—a practice used widely in the liturgy and in Sunday sermons. That the speaker or writer is being creative is taken for granted by the audience. No one is deceived or in error.

In Mk 2:26 Jesus says that David when in a difficult situation, "entered the house of God, when Abiathar was high priest." But, as all exegetes admit, not Abiathar but his father Ahimelech was in charge of the temple when David came (1 Sm 21:1-6). So, was Jesus ignorant? To reply we need to look carefully at the phrase, "when Abiathar". That is the RSV translation; other versions use phrases such as "in the days of..." or "at the time...." These translations are faithful to the Greek *epi Abiathar archiereos*. For the Greek *epi* with genitive of the person can readily have such a generic time meaning.(10) The usage occurs in pagan authors, e.g., Thucydides uses *ep' emou* to mean "in my time."(11) The New Testament uses the same structure in the same sort of sense in Lk 3:2, 4:27; Acts 11:28; and substantially in Mt 1:11. So Jesus actually says only that David entered the temple during "the life and times" of Abiathar. The reason for using Abiathar's name rather that Ahimelech's is obvious: he was much more prominent and better known to readers of the Old Testament than his father, because of his close association with David under whom he became chief priest along with Zadok. So there is no mistake. (Analogously the astute Annas is called high priest at the time of Jesus even though his successor Caiaphas held the office.)

A problem is raised because Jesus at times compared Himself to the prophet Jonah (Mt 12:39-41; 16:4; Lk 11:29-32). Most scholars today classify the book of Jonah as a sort of extended parable rather than as an historical account. Can Jesus, therefore, be charged with error or ignorance? Not at all. Both in Scripture and in everyday speech today people can quote, explicitly or implicitly, from writings purely fictitious, such as *Alice in Wonderland*, to make a point, or to illustrate. St. Paul acted similarly in recalling the rock that *followed* the Israelites (1 Cor 10:4). He had in mind a rabbinic legend, and used it to make an illustration, without intending to guarantee the truth of the legend. Similarly in Jude 9, Michael the archangel is spoken of as disputing with satan over the body of Moses. Yet the writer of the Epistle would not necessarily have believed that fiction. Similarly with Jesus in His references to Jonah.

A double charge is raised from the use Jesus makes of Psalm 110 in arguing with the scribes (Mk 12:35-37; Mt 22:41-46; Lk 20:41-44), "How can the scribes say that the Christ is the son of David? David himself, inspired by the Holy Spirit, declared, 'The Lord said to my Lord....' David himself calls him Lord; so how is he his son?"

The first objection is parallel to what we have just observed about Jonah, i.e., Jesus seems to attribute the composition of the psalm to David. In that day, everyone was accustomed to refer to all the psalms as "by David". Actually, Psalm 110 is probably by an unknown tenth century author.(12) But just as Pius XII, quoting St. Augustine wrote: "...the Spirit of God, who spoke through them [the inspired writers] did not intend to teach the inner make-up of things, for that has no bearning on salvation,"(13) similarly, Jesus did not come to make corrections in accord with current, critical views on literary authorship. Or, to phrase it more philosophically, the precise formal object of Jesus' judgment did not bear *per se* upon authorship; rather, the reference to David was merely *an accepted form of reference*, when quoting from the psalter, and as such the phrase was used in the judgment of Jesus. Hence, there is no attribution of authorship to David and no possibility of genuine error.

The second charge against Jesus from His use of psalm 110 is this: His argument takes for granted that the Lord (Yahweh) spoke thus to "my Lord," who is the Messiah. Scholars today, however, are disinclined to think there was an expectation of the Messiah at the time this psalm was written.(14) But even so, there is no problem. It is quite a legitimate practice, one often used today, to argue against an opponent by using the opponent's own principles or framework of thought against him, even though the speaker does not agree with his opponent's ideas. This is the *argumentum ad hominem*. Jewish commentators at the time of Jesus were not very concerned about original historical sense of Scripture in their arguments. The Targums attribute messianic meanings to many passages. So if Jesus followed the then current, and still current pattern of the *argumentum ad hominem*, it gives no ground whatsoever for a charge of ignorance. And, of course, no one is absolutely sure of the date of this psalm, nor whether messianic content was not injected into composition at the time of its acceptance (centuries later) into the psalter. Critics forget to distinguish: a composition in the Old Testament may originally and historically have been Canaanite in whole or in part; it becomes inspired and canonical only later when accepted as such; and at this later point its message often is radically changed.

In Mt 23:35 Jesus refers to all the innocent blood that was shed from the blood of Abel to the blood of Zechariah son of Berechiah "whom you murdered between the sanctuary and the altar." It is charged this is a mistake: the son of Berechiah did not perish that way; it was Zechariah the son of Jehoiada who died in the temple around 825 B.C. (see 2 Chr 24:20-22). There are several possible answers. First, the words "son of Berechiah" are missing in one of the most important manuscripts, that of Sinai, and in some lesser ones as well. Perhaps an ancient copyist had written these words in the margin and later they were put into body of the text (such interpolations are not part of the Bible). St. Jerome, in his commentary on this passage, reports that the "Gospel of the Nazarenes", which he thought to be the original Aramaic of St. Matthew, had "son of Jehoida." St. Luke's version (Lk 11:51) omits "son of Berechiah."

However, another answer is possible, and seems preferable. Luke 11:49 introduces this account by saying, "Therefore also the Wisdom of God said, 'I will send'...," and then he continues with the passage. So it seems from St. Luke that Jesus was quoting some work, then in circulation, which contained these words. there were extant many such works, which did not become part of Scripture. Jesus could quote from them much as he could refer to Jonah without guaranteeing the historical character of the book in question. St. Matthew does not clearly indicate that Jesus was quoting, yet could be easily taken thus, if we punctuate as follows: "For this reason: 'Behold, I send....'"

Finally, some object that Jesus, in Jn 10:33-36, to answer Jews who accuse Him of making Himself God, quotes Ps 82:6, "Is it not written in your law, 'I said, you are gods?'" The psalm seems to refer to human judges and calls them gods. The Hebrew *elohim*, which can mean *God*, can also be used for human judges. Jesus draws an argument from that loose usage—following rabbinic precedent. If Jesus remained within actual Old Testament usage (cf. Ps 138:1; 8:5; 1 Sm 28:13), and argued in the manner usual among rabbis of His day, there can be no charge of error. And of course, the passage is from John, and so may be part of the author's theological construction. In either case the force of the critic's argument escapes us; they have not identified the precise, formal object of judgment prerequisite for a claim of error.

3. Jesus' Knowledge of Demonology

In Mk 9:17-19 Jesus meets a boy who is said to be possessed. His disciples had tried to cure the boy, but failed. Jesus Himself commands the spirit to go out. It does so, convulsing the boy. Some have noted that convulsions, becoming rigid, and foaming at the mouth could be symptoms of something like epilepsy, and charge Jesus knew no more of such physical conditions than His unenlightened contemporaries.

We reply: yes, the symptoms are like those of epilepsy, but they also occur in cases of possession. No proof is offered by the critics that it was epilepsy and not possession; accordingly it is not scholarly to charge Jesus with ignorance. Yes, He did command the spirit and it went. He could have cured epilepsy by a command too. We may surmise that just as Genesis was not written to teach cosmology, so Jesus did not opt for making medical diagnoses. He could have adapted Himself to the thought patterns of the time and cured whatever needed to be cured, without explaining. The Fathers, as we shall see in chapter 6, often speak of such *adaptation* on the part of Jesus. They call it *oikonomia* in Greek; *dispensatio* in Latin. The objection limps seriously as a proof of ignorance in Jesus.

A similar objection is raised from the incident of the Gerasene demoniac (Mk 5:1-20). It is suggested the man was merely violently insane. We reply: If so, then Jesus reacted as in the incident just discussed. But that seems not the case here: for the demons did seek and got His permission to go into a herd of swine, with very visible results. A mere cure of insanity would not have produced such an aftermath.(15)

In Mt 12:43-45 and Lk 11:24-26 we meet an interesting passage, almost word for word in the two Gospels: "When the unclean spirit has gone out of a man, he passes through waterless places seeking rest, but he finds none. Then he says, 'I will return to my house from which I came.' And when he comes, he finds it empty, swept, and put in order. Then he goes and brings with him seven other spirits more evil than himself, and they enter and dwell there; and the last state of that man becomes worse than the first. So shall it be also with this evil generation."

In both Matthew and Luke the passage comes at once or shortly after the charge of the Pharisees that Jesus cast out devils by the power of Beelzebul. Jesus presents a sort of parable on the state of the Jews; Jesus came to them, cast out devils among them. But because of their wickedness, which went so far as to say He cast out devils by the aid of the prince of devils, the devils would return with reinforcements so that the adversaries of Jesus will end up worse off than before, having rejected Him and attributed to satan what was really the work of the Holy Spirit in Jesus. So "the last state of that man becomes worse than the first." Their sin became unforgiveable (Mt 12:32).

The chief point of the parable is quite clear. What of the mention of demons striding through deserts? This has occasioned charges, such as that by Fr. Brown:(16) "I do not believe the demons inhabit desert places or the upper air, as Jesus and Paul thought...I see no way to get around the difficulty except by saying that Jesus and Paul were wrong on this point. They accepted the beliefs of their times about demons, but those beliefs were superstitious."(16) Fr. Brown seems to think he is *forced*(17) to say Jesus was wrong and held superstitious views! But Fr. Brown is hardly *forced*: (1) no one presses every detail of a parable; it would then become an allegory, and no longer be a parable. (2) Jesus quite artistically embellished His parable with colorful imagery that had deep roots in the Old Testament, in poetic passages like Is 13:21 and 34:14, and in the colorful narrative of Tobias 8:3ff. Has Fr. Brown forgotten that it is impossible to speak of anything supernatural (including hell and demons) apart from the use of imagery and analogy?

4. Jesus' Knowledge of Afterlife and Apocalyptic

Jesus describes hell in terms of unquenchable fire (Mk 9:48; Mt 25:41), ravenous worms (Mk 9:48), frustrated grinding of teeth and weeping (Mt 8:12; 13:42), insatiable thirst (Lk 16:24), and with a great chasm between the place of beatitude and the place of punishment (Lk 16:26). Further, He speaks of banquets in the place of beatitude (Mt 8:11) and heaven as above the clouds (Mk 13:26; 14:62). R. Brown comments: "...we cannot assume that Jesus shared our own sophistication on some of these questions. If Jesus speaks of heaven above the clouds...how can we be sure that he knew that it was not above the clouds?''(18) Leaving aside the deep insight that Jesus was not so sophisticated as we are (which conjures up Bultmann's overweening esteem for modern man who has seen a lightbulb and the wireless,(19) we must say: These expressions certainly include some rather obvious imagery, much of it related to the apocalyptic literary genre. If Jesus wished to use imagery, adapting Himself to His hearers, and to employ apocalyptic figures, which were also current then—and precisely because current, they would be understood correctly—is that a ground for imputing ignorance? Such *oikonomia* or adaptation is really needed to enable God to meet human weakness since, as Is 55:9 reports: ''As the heavens are higher than the earth, so are my ways higher than your ways.'' We should hardly arrogantly think Jesus inferior, less intelligent than ourselves. Rather, He stooped to our dullness.

The question is raised whether or not Jesus ever definitely said (or knew) that some human beings will be eternally lost. On this topic Karl Rahner, in his article on ''Hell'' in *Sacramentum Mundi*, writes: ''Even in his 'judgment-discourse' Jesus gave no clear revelation about whether men are actually lost or how many may be. That he restricts himself to the possibility follows from the real nature of these discourses, which is to be a summons to decision.''(20) Knowing Rahner's existentialist leanings, we wonder if he is forcing the ''judgment-discourse'' to mean something similar to Bultmann's challenge to a decision for authentic existence?(21) If so, it is straining the text; it is forcing an ancient Semitic form into that of twentieth century Heidegger—hardly the proper procedure for exegesis.

But could anyone really say that Jesus does not strictly state that any are lost? It would emasculate the whole account of the judgment with so many on the left as well as on the right if there were to be none left on the left at all, after the final count. Could Jesus have been making a kind of threat, such as the prophets made, a threat understood to be conditioned, so that it might not really happen. Yes, if the situation allows for repentance.(22) However, in this instance the situation is already the parousia; the die has already been cast, the decision made on man's part. In any case there would be no grounds for a charge of ignorance in Jesus—nor does Rahner suggest that. Jesus may well have had excellent reasons for not giving us a more definite revelation on "the number of the saved."

NOTES

1 KM 11.
2 JGM 45.
3 JGM 46. Could the growth in wisdom in Lk. 2.52 mean growth in *experimental* knowledge (received through the senses, as we mentioned above)? No, for *wisdom* is not the same as sense knowledge. Luke, an educated Greek, would not have used *sophia* that way. Jesus did, of course, have an increase in sense knowledge. The fact that He already knew, even in His human mind, thanks to the Beatific Vision, the same things, would not prevent His acquiring the same information *via another channel.* Further, we would speak of His *body* as acquiring certain *habits.* Thus when Heb. 5:8 says He learned obedience from suffering, it must mean His body gradually acquired the habituation to tolerating that from which the flesh instinctively shrinks—just as a person who has long been ill gradually learns to settle down, as it were, to acquiesce on his bodily side, even though in his spirit he may have had full conformity with the will of God from the start. (*Cf.* W. Most, "On Jesus Learning Obedience: Hebrews 5:8" in *Faith & Reason* 3 (1977) 6-16). Thus His body could acquire the habitual skill of walking and of forming the sounds of His language. His *divine power* could have produced that facility in the body instantly—but just as He made it a policy (*cf.* Phil. 2:7) not to use divine power for His own comfort, and just as He treated the suggestion to turn stones into bread as a temptation, so too He would not use that power to create bodily facility. His *mind,* however, did not have to labor to retain vocabulary and inflections of His language.
4 Pity is reported in Mk. 1:41 and parallel passages: Mk. 6:34 and Mt. 14:14; Mk 8:2 and Mt. 20:34. Anger is mentioned in Mk.3:5 and is implied in the cleansing of the temple: Mk. 11:15-17; Mt.21:12-23; Lk. 19:45-46.
5 W. Arndt, F. W. Gingrich and F.W. Danker, *A Greek-English Lexicon of the New Testament,* University of Chicago Press, Chicago, 2nd ed. 1979, 240.
6 KM 8.

7   F. Pitts, "The Biochemistry of Anxiety" in *Scientific American,* February 1969, 75.

8   The Greek would actually allow three translations, as Brown points out in *The Gospel According to John, Anchor Bible* 29, Doubleday, Garden City, N.Y., 1966, 320-24.

9   JGM 51.

10 *Cf.* H. W. Smyth, *A Greek Grammar for Colleges,* American Book Co., N.Y., 1920, Art. 1689.

11 Thucydides 7.86. *Cf.* Aeschines 3.178. J. Jeremias in *New Testament Theology* (Charles Scribner's Sons, N.Y., 1971, tr. J. Bowden) notes: "Semitic languages have no regular word for 'time' in a durative sense, and use the phrase 'the days of x' as an expedient for describing a life-time, reign or period of activity," 47.

12 *Cf.* M. Dahood, *Psalms III,* in *Anchor Bible,* 17a, Doubleday, Garden City, N.Y. 1970, 112.

13 *De Genesi ad Litteram* 2.9.20. PL 34:270-71.

14 *Cf.* J.A. Fitzmyer, "The Son of David Tradition and Matthew 22:41-46 and Parallels" in *Concilium* 20 (1967), *The Dynamism of Biblical Tradition,* 75-87.

15 *Cf.* H. Thurston, *Ghosts and Poltergeists,* Regnery, Chicago, 1954.

16 In *St. Anthony's Messenger,* May 1971, 47-48.

17 For a remarkable case in which a famous scholar, Norman Perrin, thought he was "forced", but was really not, see Appendix, pp 195-98 below.

18 JGM 56.

19 KM 5.

20 *Sacramentum Mundi,* ed. Karl Rahner and others, Herder and Herder, N.Y., 1969, III, 8.

21 See Appendix, p. 180 below.

22 *Cf.* Thomas Aquinas, *Summa Theol.,* Suppl. 99.3 ad 3.

2. Lack of Foreknowledge

Since, in the course of our analysis of form criticism (see Appendix 3), we answer the chief charges that the predictions of the passion and resurrection were forged by the Church, here we need only consider the special type of prediction contained in the words of Jesus about destroying and rebuilding the temple, and about the destruction of Jerusalem.

Here Fr. Brown sees a problem:

> Far from being a clear prophecy, this saying seems to have been an embarrassment in the Synoptic tradition: Jesus had spoken about the destruction and rebuilding of the Temple, but he had died without the Temple being destroyed or his rebuilding it. Lk. omits the saying.... Mk. 14:58 adds qualifications '...made with hands...not made with hands.' Mt. 26:61 reduces the prediction to a possibility: *'I am able* to destroy....' Jn. is giving us still another reinterpretation designed to remove the difficulty.(1)

Fr. Brown must think Jesus terribly stupid (as well as superstitious).(2) Jesus must have been a deluded visionary to make such a prediction—if indeed it was a prediction—that the Temple would be destroyed, and that He would rebuild it! We say "deluded" since it did not come true. But, is it really necessary to suppose that Jesus really made that type of a prediction? Jn 2:21 said Jesus was speaking about "the temple of His body" which was to be destroyed by His death, but raised up in three days. Do we have to call that a Johannine "reinterpretation", which is a subtle way of saying that it was a falsification, since originally the saying, according to Brown, did not mean what John said it meant? I find no evidence to ''force'' me into accepting such a view. So I refuse to think of Jesus as a deluded visionary.

Note, moreover, how the saying as found in Jn. 2:19 uses the imperative form of the verb: ''Destroy this temple, and in three days I will raise it up.'' Martin Luther has been much maligned, unjustly, for a famous line: ''Sin mightily, but believe more mightily.''(3) It is erroneous to think Luther was really urging anyone to sin, and sin greatly. Rather, he was using a paratactic structure, one known in Greek, Latin and Hebrew. In parataxis one puts two clauses side by side. *Gramatically*, each seems independent, for there is no subordinating conjunction. Yet *in sense*, the normal listener recognizes that a conjunction is meant. So the real sense of Luther's words was: ''Even if (or: although) you sin mightily, believe still more mightily.'' Now if we allow to Jesus what we extend to Luther, we will understand His saying to mean: ''Even if you destroy this temple, I will raise it up in three days.'' Theoretically such a saying would be quite valid whether it referred to the Herodian temple at Jerusalem—Jesus could miraculously restore it in an instant—or to the temple of His body, as John understands it.

Further, Fr. Brown fails to notice that he is raising an objection against Jesus by depending on the precise wording used by *false witnesses* at Jesus' trial, and by those who meant to *ridicule* Him on the Cross. It is hardly common decency to make charges against Jesus based on wordings that come from those who intended to destroy Him by false testimony at an illegal trial or by ridicule as he was dying—crucified on Calvary. We hardly expected so low a blow.

Jesus' prophecy regarding the fall of Jerusalem is recorded in all three Synoptics. St. Matthew reports it in chapter 24, which opens with two questions by the disciples, first about the fall of Jerusalem, then about the return of Jesus at the end. It is likely that St. Matthew is following a multiple fulfillment pattern, i.e., that he wants the very same words to apply to both events, on the whole, even if not to absolutely every detail. Matthew does seem to use such a pattern elsewhere; e.g., in 2:15 he tells us that the Holy Family stayed in Egypt until the death of Herod, and then returned, "This was to fulfill what the Lord had spoken by the prophet, 'Out of Egypt have I called my son.'" The allusion is to Hosea 11:1. But in the original setting, Hosea clearly meant Israel as the son whom God called out of Egypt in the Exodus.

Another multiple fulfillment pattern is probably found in Mt 1:22-23 which cites the prophecy of Is 7:14, "All this took place to fulfill what the Lord had spoken by the prophet: 'Behold, a virgin shall conceive and bear a son.'" The identity of that child has been widely debated. Yet Matthew, who surely was aware of divergent opinions, did not hesitate to say it was fulfilled in the conception of Jesus. Exegetes today commonly admit that the prophecy of the terrible moral disorder "in the last days" in 2 Tm 3:1-9 refers both to the entire Messianic period and also, more specifically, to the final days before the parousia.(4) The same is said for the prophecy of 2 Tm 4:1-4.

There is, then, such a thing as a multiple fulfillment pattern. And we think that in chapter 24 Matthew is following that pattern, so that the signs described refer to both events, the fall of Jerusalem and the parousia. The following are the chief points: false Messiahs (Acts 5:36-37 tells us of such, Theudas and Judas of Galilee, who led revolts.(5) Acts 21:38 reports still another, without giving his name); wars and rumors of wars (the Jewish revolt of 66, which Nero sent Vespasian to quell in 67 would be enough for this prediction, but there were also many other wars, especially in the year of the four emperors, 69 A.D.); pestilences, famines, and local earthquakes (Acts 11:28 tells of a famine in the time of Claudius, predicted by Agabus, Tacitus, *Annals* 16:13 says 65 A.D. was marked by storms, pestilence, hurricane, plague. Tacitus also reports other earthquakes in the years 51, 53 and 62 A.D., in *Annals* 12:43; 12:58; 15:22); persecutions (there were many for the church before 70 A.D.); evil will reach its peak and the love of many will grow cold; the Gospel will be proclaimed in the whole world (it was proclaimed in most of the Mediterranean world, the world envisioned by the contemporaries of Jesus, by 70 A.D. Cf. Col 1:23; the abomination of desolation (perhaps referring to Jewish Zealots turning the temple into a fortress in 68 A.D., but it could also refer to Roman arms on the holy soil); false prophets working great signs; signs in nature (here we are dealing with apocalyptic language).

It is easy to see that many details in Jesus' prophecies on the fall of Jerusalem were fulfilled before 70 A.D. Presumably, if we are right about the multiple fulfillment pattern, similar phenomena will occur again before the parousia.

In their report of the same prophecies Mark and Luke show the multiple fulfillment pattern less clearly than does Matthew. It is because they wrote for Gentiles, for whom such a pattern would be hard to understand. Mark 13:1-37 mentions only one of the two questions asked by the disciples, the one about the fall of Jerusalem. Yet he does seem to have the parousia in mind, for in verses 24-25 he speaks of signs in the sun, the moon and stars, and verse 26 mentions the Son of Man coming on the clouds. Luke 21:5-36 also opens with the same question. He too mentions fearful things and portents in the sky in 21:11 and in 21:25-27, "there will be signs in sun and moon and stars...the powers of the heavens will be shaken.... And then they will see the Son of Man coming in a cloud with power and great glory."

Luke accordingly has much the same matter and pattern as Mark. But Luke adds a vivid detail in 21:20, "When you see Jerusalem surrounded by armies, then know that its desolation has come near." Some have said this is so vivid that it must have been faked after it happened. We reply to that charge in part 2 of the Appendix, pointing out that it merely reflects the general prejudice of form critics who gratuitously deny the very possibility of prophecies and miracles. Further, the charge here is equivalent to an accusation of dishonesty against Luke, another inadmissible ploy.

R. Brown, however, tries to eviscerate the prophecy by saying: "Its vocabulary is that of the prophetic description of the fall of Jerusalem to the Babylonians in the sixth century B.C..... Like Jeremiah and Ezechiel, Jesus would be threatening disaster to a rebellious Jerusalem, and he would be using traditional language to do so."(6) We have no objection to supposing Jesus deliberately borrowed language from the Old Testament. But that would not prove He had no knowledge of the future. Many an Old Testament prophet re-used the imagery of previous seers to express his own understanding of the future. How tendentious the critics are!

Brown adds still another charge, speaking of the prediction that *not a stone would be left upon a stone*: "If anyone would propose that this represented an exact fore-knowledge of what would happen in A.D. 70, he need simply be reminded that the gigantic blocks of the Temple foundation are still standing firmly one upon the other in Jerusalem."(7)

We find this assertion really astounding. First, the tendency to hyperbole in Hebrew (and other) literature is well known. Second, if Matthew and Luke were composed after 70 A.D., as so many scholars like to say, then both of these evangelists would have known the point Brown mentions. But then, would they not—if they were as dishonest as the critics claim they were—have glossed it over, or, more simply would they not have merely omitted the words? The fact that they did not means that, if they wrote after 70 A.D., they saw no problem, for they recognized as all natives would, a common Semitic exaggeration. The words implied total destruction, which did take place. If they wrote before 70 A.D., then we would still repeat our first point, that Semites commonly used picturesque exaggerations, so that the words, "not a stone upon a stone" would be fulfilled perfectly by the city's total destruction, even if some few rocks were still in place upon others in the ruined, desolate foundations.

NOTES

1 JGM 63, n. 37.
2 Cited on p. 5 above.
3 *Letter* 501, to Melanchthon, Aug. 1, 1521, in *Luther's Correspondence*, Lutheran Publication Society. Philadelphia, 1918, II, 50.
4 *Cf.* George Denzer in JBC II, 359.

5   As to the dates of Theudas and Judas: Josephus puts Theudas in
    middle 40's—early enough to be a sign for 70 A.D. (I believe
    Josephus, writing much later, erred: Theudas belongs in the 30's.
    Judas began his revolt about 7 A.D.—but his followers were active
    until 70 A.D.
6   JGM 69.
7   *Ibid.* 69-70.

3. The Problem of the Parousia

One of the more difficult problems about Jesus' knowledge of the future stems from the many passages about His return at the end, the parousia. It is argued that some texts imply He expected the parousia early in His public life, without dying; that some imply a parousia immediately after His death—or within the lifetime of His hearers; or a delayed parousia with apocalyptic signs, perhaps indefinitely delayed. We will examine each group.

1. Parousia early in His public life, without death

The illustrious Albert Schweitzer was about the only one to favor this view. He was strongly impressed by the words of Jesus in Mt 10:23, "When they persecute you in one town, flee to the next; for truly, I say to you, you will not have gone through all the towns of Israel, before the Son of man comes." Schweitzer tried to identify this passage with Mk 6:7-13, in which Jesus sent His disciples on a trial mission throughout Galilee. If his contention were true, Mt 10:23 would seem to make parousia imminent, even before His death.

Two observations. First, Schweitzer must have thought Jesus was some sort of a silly deluded visionary. For he did not think Jesus knew Himself as divine, yet Jesus would think He was to appear in heavenly glory, and soon. For what reason would Jesus think that? The fact that He had worked miracles would not warrant such a belief—Moses and other prophets had done such things. So Jesus would have had no sound reason for such a hope, and thus would have been a deluded visionary. Second, as already implied, almost no one today thinks the two passages refer to the same situation.

To what does Mt 10:23 actually refer? One view holds that Jesus was speaking of the time of persecution to come after His death. He said the disciples would not run out of places to flee to before He would return. The *coming* is best understood within the common Scriptural concept of *visitation*, God intervening to help, to save, to punish.(1) The intervention of Jesus, His coming, probably refers to the wars of 66-70 A.D. and the fall of Jerusalem, which put an end to the Jewish persecutions before the disciples ran out of places in which to preach. In the city's destruction, Jesus "visited Jerusalem," as we gather from chapter 24 of Matthew.(2) Further, in view of the fact that Scripture often utilizes multiple fulfillments of prophecies (and Mt 24 is a specially good instance),(3) this saying may also have another fulfillment—at the end-time. During that final persecution there still will be places to flee to when the last visitation of the Son of Man is taking place in the parousia.

2. Parousia Soon after Christ's Death

At the last supper Jesus says: "And when I go and prepare a place for you, I will come again and will take you to myself" (Jn 14:2). Brown comments: "This [a parousia right after His death] seems to be the import of Jn 14:3 where Jesus says that he is departing but will return to take his disciples along with him. A comparison with 1 Th 4:16-17 suggests that Christians would have understood this return in terms of the Parousia."(4)

We find the reasoning quite unconvincing. First, the Gospel text contains no specific indication of *when* Jesus would come for His disciples. Nothing in Jn 14:3 points to a time soon after His death. Second, if we were to use 1 Thess 4:16-17 as a confirmation, we would have another puzzle, for that Epistle was written in 51 A.D., which is not at all *right after* the death of Jesus.

Furthermore, we do not admit that 1 Thess 4:15-17 indicates Paul expected the parousia in his own lifetime. It reads: "For this we declare to you by the word of the Lord, that we who are alive, who are left until the coming of the Lord, shall not precede those who have fallen asleep. For the Lord himself will descend from heaven with a cry of command, with the archangel's call, and with the sound of the trumpet of God. And the dead in Christ will rise first; then we who are alive, who are left, shall be caught up together with them in the clouds to meet the Lord in the air; and so we shall always be with the Lord." The point is that Paul says twice, "we who are alive." Yet there are several reasons for rejecting the view that Paul expected the parousia soon. First, this type of language is merely a way of making things vivid. Many classroom teachers, (including myself) often speak in the first person, saying *I* or *we*, with no notion of giving any information about themselves: it is just a way of making things concrete. Similarly, Paul in 1 Cor 4:6 explicitly says he is using the names Paul and Apollos merely for such a purpose. So the use of the first person, or Paul, proves nothing.

Secondly, if one wants to say Paul did expect the parousia soon, he must deny that Paul wrote 2 Thessalonians, for it was written precisely to quiet the vain notions of the Thesslonians on this score. To do so, in chapter 2, Paul says the end will not come unless first the antichrist appears and the great apostasy takes place. But no apostasy was in sight then: instead, the Church was growing rapidly. Form critics do not mind denying the authenticity of 2 Thess, for they prefer inconclusive internal evidence to external witnesses. But we note that the ancient testimony for Pauline authorship of 2 Thess is just as good as it is for 1 Thess. So we find the claim that Paul expected the end soon to be quite groundless (see specifically 2 Thess 2:2-3).

Hence, we need not strain our interpretation at all if we take Jn 14:3 to refer to the meeting with Jesus at the parousia at the end, whenever that might be, and add that all meet Him right after their deaths as well.

During His trial, Jesus said to the high priest: "You will see the Son of Man...coming with the clouds of heaven" (Mk 14:62). Although this pronouncement refers to the parousia, there is nothing in it to indicate when it will happen. The high priest will see it, he is not told when.

At the Last Supper Jesus said: "I shall not drink again of the fruit of the vine until that day when I drink it new in the kingdom of God" (Mk 14:25). Actually, the kingdom was established with power, i.e., by miraculous displays, after the death of Jesus.(5) True, its formal expansion had to wait until Pentecost. Yet since the "kingdom [was] present in Jesus in some mysterious manner during his public ministry,"(6) surely it was present all the more in Him in His risen appearances, for then He had won the victory over sin and death. If then, as is most likely, He also drank some wine when He ate with the disciples after the resurrection, he would be really drinking it in the new phase of the kingdom.

While on the Cross, Jesus promised the good thief: "Today you will be with me in Paradise" (Lk 23:42-43). Could that mean Jesus expected resurrection on the very day of His death ("today")? By no means. He had predicted resurrection on the *third* day. The promise simply means what it says, i.e., the thief was to be with Jesus in paradise, that is, in heaven immediately upon dying.

3. Parousia in the Lifetime of His Hearers

We analyzed Mk 9:1, which N. Perrin and others think refers to an early parousia in the lifetime of Jesus' hearers, in the Appendix.(7) There are a number of other texts that deserve consideration here.

At the end of the long discourse in which Jesus answered questions from the disciples about the signs that would come before the fall of Jerusalem and before the parousia, we find this saying: "This generation will not pass away till all these things take place" (Mt 24:34; cf. Mk 13:30; Lk 21:32). As we already saw above(8) Matthew seems to be writing in a multiple fulfillment pattern in chapter 24, so that details may in general refer to both events. Mark and Luke seem to be cast in a similar pattern, though they each explicitly mention only one question by the disciples, that about the fall of Jerusalem. We think this saying refers most easily and clearly to the fall of Jerusalem. Yet if we wanted to take "this generation" to refer not to the whole of mankind, but just to the Christian generation or regime, since there is to be no new dispensation to replace the Christian regime (cf. Gal 1:8-9), the second fulfillment of the saying would consist in the fact that the Christian regime will not pass away before the parousia.

Early in St. John's Gospel we find Jesus speaks to Nathanael. Jesus had impressed him by saying: "Before Philip called you, when you were under the fig tree, I saw you." Nathanael replied: "Rabbi, you are the Son of God! You are the King of Israel!" Then Jesus spoke the line that concerns us here: "Truly, truly I say to you, you will see heaven opened, and the angels of God ascending and descending upon the Son of Man" (Jn 1:51).

Could this refer to the parousia, and mean that it would come in Nathanael's lifetime? No, for two reasons: (1) Nathanael was almost certainly dead before the Fourth Gospel was written. But since John wrote near 90-100 A.D., the prediction, if it meant the parousia would come in the lifetime of Nathanael, would have been shown false; in which case would John have mentioned it? No, it must have implied something else. (2) There is an abrupt shift from the singular *you* in v.50 to the plural *you* in v. 51, suggesting this saying was actually given not just to Nathanael, but to a group or crowd.

What positively did the verse mean? Before answering, we must recall that this is John's Gospel, one which seems to be of a very different genre from that of the Synoptics. John may just be creating a special "theological construct" here. F. J. Moloney suggests(9) that John was using a then current rabbinic understanding of the dream of Jacob (Gen 28:11-12), which spoke of the angels of God as standing for Moses and Aaron on Sinai. The sense would then be that Jesus, the Son of Man, would be the new means by which God communicates with man.

And of course there could have been a special vision to Nathanael and/or others, which is not recorded in Scripture.

In the final episode of the last chapter of John (21:15-23), after Jesus had asked Peter three times, "Do you love me?" and had given him charge of His lambs and sheep, Jesus foretold Peter's death. Immediately thereafter, "Peter turned and saw following them the disciple whom Jesus loved.... When Peter saw him, he said to Jesus, 'Lord, what about this man?' Jesus said to him, 'If it is my will that he remain until I come, what is that to you? Follow me!' The saying spread abroad among the brethren that this disciple was not to die; yet Jesus did not say to him that he was not to die, but, 'if it is my will' that he remain until I come, what is that to you?'''

R. Brown comments: "The obvious import of the saying (v.22) is that Jesus will return during the Disciple's lifetime, and this is how Christians interpreted it (21:23). But since the Beloved Disciple was dying or dead, the Johannine author of Chap. 21 employs casuistry to show that Jesus' promise was not absolute."(10)

We grant that this saying of Jesus, being enigmatic, as many of His saying were, could have been misunderstood. However, is it really "obvious" that Jesus' words actually foretold the parousia as coming during John's lifetime? Not at all. If it were as obvious as Brown thinks, would John have recorded the unfulfilled prophecy, especially since John so plainly attributes to Jesus divinity, consciousness of His own divinity, and its concomitant boundless knowledge? Or is it "obvious" that the explanation given in the Gospel is mere "Casuistry?" By no means. Jesus often used enigmatic forms of speech, e.g., He told the crowds to call no man father or teacher (Mt 23:8-10). Father Brown does not object to such titles publicly. Again, the mysterious words of Mt 19:12, "There are eunuchs who have made themselves eunuchs for the sake of the kingdom of heaven. He who is able to receive this, let him receive it." Only Origen, it is said, interpreted these words literally and proceeded with self-castration. And there are more examples (e.g., Mt 19:17; 19:24; 20:16; 13:12). In speaking enigmatically, Jesus was following in the tradition of the ancient prophets. Let us picture the situation realistically. Jesus had just predicted Peter's martyrdom. Peter notices John. (Peter is frequently depicted in the Gospels as impulsive.) So he asks: "What about him?" No one likes to be manipulated—Jesus refused to be put "on the spot." A kindly sympathetic but enigmatic reply is given. In effect Jesus says: *If* I would want him to remain, that is none of your business. Considering the evidence in this light, could a jury be found to enter a verdict of ignorance and error against Jesus?

4. The Parousia Indefinitely Delayed

In our examination of Matthew 24 we tried to point out how it utilizes a multiple fulfillment pattern so that certain signs apply both to the fall of Jerusalem and to the parousia.(11) Do these signs signalize a definite time, or at least do they enable a person to be certain about it when it is close? It seems not, for two reasons. First, Jesus often said His return would be like that of the "thief in the night," that is, quite unforeseen (Mt 24:43-44; Lk 12:40; cf. 1 Th 5:2-4), or like the unexpected return of the master (Mt 25:13-30; Mk 13:33-37; Lk 19:12-26; Mt 24:50; Lk 12:46), and again that, as in the days before the deluge, they were marrying and giving in marriage (business as usual) and they did not know until the flood was upon them, so it will before the parousia (Mt 24:37-39; Lk 17:26-27). A few, like Noe, might read the signs; but most men will not. Secondly, for the most part, the signs given in the Gospels are rather vague and hard to interpret precisely because of apocalyptic coloring.

More importantly, it is even charged that Jesus Himself did not know the day, since in Mk 13:32 He said: "But of that day or that hour no one knows, not even the angels in heaven, nor the Son, but only the Father."

Many commentators take this text at what seems face value and insist Jesus was ignorant on the matter. E. Haenchen proposes that only later did the Church become opposed to admitting ignorance in Jesus; earlier it accepted that inferiority in line with the mentality of 1 Cor 15:28 according to which at the end "the Son Himself will also be subjected to him who put all things under him."(12) B. Rigaux holds that Jesus *taught* that He did not know the time, but *hoped* it would be soon.(13) R. Brown, after reviewing the different possible times for the parousia proposed by the exegetes, adds:

> Since it is not reasonable to suppose that he knew about the Parousia but for some mysterious reason expressed himself obscurely, one is almost forced to take at face value the admission of Mk. 13:32 that Jesus did not know.... Is it totally

inconceivable that, since Jesus did not know when the Parousia would occur, he tended to think and say that it would occur soon?(14)

Brown must think Jesus a bit moronic! *Since* Jesus did *not* know, *therefore*, He tended to think and say the parousia would be soon. Any sane person refrains from making conclusions based on ignorance as the major premise. With such ratiocination it becomes easier to categorize the logic of Brown's initial judgment: "It is not reasonable to suppose that he [Jesus] knew about the Parousia."

Our commentators seem to have forgotten that there are two ways of writing about Jesus in the New Testament: (1) to note things associated with His divinity, (2) to note the things associated with His humanity. Since He had both a true humanity and a true divinity, both forms of speech were proper. Thus in three speeches in Acts (2:14-36; 3:12-26; 4:8-12) Peter speaks almost exclusively within the human category. Paul in 1 Cor 15:28 speaks of the Son as becoming "subject" to the Father. And John, along with evident emphasis on the divinity of Jesus, has Him say (Jn 14:28), "The Father is greater than I," speaking within the human category, of course. Therefore, it is not at all strange if Jesus, whose Spirit moved the evangelists, expresses Himself in the same way at times. Accordingly Mk 13:32 would mean: As far as human means of knowledge are concerned, I do not have that information. Pope St. Gregory the Great summed up the conclusions of the patristic thinking in these words: "[Jesus] knew the day and hour of judgment *in* the nature of humanity, but yet not *from* the nature of humanity."(15)

To obviate possible criticism a concluding observation is in place. We do not claim to have proved that Mk 13:32 conveys Gregory's conclusion. In this text, as with other texts we merely wish to show that one can *plausibly* offer an interpretation that in no way implies ignorance or error on the part of Jesus.

NOTES

1 *Cf.* Xavier Leon-Dufour and others, *Vocabulaire de Theologie Biblique*, Cerf, Paris, 1962, col. 1120-21. F. Zorell, *Lexicon Hebraicum et Aramaicum Veteris Testamenti*, Pontificium Institutum Biblicum Roma, 1961, 662-63.
2 *Cf.* Mt. 24; Lk. 19:44.
3 See pp 54-56 above.
4 JGM 71-72.
5 See Appendix, pp 196-97 below.
6 JBC II, 783.
7 See Appendix, Pt. 2.
8 See pp 54-56 above.
9 F.J. Moloney, "The Johannine Son of God" in *Biblical Theology Bulletin* 6.2-3 (June-October 1976) 178-180. On the rabbinic view see *Midrash Rabbah, Genesis* 68.12 (tr. H. Freedman) Soncino, London, 1939, II.625. *Cf.* also O. Cullmann, *The Johannine Circle* (tr. J. Bowden) Westminster, Philadelphia, 1976, 44.
10 JGM 74.
11 See pp 54-56 above.
12 E. Haenchen, *Der Weg Jesu*, Topelmann, Berlin, 1966, 452.
13 B. Rigaux, "La Seconde venue de Jesus" in *La Venue du Messie* in *Recherches bibliques* 6. Desclee de Brouwer, Paris, 1962, 190.
14 JGM 77-78.
15 See pp 122-24 below.

4. Messiahship and Divinity

Major objections to Jesus' Knowledge of His messianic dignity stem from Wrede's views on the Messianic secret, and from certain form critical analyses of Mk 8:27-33. Since we pursue these errors in the Appendix,(1) we shall here consider other charges.

John A. T. Robinson claims to have found three variant Christologies in the Gospels and Acts: (1) in the Gospels, Jesus seems to be the Messiah already during His public ministry; (2) Acts 2:36 says that "God made Him [the crucified Jesus] Lord and Messiah!" (3) Acts 3:19-21 urges: "Repent therefore, and turn again, that your sins may be blotted out, that times of refreshing may come from the presence of the Lord, and that he may send the Christ appointed for you, Jesus." Robinson comments: "Jesus here is only the Christ elect, the Messianic age has yet to be inaugurated;" Jesus will become the Messiah only at the end.(2) Thus we have, according to Robinson, conflicting Christologies, with Scripture itself featuring contradictions. And also, according to the "most primitive" Christology, the third one: Jesus did not know He was Messiah, but only thought of Himself as the "Servant".

There is some trouble here, however, we read the Acts 3:18, "But what God foretold by the mouth of all the prophets, that his Christ should suffer, he thus fulfilled." This sentence comes immediately before the passage in which Robinson thinks he can find the most primitive Christology, namely, Jesus will become

Messiah only at His second coming. Verse 18 clearly proclaims Jesus as Messiah already when He suffered. Robinson escapes the trap by saying Luke interpolated the words "that His Messiah would suffer." What an arbitrary procedure! Simply deny the evidence.

But more basically, even if the texts were as clearly in Robinson's favor as he claims, there is another solution. Paul many times speaks of Christians as sons of God (e.g., Rom 8:14; Gal 3:26; 4:6-7); yet in Rom 8:19,23 he tells us: "Creation waits with eager longing for the revealing of the sons of God...we ourselves...groan inwardly as we wait for adoption as sons." That is, we already have the beginning of sonship, but not its full possession and manifestation. Similarly, Jesus was the Messiah from the start, but came to its fuller manifestation and fruition in stages; the final, perfect manifestation of His messianic, redemptive mission is still to come at the end of time.

Similar objections surround Christ's knowledge of His divinity. For example, R. Brown raises this objection:

> ...when we ask whether during his ministry Jesus, a Palestinian Jew, knew that he was God, we are asking whether he identified himself and the Father—and, of course, he did not. Undoubtedly, some would wish to attribute to Jesus an anticipated understanding of the later broadness of the term 'God' (or, indeed, even expect him to speak in trinitarian terminology), but can serious scholars simply *presume* that Jesus could speak and think in the vocabulary and philosophy of later times?(3)

Tilt that question somewhat: Can serious scholars simply *presume* Jesus lacked divine knowledge—which would surely include the information in question? Brown himself more than once admits that the Scriptural evidence on the knowledge of Jesus is inconclusive.(4) So, until it has been *proved* that Jesus did not know who He was, it is not *presumption* to suppose Jesus knew of the Trinity and knew who He was. Further, if we press Brown's language strictly, and say *HE* did not know, it would be undiluted heresy. To be charitable, we assume Brown really means to question whether this knowledge registered on the human intellect of Jesus.

Secondly, it is not at all necessary for any person, human or divine, to use the language of the Council of Chalcedon, or later speculation, in order to know of the Holy Trinity. Semites particularly were adept at accepting several seemingly conflicting statements as true without trying to harmonize them. Jesus often taught in this pattern, e.g., in Mt 6:6 He said: "When you pray, go into your room and shut the door and pray to your Father who is in secret." Yet Mt 5:16 says: "Let your light so shine before men, that they may see your good works and give glory to your Father who is in heaven." A Westerner would want to know how to avoid the appearance of contradiction here; a Semite could comfortably believe both. Similarly, a Semite could comfortably, if assured on proper authority, accept that the Father is God and the Son is God, yet there is only one God, without endeavoring to reconcile the statements. For that matter we, with all our vaunted sophistication and speculative ability, are still unable to explain away the seeming contradiction in the Holy Trinity. We said, "if assured on proper authority", because the fact that monotheism had been hammered in for so many centuries would create a psychological difficulty unless adequate authority were at hand to assure the faithful listeners: "Thus says the Lord."

Thirdly, Brown puts the question badly when he asks if Jesus would identify Himself with the Father and replies "of course he did not." For "identify" normally means to assert there is *no* difference. But there is a difference: the Father and the Son are distinct persons, even though they, with the Holy Spirit, form only one God. Moreover (without entering the problem of the literary genre of John(5)), we read in Jn 10:30, "The Father and I are one." Jn 14:9 adds: "He who has seen me has seen the Father." Still more strongly in Jn 8:58: "Before Abraham was, 'I Am.'" We do not presume to have solved the problem of the fourth Gospel's literary genre, yet as a minimum we may say this: the writer did not consider it *presumption* to suppose Jesus knew what Brown considers too sophisticated for Jesus to have known.(6)

A further objection is raised from Mk 10:18. A young man came to Jesus and, addressing Him as "Good Teacher," asked what he should do to attain eternal life. Jesus replied: "Why do you call me good? No one is good but God alone." Lk 18:19 is verbatim the same, while Mt 19:17 is a bit different: "Why do you ask me about what is good? One there is who is good."

As Lane points out, the young man showed Jesus unusual reverence, in kneeling to Him—a deference reserved for revered teachers of the Law—and in calling Him "Good Teacher." Such a title is virtually without parallel in Jewish sources."(7)

Jesus replied by using an enigmatic form of speech, to arouse meditation on a sublime truth. Spiritual writers would probably put it this way today: (1) only God is the source of His own goodness; really, He is one with it, while humans merely participate in that goodness after receiving it. As St. Paul reminds us (1 Cor 4:7): "What have you that you did not receive?" (2) strictly, we should imitate 1 Jn 4:8 and say that God *is* goodness, rather than that He *has* goodness. (3) goodness in men is not goodness in the same sense as it is in God. The term *good* is used analogically, i.e., it applies to God and to men in senses that are partly the same, partly different.

Now it is evident that it would not fit with the divine economy for Jesus to make all these distinctions, and then formally add: "I *am* God." A revelation, so flat, so prematurely given would have been difficult for His hearers to grasp. (Think of the difficulties His disciples had in assimilating simpler things about the nature of the suffering Messiah and His coming resurrection.(8)) Yet Jesus, in that enigmatic style, partly revealing and partly ambiguous, which many skilled teachers use, did want to convey some of the ideas just sketched.(9) And He did succeed in provoking thought as witnessed by the ensuing Pharisaic opposition.

Matthew's report of Jesus saying, "Why do you ask me about what is good? One there is who is good," could be an instance of that *approximation* in reporting described in *Divino afflante Spiritu*.(10) Nevertheless can anybody actually prove that Jesus is not responsible for these words as well as the words recorded in Mark and Luke?

A statement by R. Bultman (quoted already for a different purpose) is pertinent here: "...if the Christ who died such a death was the pre-existent Son of God, what could death mean for him? Obviously very little, if he knew that he would rise again in three days?''(11) Bultmann does not believe in the incarnation at all.(12) But he does perceive, correctly, that if there had been an incarnation, then Jesus would consciously know He was God and would know He would rise again in three days.

The Epistle to the Hebrews (4:15) is often quoted as supporting a general charge of ignorance in Jesus, one which would, probably, include ignorance of His Messiahship and divinity: "We have not a high priest who is unable to sympathize with our weaknesses, but one who in every respect (*kath' homoioteta*) has been tempted (*pepeirasmenon*) as we are, yet without sinning." So, the argument goes, since *we* are ignorant, *He* must have been ignorant. The basic flaw in this line of thought is that it ignores the literary genre of Hebrews, generally admitted to be homiletic. Within that genre, it is common to speak a bit loosely, and therefore it would be out of place to attempt precise deductions from mere implications. Further, who would know just where to draw the line, if we ignored the genre? Would that text quoted refer to merely external, physical sufferings? Did He have various kinds of bodily diseases like other humans? Mental illnesses? Did He even suffer from psychoses as many persons do? And so on. Common Catholic faith and piety have provided interpretative guidelines that critical exegesis ignores to its own detriment. We are attempting to remain within this tradition.

NOTES

1 See pp 202-05.
2 John A.T. Robinson, "The Most Primitive Christology of All?" in *Journal of Theological Studies* 7 (1956) 177-189.
3 JGM 87 (italics in original).
4 *Ibid.* 42, 68, 99-100.
5 See pp 26-28.
6 JGM 56.
7 William L. Lane, *Commentary on the Gospel of Mark*, in NICNT,

Eerdmans, Grand Rapids, Michigan, 1974, 364-65.
8   See pp 205-06 below.
9   See p. 64 above.
10 *Enchiridion Biblicum* 559.
11 KM 8, cited above, pp 42-43.
12 KM 7.

5. Scripture: Support for Jesus' Knowledge

We will limit our investigation to the Synoptics, omitting St. John's Gospel, not because it has little to offer, but because the problem of its literary genre complicates the presentation of the matter.(1)

1. Extraordinary or Superhuman Knowledge in General

All Gospels report several occasions on which Jesus read the interior thoughts of others. Thus on the occasion of the healing of the paralytic who was let down through the roof, the scribes and Pharisees were grumbling interiorly because Jesus had claimed to forgive the man's sins. "And immediately Jesus, perceiving in his spirit that they thus questioned within themselves, said to them, 'Why do you question thus in your hearts:'" (Mk 2:8). With less detail, substantially the same text appears in Mt 9:4 and Lk 5:22.

On another occasion, when the disciples had been discussing among themselves who was the greater, Jesus, though not present, knew it. Lk 9:47 reports, "When Jesus perceived the thought of their hearts, he took a child, and put him by his side, and said to them...." Mk 9:33-37 does not explicitly say that Jesus knew, but indicates it in that He asked them what they had talked about; whereupon they were silent in shame. He then said (Mk. 9:35): "If any one would be first, he must be the last of all and servant of all." He then put a child in front of them and continued His reflections.

Before His triumphal entry into Jerusalem, Jesus sent on ahead two disciples after telling them where they would find a tethered colt upon which no man had yet ridden; they were to fetch the colt and if anyone should object, Jesus added, simply inform him that "the Master needs it"; and there would be no further trouble (Mk 11:1-3). Lk 19:28-31 gives almost an identical account; Mt 21:1-3 is practically the same, the detail about no one having ridden the animal before being omitted. Obviously Jesus knew at a distance what His disciples would meet with. Brown notes that in Jn 12:14 Jesus Himself finds the animal.(2) We could either recall the adage "Qui facit per alios, facit per se" (the master operates through his underlings) or we could consider this an example of Semitic approximation, of which Pius XII spoke.(3)

Again, according to Mk 14:12-16, just before the Passover Jesus sends on ahead two disciples after telling them how they would find a man carrying a jar; they should follow him into a house, and then ask the master of the house about the place where Jesus could observe the Passover; whereupon he would show them a room made ready. Brown notes that a parallel passage, Mt 26:17, has "no such hint of mysterious knowledge."(4) Neither does the passage deny or contradict Mark's report. Matthew simply opted for a briefer account—in spite of Bultmann's claim that Matthew and Luke are more detailed than Mark.(5)

Only Matthew (17:24-27) favors us with the remarkable incident in which Jesus tells Peter to go fishing, to pull up the first nibble, and, lo!, he would find a coin in its mouth sufficient to pay the temple tax for himself and for Jesus. Here we seem to have not only special knowledge, but probably the exercise of miraculous power: to cause such a coin-bearing fish to strike at precisely the right time and place. Many critics are inclined to dismiss this catch as a fake, saying it resembles things done by Greek wonder-workers. But D. J. McCarthy, commenting on the claim that literary similarities might show the Sinai covenant was modeled after Hittite treaties says: "It should be an axiom of form study that similar situations call forth similar responses, and thus formal similarity hardly proves a causal nexus between similar manifestations in different cultures."(6) He meant that literary similarities do not prove one work is based on another. The same principles apply here: similarities of Gospel miracles to Greek stories do not prove the literary form of the Gospel stories was patterned after that of the Greeks, still less that the Gospel incidents were just invented. Furthermore, as we see in the appendix, the similarities between Gospel miracles and alleged wonders by pagans are not nearly so great as the critics claim.(7)

We could list more instances of special knowledge on the part of Jesus, but these should suffice. Could we say that some of these cases, such as those in which Jesus knows the thoughts of others, are merely instances of keen human perception involving nothing necessarily divine? Yes, to some extent it could be successfully argued. Such perceptiveness, however, could not reasonably account for all the details mentioned. Does such knowledge prove divinity? Clearly not. Some Old Testament prophets, Ezechiel, for instance, had similar powers: while in Babylon he knew what was going on in Jerusalem. In fact, there are cases today of otherwise ordinary persons who claim they have extra-sensory perception. Are there at work merely natural powers which we do not yet understand? Even though these cases do not prove divine knowledge in Jesus, divine knowledge could, as a matter of fact, have been involved. The evangelists do not explicitly assert the supernatural character of such knowledge, though they seem to imply it.

2. The Evidence of the Special Titles: Son of Man, Messiah, Son of God

Before considering separate titles, we should recall the conclusion to our treatment of retrojection in the Synoptics.(8) Under certain conditions retrojection is possible without falsification. The retrojection of a name or title is possible, provided that the agent in some way revealed himself to be or do what the title indicates. In general, however, the Synoptic genre is such that even this retrojection is unlikely; it could be allowed more easily in John.

Jesus spoke of Himself as the Son of Man in three respects: earthly, suffering, eschatological.(9) Could the Church have retrojected this title? It is unlikely because of the genre proper to the Synoptics; it is still more unlikely in that the title is found exclusively on the lips of Jesus. There are only two exceptions, its use by the dying Stephen (Acts 7:56) and a single use by the enemies of Jesus (echoing Him, Jn 12:34). Would it not be strange for the Church to invent a title, and then drop it so absolutely? An attempted reply argues that since the title was Semitic, it did not set well with Greek Christianity. That reason is not convincing, for Mark and Luke who were writing for Greeks did use it, while Peter (Acts 2:14-36; 3:12-26; 4:9-12) did not use it when speaking to Semites.

Much ingenuity and learning have recently been exercised on the question of whether "Son of Man" was used in the Aramaic of Jesus' time as a mere equivalent for *I*. It seems that it was.

J. Fitzmyer asserts that, "in none of the phases of the Aramaic language has one been able to show that *bar enas* was ever used in a titular sense, for some 'apocalyptic' Son of Man. The evidence that we have at present...supports the contention... that the apocalyptic Son of Man must exit from the stage of the NT study."(10)

But his argument, and the other arguments are all inconclusive: even if the phrase was often used as an equivalent for *I*, and even if we do not find it used for an apocalyptic figure in the Aramaic of Jesus' time, it does not follow that Jesus Himself could not have used it to hint that He was the one mentioned in Dan 7:13. It could well be that the very vagueness was intended by Jesus, in line with His gradual self-revelation, to provoke thought. That vagueness could then explain why the Church later dropped the use of the title, except for faithfully reporting that Jesus often used it Himself.

Our study of Wrede and our form critical analysis of Mk 8:29-33 provide sound proof for maintaining that Jesus did know He was the Messiah.(11) We see that the additions by Matthew could have been retrojected, but that this was unlikely. If the title of Messiah had been retrojected in the basic narrative of Mark, nothing would remain of the scene except the question of what people in general were saying, which would be a fringe matter, not the heart of the scene. So, to retroject the title itself would mean we would have a genre looser than midrash; for midrash requires a substantial core of factual matter, surrounded by a fringe of meditative embellishment. In Mark, since the title is the core, the whole scene, not just the fringe, would be fancy. But the genre of the Synoptics is not looser than midrash.

As to retrojection of the title in other episodes, we could admit the speculative possibility; but in practice, such a massive amount of retrojection would have been required that its consistent application would be astounding.

The title "Son of God" presents a problem of precise meaning. Hosea 11:1 speaks of all Israel as God's son. A virtuous Israelite also could be called a son of God (Sir 4:10; Ps 73:15). What did the title "Son of God" convey when used in reference to Jesus?

The demons often call Him Son of God (Mk 3:11; 5:7; Mt 8:29; 4:3,6; Lk 8:28). The disciples sometimes do so also (Mt 14:33; 16:16).

More important, Jesus applies the title to Himself, and frequently speaks of God as His Father. In itself the title Son of God is not clearly a designation of divinity, yet there is something very special about its use for and by Jesus.

The parable of the wicked tenants (Mk 12:1-12) embodies at the very least some allusion to Jesus as God's special Son. In v.6 we find the Father sending His beloved (*agapeton*) Son. It is well known that the Septuagint often uses this word to translate Hebrew *yahid*, which stands for *only* Son. In spite of this, Lane writes: "Without declaring his own transcendent sonship, Jesus clearly implies that the Sanhedrin has rejected God's final messenger."(12) We think Lane has weakened the parable's message unduly, for in the parable, the son is a natural son.

Matthew 11:27 (Lk 10:22)—the "thunderbolt fallen from the Johannine sky"—has been interpreted to stand for strict divine sonship, because it asserts that Jesus has the same knowledge of the Father that the Father has of Him: a divine knowledge implying a divine being.(13) However, this interpretation is criticized as being too metaphysical. Jeremias propoes the view that this unit is basically a Semitic proverb (with repetition, to make up for the Semitic lack of a good reciprocal pronoun) conveying the idea that only a father and a son really know each other.(14) Jeremias thinks this may have been a point of departure for Johannine theology. We think John quite capable of theologizing for himself, from his own association with Jesus. But to return to the proposal of Jeremias, it would be in place to add that even if Jeremias is right, Jesus would at least be applying the saying to Himself in such a way as to claim a special sonship beyond that which others could ever claim.

This observation is in harmony with the fact that Jesus constantly speaks of God as His father—a form of address not common in the Judaism of His time—and constantly draws a distinction between *my* Father and *your* Father, again, an indication of at least a special relationship. This special character is heightened by His use of *Abba*. Jeremias has argued forcefully how this imples a unique and familiar relationship.(15) The word seems proper to small children, like our "Daddy." No Jew would have dared to speak so intimately with Yahweh. But Jesus did.

We grant that all the above indications do not provide conclusive proof that Jesus referred to Himself explicitly as the natural, divine Son of the Father. We think this lack of precision was intended by Jesus, as part of His gradual self-revelation, and we recall the similar or greater vagueness of the term Son of Man.(16)

We come to the theophanies in which at the baptism and the transfiguration of Jesus a voice speaks from the sky (Mk 1:11): "Thou art my beloved (*agapetos*) Son; with thee I am well pleased." Lk 3:22 has the identical wording. Mt 3:17 represents the voice as speaking to the bystanders: "This is my beloved Son." In the accounts of the transfiguration, Mk 9:7 and parallels all agree in using the third person: "This is my beloved Son." The differences in the readings for the two events is not great enough for us to have to call the sayings into question: it is a case of Semitic "approximation" of which Pope Pius XII spoke.(17) We note the *agapetos* in all versions and recall again that the Septuagint often used it to render Hebrew *yahid, only Son*.

The form critics are committed in advance, by their

prejudice,(18) to reject anything miraculous or supernatural; they must deny these theophanies. That is, to say the least, a most unscholarly stance, to reject a thesis without a hearing. Those who are free of such prejudice are free to accept the theophanies.

Could the theophanies be pure fancy, to dramatize the Church's later belief in the divinity of Jesus? No, for such a dramatization would be looser than midrash; it would lack the necessary historical core to keep it within the range of the Synoptic genre.

A further objection is raised: if the crowds really heard this voice, then there could have been no gradual self-revelation. The facts? At the transfiguration only three disciples were present; we have already dealt with the question of their receptivity.(19) At the baptism many indeed were present. What actually registered on their minds? After days, weeks, years with Jesus and in spite of all His miracles, the disciples failed to comprehend the message and mission of their Master. Should we expect the crowd at the Jordan to have had a greater power of assimilating the revelations so contrary to their mental framework? Only after Easter, when Jesus opened their hearts to understand (cf. Lk 24:45) did they really grasp many things.

3. Other Scriptural Evidence

A number of other bits of evidence may be pieced together to show Jesus' knowledge. First, we may comment on exorcism as a sign that the kingdom has come. Jesus said (Lk 11:20; Mt 12:28): "But if it is by the finger of God [Mt has "by the Spirit of God] that I cast out demons, then the kingdom of God has come upon you." Strangely, Bultmann comments: "The latter [saying just cited] can, in my view, claim the highest degree of authenticity which we can make for any saying of Jesus: it is full of that feeling of eschatological power which must have characterized the activity of Jesus."(20) We note two things. First, of course, Bultmann does not really believe Jesus cast out devils, for he denies anything miraculous or supernatural. Secondly, his subjectivity is showing again, for he depends on the "*feeling* of eschatological power", which he seems to sense in this saying.

Persons who are not hampered by such unscholarly prejudices have no reason for not accepting the incident and saying as genuine. The objection is made that the people then were apt to confuse illness, especially epilepsy, with possession. There is no evidence of such confusion in this incident. Surely, whatever the man suffered from, Jesus did cure him, miraculously. Further, Jesus did it to prove the Kingdom was at hand. Now the power to work a miracle, whether healing or exorcism, must come ultimately from God Himself. But God, being Truth, cannot provide power to support a false claim. Therefore, the Kingdom really was at hand; and Jesus was aware of it, and of His power to exorcise.

Second, Jesus referred to Himself as greater than Jonah, Solomon and the Temple. On one occasion when the Pharisees had asked for a sign, Jesus refused (not, as some say, because He refused to use miracles as a support to faith, but because of the hardness of the Pharisees, who had already seen so many signs; actually, He did explicitly appeal to miracles as proof more than once, e.g., Mk 2:1-12; Lk 11:20.(21)). Jesus then said they would have the sign of Jonah, and added (Mt 12:41-42), "The men of Nineveh will arise at the judgment with this generation and condemn it; for they repented at the preaching of Jonah, and behold, something greater than Jonah is here. The queen of the South will arise at the judgment with this generation and condemn it; for she came from the ends of the earth to hear the wisdom of Solomon, and behold, something greater than Solomon is here."

We cannot gather much from the reference to Jonah, for, as we saw,(22) the fact that Jesus speaks of Jonah in this way could be mere literary allusion, which need not prove the book of Jonah to be historical. But it does show He knew He was greater than Solomon—a large claim. Nor could this text be retrojected, for it is part of a controversy with scribes and Pharisees; there were no such debates after Easter. If someone classifies the scene as entirely fictional, good only for meditation purposes, we reply that that would be looser in genre than midrash, far too loose for the genre of the Synoptics.

On the occasion of another clash with the Pharisees, when His disciples plucked grain on the sabbath, Jesus appealed to the example of David, and added (Mt 12:6) "There is something here greater than the temple."

Third, Jesus claimed authority over the Torah. On the occasion just described, Jesus proclaimed: "The Son of Man is Lord of the Sabbath" (Mk 12:8; Lk 6:5; Mk 2:28). These words were not at all spoken by Jesus, commentators say; they were a comment by the evangelists.(23) Be that as it may, there is absolutely no doubt that Jesus claimed authority to revise the Torah, as stated in Matthew 5, verses 22, 27, 32, 34, 39, "You have heard it was said to men of old.... But I say to you...." Pannenberg comments: "Jesus set his *ego* against and above the authority of Moses himself, without any kind of justification. However, the authority above Moses himself, which Jesus here claims for himself, can be none other than the authority of God. Thus...Jesus makes himself the spokesman for God himself."(24)

As Pannenberg phrases it, Jesus claims an authority which really belongs to God. Did Jesus claim to have it because of being God, or as a delegate? If we may indulge in an *argumentum ad hominem*: those who wish to limit the knowledge of Jesus greatly insist that He could not rise above the mental horizon of the times.(25) But that horizon did not envision any delegated authority that could change the Torah, as is evident from Mk 2:7 (a claim to forgiveness of sins apart from Torah procedures was considered a claim to divinity by the scribes and Pharisees). Hence this claim of Jesus must have expressed a conscious claim to divinity.

Further, if His human mind registered only a belief that He had delegated authority, where would it get such a notion? If it was by revelation, why would God have made a special revelation that was so incomplete? If the notion came from a vague self-perception, how substantive was it? To be a prophet, even to be a Moses, would not give rational grounds for the power of modifying the Sabbath. It was strictly unheard of. Really, there could be no earthly justification. The human intellect of Jesus would have been deluded in formalizing so unheard of a revolution with no real authorization. We conclude: His human intellect operated in harmony with His divinity.

Bultmann classifies the passage as a retrojection.(26) Retrojections indeed are possible under some conditions.(27) But there is no evidence; there is only the prejudice that Jesus could not have known. The following episode likewise involves the question on delegated authority; it is of such a character that no retrojection is possible.

Fourth, Jesus claimed authority to forgive sins. Seeing a paralytic let down through the roof before Him, Jesus said (Mk 2:1-12; Lk 5:17-26; Mt 9:2-8), "My son, your sins are forgiven." The scribes and Pharisees murmured in their hearts: "Why does this man speak thus? It is blasphemy! Who can forgive sins but God alone?" Knowing their thoughts Jesus said: "Why do you question thus in your hearts? Which is easier, to say to the paralytic, 'Your sins are forgiven,' or to say, 'Rise, take up your pallet and walk.'" It was as if Jesus had said: "If I say, your sins are forgiven, no one can check that. But if I say: Get up and walk, anyone can verify it." So Jesus cured the man. All three Synoptics add a line the origin of which is debated: "But that you may know that the Son of Man has authority on earth to forgive sins, he said to the paralytic...." Some label this line as a comment by the evangelists, and not spoken by Jesus. Even if that be proven, the connection between the forgiveness and the cure remains evident from the other words of Jesus (as Bultmann and Dibelius admit).(28)

The presence of this connection is of prime importance. If they were genuine miracles, the power came from God. For various reasons God might do such for a good pagan. *But He could not provide miraculous power if it were used to prove a lie.* The scribes consider that claim *a claim to divinity.* We grant that sins could be forgiven by a delegated power. But the scribes did not see that possibility (see verse 7). Hence, in that concrete situation, the miracle was used to prove a claim understood as a claim to divinity. God could not have supported such a claim by confirming it with a miracle if it were false. Jesus, therefore, did show an understanding of His own divinity on this occasion.

The supposition that Jesus' human mind thought it had only

delegated power is factually impossible for the same reasons as outlined above on His power over the Torah.

Lane(29) thinks the passive, "your sins are forgiven," is a "divine passive," employed to avoid the mention of Yahweh's name; what Jesus said would mean merely (as Nathan said to David): God has forgiven your sins. But that cannot be the case here; for the scribes (who should have known all about divine passives if anybody did) would not then have objected in the way recorded. Jeremias observes that the divine passive is almost completely absent from the Talmud; instead, the usual circumlocution is a third person plural.(30)

Fifth, we may look at a passage, also examined in the Appendix, in which Jesus reveals Himself as the eschatological judge.(31) In Mt 13:36-41 Jesus refers to Himself as the Son of Man who sows the good seed, and also as the Son of Man who at the end-time will send His angels to remove all evils from His Kingdom. The same prophecy appears in Mt 24:5, "Many will come in my name, saying, 'I am the Christ,' and they will lead many astray." But v. 27 adds that His real coming will be as clear as a lightning flash across the sky. In 25:31-46 Jesus holds judgment as the Son of Man and decides the eternal fate of men. Even Todt admits(32) that Matthew in these two passages presents Jesus as Son of Man and Judge. We examined Todt's evidence for denying the historical factuality of these texts, and found it wanting.(33)

Another passage in which Jesus refers to Himself as the final judge is Mt 7:22-23 "On that day many will say to me, 'Lord, Lord, did we not prophesy in your name, and cast out demons in your name, and do many mighty works in your name? And then will I declare to them, 'I never knew you.'"

John the Baptist is also presented as knowing Jesus is the final judge.(34) Mk 1:7-8 records how John regarded Jesus as immeasurably greater than himself: "After me comes he who is mightier than I, the thong of whose sandals I am not worthy to stoop down and untie...he will baptize you with the Holy Spirit." Lk 3:16-18 (Mt 3:11-12 is almost identical) adds to Mark's account: "His winnowing fork is in his hand, to clear his threshing floor, and to gather the wheat into his granary, but the chaff he will burn with unquenchable fire."

Mt 11:3 (Lk 7:20) is highly revealing. John the Baptist, in prison, had sent messengers to Jesus to ask: "Are you he who is to come?" John knew well who He was, as we gather from Mk 1:7-8 and parallels. John just wanted to impress the fact on his disciples dramatically. Jesus' answer implied that He was the fulfillment of several Isaiah prophecies (Is 26:19; 29:18-19; 35:5-6); and then added that John was "more than a prophet. This is he of whom it is written, 'Behold, I send my messenger before thy face, who shall prepare thy way before thee.'"

The implications are tremendous. Jesus quotes basically from Mal 3:1, which, in the Hebrew reading says: "Behold, I send my messenger, and he will prepare the way before my face." Jesus makes a modification, shifting the final pronoun from first to second person, because "in the exegetical tradition of the rabbis,(35) these texts had already been combined."(36) Is 40:3 seems to be also in mind: "A voice cries: 'In the wilderness prepare the way of the Lord, make straight in the desert a highway for our God.'" Lane also speaks of "Israel's expectation either of the eschatological coming of God himself or of his appointed representative."(37)

But note that Malachi 3:1 continued: "and the Lord whom you seek will suddenly come to his temple, the messenger of the covenant in whom you delight, behold he is coming, says the Lord of hosts." Fuller observes correctly, in regard to the expectation of Elias (Jesus in Mt 11:14 identifies John with Elias), "The starting point for this expectation is Mal 4:5f (Mt 3:23f). In this passage, an editorial note commenting on Mal 3:1, Elijah appears as the forerunner not of the Messiah but of Yahweh himself...followed by the coming of Yahweh to his temple for the eschatological judgment...."(38)

So we have a fascinating picture. In the midst of an expectation that Elias would come, followed by Yahweh Himself, Jesus quotes the key prophecy of Malachi 3:1 in which God clearly says He himself will come to His temple, preceded by His messenger. Now if John is the messenger, then Jesus, it is plainly implied, is

Yahweh Himself!

Of course, Jesus makes clear that John is Elias only in an extended sense, "if you are willing to accept it...." However, we note two things. First, would Jesus dare to apply to Himself words referring to Yahweh if His human intellect were not registering the fact that He was divine? No Jew would dare to do that for fear of blaspheming. Secondly, we may well be dealing here with a multiple fulfillment pattern in prophecy.(39) Consequently, in both fulfillments, there will be a messenger, followed by the Lord Himself coming to His temple. The messenger is in the one case John, in the other, Elias literally. In both instances, Jesus is the Lord. Objectively we know such was and will be the case. Could Jesus have dared to speak in this manner if His human intellect did not register the objective fact?

Bultmann regards Mt 11:2-19 as a sort of scholastic dialogue and concludes: "Passages like Matt. 11:2-19...can on quite other grounds be seen probably or surely to be formulations of the Church,(40) that is, faked in by the Church. Such a connection clashes with the honesty and genuine historical concern of the early Christian churches.

If we wanted to be as subjective as Bultmann, we could very reasonably claim for this passage what Bultmann said of Mt 12:28 (exorcism as a sign the Kingdom had come): "[this saying] can, in my view, claim the highest degree of authenticity which we can make for any saying of Jesus; it is *full of that feeling of eschatological power* which must have characterized the activity of Jesus."(41)

But we prefer to be objective, and place our emphasis on the genre of the Synoptics. Abstracting for the moment from the infancy narratives, the Synoptics are not midrashic in character, they are far too factual. At very most, Mt 11:2-19 might synthesize sayings of Jesus given on more than one occasion. But the ideas that John is the forerunner and that Jesus is the final judge are too well attested in many other texts.

We conclude, for a twofold reason, that Jesus shows an understanding of His divinity in the sayings about Himself as eschatological judge. There is, first of all, the passage we have just studied, with the implications of the citation from Mal 3:1. Secondly, the function of the eschatological judge is so momentous that it is hardly conceivable that any mere human could exercise it. The judge must know all the secrets of all hearts of all men of all times—otherwise, the principle proclaimed by Jesus Himself would condemn the judge (Mt 7:1): "Judge not, that you may not be judged. For with the judgment you pronounce you will be judged."

The reason why we creatures should not judge is our lack of knowledge of the secrets of hearts, e.g., I could see a man kill another, and could say *objectively*: this is murder. Yet I could not judge the killer guilty of mortal sin, for I do not know what is in his heart. In addition to this knowledge, the heavenly judge needs absolute infallibility in giving the sentence based on that knowledge, for his sentence is eternal bliss or eternal misery. Nothing short of full infallibility could satisfy as qualifications for such a judge. Could God endow a mere man with all these qualities? Theoretically, perhaps. However, if, for the sake of argument, we entertain the thought that it did not register on the human mind of Jesus that He was God, yet that mind would know itself to have phenomenal qualities, it would have a brilliance such that it would be inexplicable how that same brilliance could fail to perceive the secret of His own being, namely, His own divinity.

Actually, Jesus did manifest at least some facet of what seems to be divine omniscience when He read the hearts of others and exercised judgement dependent upon such knowledge, i.e., He condemned the Pharisees fiercely even though their works outwardly seemed righteous, for He knew their hearts were corrupt.

As to the role the apostles will play in judging with Jesus, that is wholly honorary. Only the chief judge, the real judge Himself needs to have the qualities enumerated.

Finally, Jesus' institution of the Eucharist deserves comment. Not all scholars agree that Jesus willed a real, substantial presence of Himself in the Eucharist. Mere human exegetical techniques alone can neither prove nor disprove Christ's Real Presence on the altar. But if one has arrived at the intellectual conviction that He did institute a body, His Church, to continue His teaching, and promised it providential protection in that teaching, such a person not only may, but intellectually is compelled to hold Christ's Real Presence in the Eucharist, for the Church, protected by His promise, so teaches.(42) If we think of His divine person, there is no problem: a divine person can dare to promise such a presence as that. Did the fact of His divinity register also on His human intellect? If it did not, then that human mind could never have dared to entertain such a thought as the actual institution of the holy Eucharist. A human mind that was unaware of its forming part of a God-man would have had to be utterly mad to dream of such a presence, a presence so marvelous if it occurred even once, and yet a presence multiplied countless times over. Of course, no one charges that the human mind of Jesus was so totally bereft of reason. Therefore, the fact that His divinity registered in His human intellect is completely inescapable.

4. Conclusions from the Scriptural Evidence

1. The objections in general. We have seen in detail that a plausible solution without implying ignorance in Jesus can be offered for each text that has been proposed as an objection. It is not necessary to prove what each text must contain. And we are pleased to record that even R. Brown, who seems so predisposed to find ignorance in Jesus, admits that the biblical evidence does not prove his case.(43)

2. Extraordinary knowledge. The Gospels repeatedly report how Jesus exhibited special knowledge of remote or future events (such as Palm Sunday and Passover preparations) and of the inmost thoughts of men. The evangelists seem to imply that this was actually supernatural knowledge, though parallel phenomena have been found today in extra sensory perception, which some think have a natural explanation.

3. Special titles: Son of Man, Messiah, Son of God. While it would not have been impossible, even within the genre of the Synoptics, for the Church to have placed the titles Son of Man, Son of God, and Messiah on Christ's lips, yet the reason for doing so must revert back in some substantial way to His self-revelation by words or deeds, during His earthly ministry. The title Son of Man is unclear as to content, and is probably part of His method of gradual revelation, which necessarily involves partial or temporary concealment.

There is no doubt that Jesus accepted the title *Messiah*. It is also certain He used the title *Son of God*, in a very special way, and repeatedly; He likewise distinguished His own case from that of men in general (Abba; *my* Father vs. *your* Father; the Son in the parable of the wicked husbandmen). The theophanies make it certain that His divine Sonship registered on His human mind.

4. Exorcism as a sign the kingdom had come. Exorcisms prove that Jesus knew He had power over demons, and that the kingdom was really at hand.

5. Greater than Jonah, Solomon and the Temple. Uncertainty about the precise literary genre proper to the Book of Jonah makes it difficult to determine the measure of Jesus' claim to be greater than Jonah. But it is clear that His human mind registered the fact of being greater than Solomon and the Temple. These claims happened in a setting of controversy, which could not have occurred after Easter. Therefore no retrojection is possible.

6. Authority over the Torah. Jesus claimed a power over the Law superior to that of Moses. Since the concept of such delegated power was unknown even to the greatest theologians of the time, those who want to limit His mentality to that of a man of His time leave no possible explanation for a claim so unheard of. But further we must ask: If His human mind registered only a belief in delegated authority, where would it get such a notion? Not by a special divine revelation, for why would God have made a special revelation so incomplete? Nor from thinking He was a prophet, for being a mere prophet would give no grounds for such a power. So, since there would be no justification for the belief, either He was silly and deluded (which is impossible) or He knew He had the power from His divinity.

Retrojection of this claim is not impossible, but is highly unlikely.

7. Authority to forgive sins. The scene of the cure of the paralytic (Mk 2:1-12) cannot be retrojected: no such cures occur after Easter, nor debates with scribes. In the context, objectively, Jesus made a claim understood to be one implying personal divinity (delegated power to forgive sins was unknown to Jewish thought). God could not have supported such a claim, if false, by a miracle. The concept of merely delegated power is ruled out as above. Hence, His human mind must have been aware of His divinity as the source of power to forgive.

8. *Eschatological Judge.* Several times Jesus called Himself the final judge. Of special import in His quotation of Mal 3:1 (in Mt 11:10), a text foretelling a forerunner to the visit of God Himself. Jesus identifies the forerunner as John, implying He Himself is God. Since Jesus indicates John is not primarily meant, we could either say we have another instance of a multiple fulfillment prophecy, in which case Jesus still is presented as God; or a case of an accomodative sense for John. But, it would be unthinkable boldness of Jesus to even apply to Himself a text that objectively means God if He in His human intellect did not know He was God. No Jewish intellect would be so bold.

Although it is not inconceivable that God could make a mere man competent to be the final judge, yet that person would have to have prodigious power: to know all secrets of all hearts of all ages, and then to pass sentence infallibly. It is inconceivable that the human mind of Jesus should have been so equipped as to know all hearts, and yet not know the secret of His own heart, His divinity.

9. *The Eucharist.* Without knowledge of His divinity, only the mind of an utter madman could have entertained a thought of instituting such a presence. So we have a most conclusive proof that His divinity did register on His human intellect.

Summation

We have, on the negative side, answered all objections. Positively, we have proved that the human mind of Jesus registered that He was God's Messiah and Son in a special sense, even in the ontological sense if we accept the theophanies, which we do. It is clear also that that human mind registered the fact that He had not just delegated power, but power as God to change the Torah and to forgive sins. It also knew He was eschatological judge.

With such evidence, much of which is conclusive by itself, and with all of it converging on the same point, it is not possible to deny that His divinity registered on His human mind. Of overwhelming significance is the argument derived from His institution of the Eucharist; no human mind could have dared to do that without conscious awareness of divinity.

NOTES

1 See pp 26-28 above.
2 JGM 48.
3 *Enchiridion Biblicum* 559.
4 JGM 48.
5 See Appendix, pp 218-19 below.
6 Dennis J. McCarthy, *Treaty and Covenant*, 58 in *Analecta Biblica* 21, Pontifical Biblical Institute, Rome, 1963.
7 See Appendix, pp 218-19 below.
8 *Cf.* pp 27-28 above.
9 *Cf.* Appendix, pp 207-09 below.
10 Joseph A. Fitzmyer, S.J., "The Aramaic Language and the Study of the New Testament" in JBL, March, 1980, pp. 5-21, at p. 21. *Cf.* also R. Leivestad, "Exit the Apocalyptic Son of Man" in NTS 18 (1971) 243-67; B. Lindars, "Re-enter the Apocalyptic Son of Man" in NTS 22 (1975) 52-72; M. Black, "Jesus and the Son of Man" in JSNT 1 (1978) 4-18; G. Vermes, "The Son of Man Debate", *ibid.* 19-32; J. Fitzmyer, "Another View of the 'Son of Man' Debate" in JSNT 4 (1979) 58-68.
11 See Appendix, pp 202-209 below.
12 William L. Lane, *Commentary on the Gospel of Mark,* in NICNT, Eerdmans, Grand Rapids, Michigan, 1974, 419.
13 *Cf.* P. Benoit, *Exegese et Theologie*, Cerf, Paris, 1961, I, 130-31; Manuel de Tuya, *Evangelios,* in *Biblia Comentada* V, BAC, Madrid, 1964, 274.
14 J. Jeremias, *New Testament Theology*, tr. John Bowden, Charles Scribner's Sons, N.Y., 1971, 56-61.
15 *Ibid.*, pp. 67-68.
16 *Cf.* pp 76-77 above and pp 207-09 below.
17 *Enchiridion Biblicum* 559.
18 See Appendix, pp 175-78 below.
19 See Appendix, pp 205-06 below.

20 HST, p. 162; *cf.* N. Perrin, *Rediscovering the Teaching of Jesus*, Harper and Row, N.Y., 1967, 65.
21 *Cf.* p. 33 above and 214-15 below.
22 See p. 10 above.
23 *Cf.* Appendix, pp 214-15; Lane, *op. cit.*, 120.
24 W. Pannenberg, *Jesus—God and Man*, tr. L. Wilkins and D. Priebe, Westminster, Philadelphia, 2nd ed. 1977, 56. *Cf. 251.*
25 *Cf.* pp 47-48 above.
26 HST 149.
27 See pp 27-28 above.
28 See Appendix, pp 214-15 below.
29 Lane, *op. cit.*, 94, n.9.
30 Jeremias, *op. cit.*, 12. Jeremias notes that the passive is found in Paul and in the LXX, but thinks it unlikely that this explains the divine passives in the Gospels.
31 *Cf.* Appendix, pp 207-09 below.
32 H.E. Todt, *The Son of Man in the Synoptic Tradition*, tr. D.M. Barton, Westminster, Philadelphia, 1965, 77-78.
33 Appendix, pp 207-09 below.
34 *Cf.*, Todt, *op cit.*, 195: "...the Christians certainly identified the Baptist as the forerunner of the judge of the last days as Matt. 3:12 and par (Q) prove, but precisely because of that he was seen as the forerunner of Jesus; for Jesus was not only acknowledged as the authorized proclaimer of God's final judgment, but he was also expected from the primitive community as the coming executor of that judgment."
35 *Cf.* H.L. Strack and P. Billerbeck, *Kommentar zum Neuen Testament aus Talmud und Midrasch*, I, Munich, 1922, 597.
36 Lane, *op. cit.*, 45.
37 *Cf.* Lane, 51.
38 R. H. Fuller, *The Foundations of New Testament Christology*, Charles Scribner's Sons, N.Y., 1965, 48. Fuller uses the numbers 4:5 of Mal., following some English versions and the Vulgate. The Hebrew has the same wording at 3:23-24 (LXX is 3:22-23).
39 *Cf.* pp 54-56 above.
40 HST 54; *cf.* 164-65 and 23.
41 *Cf.* note 33-34 above.
42 *Cf.* pp 33-34 above.
43 JGM 42, 68, 99-100.

6. Patristic Evidence

The Fathers of the Church faced a difficult problem when they considered the question of the knowledge of Jesus. First, Semites had very different ways of speaking. Paul often taught by sets of statements that seemed contradictory, e.g., he often said that the law could not be kept, that it brings only death and a curse (1 Cor 15:56; Gal 3:10; 2 Cor 3:6, 9). Yet he also wrote that it is good, spiritual, and a great privilege (Rom 7:12, 14; 9:4). Again, he said that we need not keep the law (Rom 3:21, 28; Gal 2:16; 5:18); yet he also said if we do not keep it we will not be saved (Rom 3:31; 2:13; 2:6, 25; Gal 5:19-21; 1 Cor 6:9-10; Eph 5:5). Jesus too used such pairs of seeming opposites. Thus Mt 6:6 tells us to pray in secret, while Mt 5:16 says men must see our good works and so glorify the Father. The Semitic mentality could calmly take in and believe both parts of the these pairs, without asking how to reconcile them. But Greeks and Westerners are of a different disposition: they want a logical synthesis.

There is, of course, a special basis for some seemingly contradictory pairs of statements about Jesus: His two natures, divine and human. The New Testament follows up the implications of both natures with vigor, so that some texts refer to Him in the fully divine category, while others, to a surprising degree, speak of Him entirely within the human category, e.g., most of Peter's address on the first Pentecost (Acts 2:14-36). Even Jesus Himself is reported to have said (Jn 14:28), "The Father is greater than

I''—and this in John's Gospel, which shows Him speaking so clearly of His own divinity as to say (Jn 8:58); ''Before Abraham was, I Am.''

The most acute part of the problem comes from two synoptic texts; Lk 2:52 asserts that Jesus grew in age and wisdom and grace, while Mk 13:32 has Him say: ''But of that day or that hour no one knows, not even the angels in heaven, nor the Son, but only the Father.''

The Fathers, not being Semitic, wanted to know how to reconcile these two texts with their scripturally based belief in His divinity. But before they had time to give unbiased study to the question, the Arian and Apollinarist heresies arose. The practical need to combat these, of course, came first. It was so easy, and almost necessary, to say to the Arians that these ''lowly sayings'' referred to His human nature—otherwise the Arians would refer them to the Word, and so deny the divinity of the Word. Similarly, when Apollinaris denied that Jesus had a human rational soul, it was temptingly easy to assert that the ''lowly sayings'' proved He did have a human rational soul—for Apollinaris would not dare to refer these sayings to the divinity. So, not surprisingly, some Fathers did say that *humanly* Jesus could grow, and *humanly* did not know the day and hour of the end.

Eulogius, writing around 600 A.D., labelled assertions that attributed ignorance to His humanity as *tactics* in the controversies, tactics that should be discounted. His view does seem at least plausible, for the situation, as we said, was tempting, almost compelling. We have further evidence for his view in the fact that eight Fathers clearly, and two others less clearly, beginning with St. Athanasius, and running as late as the Venerable Bede, said that humanly Jesus might grow or not know the day; yet they also made other statements clearly holding for no ignorance and no growth at all—a pattern that reminds us of the seemingly contradictory pairs in the Bible.

But these seemingly opposite statements found in patristic writings were not *mere* tactics. The Fathers seem to have recognized that both statements were strictly true. And they are true, if the proper distinctions are made, even though it took some time before the Fathers saw how to make the needed distinctions. They succeeded rather early in their resolution of Lk 2:52 (Jesus' growth in wisdom). Already for St. Athanasius that growth was only a growth in *manifestation*. (Thus He would be said *not* to know something when He did not manifest it; while He really *did* know it). It was only later that they discovered the complete answer to the problem of Mk 13:32 (ignorance of the day of the parousia). That full explanation came with Eulogius and Pope St. Gregory the Great; they explained how Jesus could know the day *in* His humanity but not *from* His humanity. However, long before that, beginning explicitly in St. Basil, we find the statement, which is correct, that His avowal of ignorance was only *feigned* ignorance as part of His *oikonomia*—His adaptation to human conditions. A bit earlier, St. Athanasius, though he does not actually use the words *feigning* or *oikonomia*, seems to have the same ideas in mind.

The Fathers, then, deserve great credit for struggling hard to find ways of presenting the truth even before they found all the needed distinctions. They did far better than many modern scholars who shockingly ignore all that has been learned during centuries of patristic labor. Instead, they insist simplistically: Mk 13:32 and Lk 2:52 (along with other texts whose problems the Fathers solved readily) do say He was ignorant; so one had better believe it. Scripture says so. Such simple-mindedness reminds one of the fundamentalists, especially of some of the Jesus-people who demand that teenagers actually hate their parents because Jesus said (Lk 14:26): "If anyone comes to me and does not hate his own father and mother and wife and children and brothers and sisters...he cannot be my disciple."

We now proceed to the evidence.

1. Before the Golden Age of Patristic Literature

St. Justin Martyr. In explaining Psalm 22, Justin comments on the words:

"O my God, I cry to you by day, and you will not hear, and at night, and not unto ignorance on my part." ....It is clear through these things that He really became a man subject to suffering.

But so that someone might not say: he did not know that He was about to suffer, He continues right away in the psalm: "and not unto ignorance on my part." In the same way it was not ignorance on the part of God to ask Adam where he was, nor Cain where Abel was....(1)

Justin does not have occasion to take up the question of the knowledge of Jesus in general, nor of His knowledge in respect to the two critical texts we have mentioned. Yet Justin does show the desire to reject ignorance in Jesus, even on the human side, since he rejects the idea of ignorance right after noting that "it is clear... that He really became a man subject to suffering." Note too the first patristic occurrence of the argument that Jesus might appear not to know, yet really know, just as Yahweh could ask where Adam was.

St. Irenaeus. Similarly, St. Irenaeus does not really take up our question. He is writing against the Gnostics who pretended possessing great knowledge; in a polemic way he could not resist saying: "Irrationally, moreover, and proudly and boldly you say you know the unspeakable mysteries of God, while even the Lord, the Son of God Himself, admitted that only the Father knows. For He says clearly, 'About that day and hour no one knows, not even the Son, but the Father only.' If then the Son was not ashamed to refer to the Father the knowledge of that day while saying what is true, neither should we be ashamed to refer to God the more difficult questions that plague us. For 'No one is above his teacher.'"(2) The remarks of Irenaeus are, as already pointed out, made in polemic, and in passing, without real consideration of the problem. We may note he did not say flatly that the Son did not know, but rather that "the Son was not ashamed to *refer* to the Father the knowledge of that day...." A bit later Irenaeus adds: "For if anyone asks the reason why the Father, who communicates with the Son in all things, alone knows the day and the hour according to this statement by the Lord, he would not find a more fitting and becoming reply...than that we should learn through Him that the Father is above all. For, he said, 'the Father is greater than I.'"(3) Notice, Irenaeus says the Father really did communicate "with the Son in all things."

Clement of Alexandria. Quite the opposite position appears in *Clement's Paedegogus,* written after 195 A.D., "It was proper that He learn nothing, since He was God. For no one is greater than the Word. Nor is there a teacher for the one teacher."(4) Clement is influenced partly by Scripture, partly by Stoicism. He clearly alludes to the Gospel verse that there is only one teacher, and notes that Jesus is the Word, who cannot be ignorant of anything. The Stoic influence shows in a statement in his *Stromata* (208-11 A.D.): "He was simply free of passion, into whom no movement of passion came, nor pleasure nor grief."(5) We wonder how Clement could have made such a judgment in view of the Gospel descriptions of Gethsemani, and of the many passages which portray Jesus as having human feelings. Here we clearly have a case of Stoicism deciding, a priori, what is true, so as to blank out the Gospel message.

Surely Clement could not hold for ignorance in the humanity of Jesus when he sought to exclude human emotions.

Origen. Stoicism dictated conclusions for Clement; Platonism seems to have dominated Origen. He thought that the human soul of Christ, before His birth, had existed as a spirit in the world of all other spirits.(6) While there, that spirit earned, by ethical means, especially by love, to be united with the Word.(7) In becoming man Jesus did empty Himself, but there was no complete darkening of consciousness as in other spirits that became souls.(8) However, because of this emptying He could grow: "Human nature does not permit this, that it be filled with wisdom before the age of twelve.... For He had lowered Himself, taking the form of a slave, and had grown in the same virtue in which He had lowered Himself."(9) But "...in advancing He advanced beyond all in knowledge and wisdom; however, in such a way that perfection did not come until He had fulfilled His own dispensation."(10) That is: comparing Mk 13:32 and Acts 1:7, Origen thinks Jesus after His resurrection knew "The Day," but not before. Before His death he had advanced so far that there was only one thing He did not know: "He did not know this one thing out of all, that is, the day and the hour of the consummation."(11)

Obviously, Origen is not here a witness to the tradition of the

Church. He is rather a bold Platonic speculator.

Fondness for allegory led Origen to propose an alternative view: "For as long as the Church, which is [His] body, does not know that day and hour, so long neither is the Son Himself said to know that day and hour; he is then understood to know when all His members know."(12)

We also find in Origen the first clear occurrence of what later writers will speak of as *oikonomia*, Jesus adapting Himself to the ways of men.(13) For in his commentary on Matthew, Origen says: "[Jesus] did not ask because He did not know, but once having taken on man, He used all his [man's] characteristics, one of which is to ask."(14) Origen continues, noting that the Father did the same when He asked where Adam was or where Abel was. In this *oikonomia*, Jesus really did know, but acted as though He did not, in order to adapt to our condition.

2. The Golden Age: Eastern Writers

Emperor Constantine. Eusebius reports that Constantine spent much of his time composing and delivering sermons.(15) Manuscripts of the Emperor's *Life*, by Eusebius, have an appendix to the fourth book with the title *Oration to the Assembly of the Saints.* Its authenticity is debated, with good authorities on both sides. In it we read: "The wisdom of God [was in Him] from [the time He was wrapped in] swaddling clothes. The Jordan, which provided the bath, received Him with reverence. Moreover, [there was] the royal anointing, joined with knowledge of all things."(16)

Eusebius of Caesarea. At and after the Council of Nicea, Eusebius seemed to be soft on Arianism—perhaps as a matter of peacemaking tactics, coupled with a lack of full understanding, and a fear of Sabellianism. However, in his *Demonstratio evangelica*, written well before Nicea (perhaps 315-20 A.D.), he shows no traces of Arianism: "But then, in that period when He lived among men, He filled all things and was with the Father and was in Him; likewise He took care of all things, those in heaven and those on earth, by no means being locked out, as we are, from the presence everywhere, nor being impeded from carrying out the divine activities as usual."(17) Now Christ's humanity did not fill all things, nor as such, did it carry on divine activities. On the other hand it was perfectly obvious without any need to say so that His humanity could not lock His *divinity* from the divine presence. So the fact that he mentions this item may well mean that the human nature did share in that presence—perhaps by the beatific vision.

Eustathius of Antioch. Though of Antioch, he was clearly anti-Arian. Out of fear that the Arians might speak of the Word as assuming a body without a soul and so might attribute the human reactions of Jesus to the Word, Eustathius preferred a Word-man Christology. Resultant expressions have caused some to ask if he might not have been of Nestorian tendencies. Probably he was not. In a fragment of his work *Against the Arians* we find:

> Let us point out the reason why the Son of man did not know the day of His own coming. There is no doubt that the Creator of all and maker of our race, God, providently devised this for the utility of men. For just as He fitted man to the Word and God for the salvation of men, so He suitably hid the day of judgment from man for the divine benefit, lest perhaps man, making known the unspeakable mysteries of this kind to men, might also reveal the day of the second coming.(18)

It is difficult to interpret this text. We note the strange expressions, viz., God "fitted man to the Word" and hid the day "lest perhaps *man*, making known the unspeakable mysteries... might also reveal the day of the second coming." These expressions have caused some to suspect Eustathius had Nestorian tendencies. We propose as more likely that Eustathius spoke this way as a tactic against the Arians. If so, he would be doing what Eulogius asserts many Fathers did. Then we would not have to count it as a real attribution of ignorance, even to the humanity. Furthermore, on any view, we can hardly suppose Eustathius really meant to say the Father feared His Son might act contrary to His will and reveal the day if He knew it! So, more likely, this is written as an expression of *oikonomia*, the adaptation made by Jesus to the ways of men, so that He really knew even as man, but did not reveal the day to men.

St. Athanasius. Although Athanasius does not use the words *feigning* and *oikonomia*, it seems clear that he did have these concepts in mind. For Athanasius says quite flatly: "Though He knew, He *said*, 'Neither does the Son know!...because of the flesh, as man. For *this is not deficiency of the Word, but of human nature*, to which not knowing is proper."(19) And a bit farther on: "It is clear that as the Word He knew the hour of the end of all, but as man He did not know."

On the contrary, Athanasius at least three times clearly states that Jesus did know even as man. First, Athanasius draws a parallel between Jesus and St. Paul. In 2 Cor 12:2, Paul says he had a marvelous vision, and adds that he did not know if he was in the body during it or not. Athanasius refuses to accept Paul's statement of not knowing, and says that then Paul would be like the mindless pagan prophets. He continues:

> but if he [Paul] knew, though he said, 'I do not know'—for he had Christ within his soul making all things clear—how is not their heart turned inside out, and self-condemned when they [the opponents of Athanasius] say that the apostle in saying 'I do not know' *did* know, while the Lord in saying 'I do not know' *did not* know.(20)

We must follow the parallel. Paul and Jesus both said they did not know. Paul really did know, for Christ in him made it known to him. The Christ in Paul was, of course, the divinity of Christ. That divine nature within Paul caused Paul's human mind to know. If the same divinity within Jesus did not cause His human mind to know, then Jesus would be inferior to Paul. Athanasius vigorously rejects this. So the parallel must mean that Jesus knew even in His humanity, else Paul would be superior and the divinity of Jesus would do more for Paul than for His own humanity.

Secondly, Athanasius observes that after the resurrection (Acts 1:7) Jesus said, "It is not for you to know times or seasons which the Father has fixed by his own authority," and adds: "Then [after the resurrection] He did not say 'Neither does the Son know,' as He had said before in a human way, but, 'It is not for you to know.' For as to the rest, His flesh was risen, and had put aside mortality and was made divine, and...*it was no longer fitting* [*ouketi eprepe*] for Him to answer in a fleshy way."(21) The key expression is, "it was no longer fitting." So, before the resurrection, it was *fitting* for Him to say he did not know. But it was a matter of *fittingness, not of ability*. Had Athanasius meant that after the resurrection Jesus was *able* to know, while before He was *not able*, he hardly would have reduced the distinction to a matter of fittingness. So again, Athanasius means Jesus knew even humanly before the resurrection.

Thirdly, Athanasius argues: "He explained to the disciples the things before the day saying, 'These things will be, and these, and then the end.' But He who tells the things that come before the day, fully knows also the day, which will appear after the things predicted."(22) Now Jesus spoke these predictions *humanly*, and so, in the thought of Athanasius, *humanly* He knew the things before the end. But this knowledge in turn had to imply knowledge of the end, thinks Athanasius. So, according to our saint, Jesus' knowledge of the end was also human. (Really, one might have a revelation of the *signs*, without a knowledge of the *date* of the signs, and so not know the date of the end. Yet, the fact that Athanasius uses the argument proves Athanasius believed Jesus, as man, knew the day when the end will come).

The comments of Athanasius on Lk 2:52 also show the seemingly contradictory pairs. On the one hand he speaks of growing in a human way (though less forthrightly than he spoke about not knowing the day: "The words 'making progress' are said from the human vantage point, since it is for men to make progress."(23) On the other hand, a bit later he adds: "Gradually as the body grew and the Word *manifested itself in it*, He is acknowledged first by Peter, then by all." So it is primarily a question of gradual manifestation: "The humanity advanced in wisdom, gradually going beyond human nature and being divinized and *appearing to all* as its instrument, for the working and manifestation of the divinity."(24)

When we find Athanasius bringing the question of knowledge into relation with the physical-mystical solidarity explanation of the redemption,(25) we should understand his statements to be in harmony with the clearer patterns just examined: "Being made man, He exhibits [*epideiknutai*—need not mean He actually possesses the item in question, rather He manifests it in *oikonomia*] the ignorance of men, first, in order to show He had a real human body, then, that by bearing the ignorance of man in His body, He might free and cleanse human nature from all these things.''(26)

Athanasius, accordingly, clearly denies any real growth: there is growth only in manifestation. And he implies that Jesus said He did not know the day only by *oikonomia:* He really did know.

St. Epiphanius. Again we meet the same sort of seemingly opposite pairs of statements. On the one hand: ''And Jesus advanced, it says, in age and wisdom.... If he did not have a human mind, how could He advance?''(27) Epiphanius is here arguing against Apollinaris, who denied a human mind in Jesus. Similarly: '''He advanced in wisdom and age.' Neither did the divinity grow in age, nor did that which is wholly wisdom lack wisdom. The humanity of the Savior advanced in wisdom.''(28) Yet, on the contrary: ''The Father knows the day and hour in two ways, in knowledge and in action; for He knows when it is coming, and as He has already given judgment in appointing the Son to judge, He knows it in action. The Son of God knows when it is coming; and He Himself is bringing it on, and He is not ignorant. But He has not yet carried it out according to [His] knowledge, that is, in action.''(29) In this sense He can *say* He does not know. The distinction in question must refer to His humanity—in His divinity there can be no distinction from the Father in knowledge or in action. Epiphanius therefore means that Jesus even in His human nature does know, but can say He does not know because He knows it in one way, not in the other.

St. Basil. In *Epistle* 236 we read:

> ''As the Father knows me, I also know the Father.'' If the Father knows the whole Son wholly, so as to know even all the wisdom stored up in Him, it is clear that He [the Father] is known in the same measure by the Son, with all the wisdom within Him, and the knowledge of future things.... Regarding the saying of Mark...''No one knows, neither the angels of God, nor the Son, but only the Father''...we understand it thus: the *cause* of the Son's knowing is from the Father.(30)

So, Basil clearly says: the Son knows. In His divinity or in His humanity? To say the Father *causes* something in the Son is out of place for His divinity, in which He is incapable of being acted upon, and has no void, as it were, to be filled by the action of any cause. So it refers to His humanity, and Basil is saying that even humanly Jesus knew.

Still more forceful is a statement in *Epistle* 8:

> For your sake He does not know the day and the hour. Yet nothing escapes the true wisdom, for all things were made through Him. No man ever fails to know what he has made. But He [Jesus] handles this by dispensation [*oikonomei*] because of your weakness...by dispensation He provides for each of these [two classes, i.e., sinners tempted to despair by the scant time remaining, and those weary from long battle] through His *feigned ignorance* [*dia tes prospoietes agnoias*].(31)

In other words, He did know, because He made all things, including that final day. But by adaptation to our condition (*oikonomia*) and by *feigning* He speaks as though He did not know. The critical words are *feigning* and *oikonomia*. Of course, the action of *feigning*, as all other actions, is attributed to the Person. yet when we ask which nature Basil refers to as acting, we must say that *the divinity as such does not feign, but humanity does. Now if humanly He did not know, there would be no point in feigning.* So Basil says that when Jesus said He did not know, he was feigning by reason of *oikonomia*. It is important to note that in the very same passage Basil can also state flatly: "For your sake He does not know the day and hour." So we have another instance of seemingly contradictory twin statements.

An objection is sometimes raised from a passage that follows somewhat later in the same *Epistle* 8.(32) It is completely allegorical. Basil says that the disciples, after coming to the highest degree of contemplation possible in this life, desired the final beatitude, and this

> our Lord made clear He did not know, and His angels did not know. By 'day' He meant full and precise comprehension of the plans of God, by 'hour' He meant the knowledge of oneness and aloneness, which He [in the allegory] attributed to the Father

alone. ...if then...Our Lord, in regard to the incarnation and grosser(33) knowledge is [in the allegory] not the ultimate desired end, our Savior did not know the final happiness. But neither do the angels know, He says, that is, neither is the vision that is in them and the principles of their ministeries the final end. For even their knowledge, in comparision with face to face knowledge, is dim and obscure.... But only the Father knows, He says, since He is the end and final blessedness. But when we no longer know God in a mirror and through other things...then we too will know the final end.... But inasmuch as He is the Word, Our Lord is also the end and the final blessedness.

Because the entire passage is allegorical and its message less than clear, it should not be accepted as contradicting the other testimonies of Basil, including that in the same Epistle.

Certainly, just as the angels in the allegory do not *stand for* the vision, though they *have* it, so too Jesus, though He did not stand for the vision, could still have it.

Didymus the Blind. Didymus is of special interest at this point for his interpreation of St. Basil:

No one knows the Father but the Son," and "Just as the Father knows me, I also know Him." It is evident that He knows it [the day] through the knowledge the Father has. But if [someone says] it is one thing to know the Father, another to know the things of the Father, [we reply] it will be greater to know the Father than to know the things of the Father, e.g., the last day.... But that [text on the last day] also can be [understood] as one of the holy Fathers, full of wisdom, taught (Basil was his name)... "If the Father did not know, neither would the Son know.".... So, He says, for you I do not know, even though in truth I do know.(34)

Didymus refers to the notion that the Father causes the Son to know; in a patristic context this would mean that the Father causes the Son to know in His human nature.

A few paragraphs before the passage just cited, Didymus also wrote: "Just as He willed to take on the form of a slave for us, so also He willed to *say* He did not know; He used this as a medicine, because it is beneficial for humanity not to know everything about which it is curious [the day of the end]."(35)

St. Gregory Nazianzen. This great personal friend and

associate of St. Basil agrees, as we would expect, with the thinking of Basil: "How could Wisdom, the maker of the ages, not know anything, He the maker and consummator of the ages, the end of all things created, who knows the things of God as the spirit of man knows the things of man? What is more perfect than this knowledge! How now would He know precisely the phenomena before that hour and those at the end, but not know the hour itself? This is like a riddle, as if someone said he knew in detail the items in front of a wall, but did not know the wall; or that he knew well when the day ended but not when the night began...is it not clear to all that Jesus knew as God, but *said* He did not know as man, if one separates what appears from what is mentally under- stood?"(36) The last sentence became almost classic in later theology. St. Maximus and St. John Damascene interpret it to mean that only by prescinding from His divinity, i.e., by considering His humanity as it *would be* if it were not joined to the divinity, could the humanity be said not to know.(37)

More importantly, Gregory uses the same argument as that which we met in Athanasius: to know the signs preceding Judgment Day implies knowledge of that day. Since Jesus knew and revealed those signs through His human nature, then, in the thought of Athanasius and Gregory, that implied that *humanly* Jesus did know the day. (The argument may not prove what Athanasius and Gregory thought it proves, but it does prove that they held that Jesus knew the day humanly).

Our understanding of Gregory is confirmed by statements in his remarkable *Eulogy* over St. Basil: "Jesus made progress, it says, as in age, so also in wisdom and grace—not, however, in experiencing an increase in the latter (for if one is perfect from the beginning, how can he become more perfect?) but *in its revelation or gradual manifestation.* Similarly, I believe that the virtue of the man [Basil] then experienced, not an increase, but a greater scope, having more abundant material on which to use his power" when he became a bishop.(38) So, Basil resembled Jesus in that he only seemed to mature; really he was quite perfect already. He means, of course, Basil was perfect not from the first moment of his existence, but before he became bishop.

St. Gregory of Nyssa seems to say that Jesus really did grow in wisdom: "Who is so childish as to think that the divine passes to perfection by additions? But to think in this way about human nature is, indeed, plausible, because the voice of the Gospel speaks clearly of an increase in the human dimension of the Lord. For Jesus advanced, it says, in age and wisdom and grace."(39) In a like view, speaking of the day, he wrote:

> How does God in the flesh [without a human mind, as Apollinaris said] not know the day and the hour? How does He not know the time for figs.... Who is the one who does not know? Let him [Apollinaris] speak. Who is the one who is grieved? Who is the one who groans in powerlessness...? How is the one substance of the divinity divided in the Passion [so] one forsakes, one is forsaken?(40)

It is difficult to evaluate these statements. In the first, Gregory is arguing against Eunomius the Arian, and attributes growth to the humanity in Jesus in order that Eunomius may not attribute it to the Word, and so call the Word created. Similarly, in the second text, he is laboring against Apollinaris who denies a human rational soul in Jesus. Gregory insists that without a human soul, there is no way to account for the "lowly sayings". Should we, on the one hand, say that these statements are tactics against the heretics, and conclude that just as Basil his brother could use such language and still not attribute ignorance to the humanity of Jesus, so Gregory too did not mean to do so? The fact that he says Jesus was ignorant of the time for figs—something a plain peasant would know—surely suggests the tactic approach. Or should we, on the contrary, note that Gregory was under the influence of Origen (to such an extent that he too denied the eternity of hell?), and then say Gregory is probably following Origen in attributing real ignorance to the humanity of Jesus? Both interpretations are plausible; neither can be proven.

St. Amphilochius of Iconium. It is not surprising that this intimate friend of Basil and the two Gregories presents us with seemingly opposing pairs of assertions, as Basil also did. On the one hand: "So, after assigning the passions to the flesh, assign also the lowly words to it."(41) On the other hand: "He advanced in age, growing to manhood according to the nature of the body; *in wisdom, through those whom He made wise....*"(42) So Jesus did not really grow in wisdom Himself, not even humanly; Lk 2:52 means merely that He caused others to grow.

St. Cyril of Alexandria's views have been much debated. According to E. Schulte, Cyril, before the rise of Nestorianism, admitted real human ignorance in Jesus; afterward, he maintained only an apparent ignorance.(43) J. Mahe thought Cyril at no time attributed ignorance to Christ. J. Lebreton interprets Cyril as believing there was real ignorance in His humanity, and real growth: the growth in manifestation mentioned by Cyril was in a manifestation of His knowledge *as God*; (His human knowledge actually did grow). Lebreton explains how the ignorance in the humanity was "real, but so to speak, at the surface of the life of Christ."(44) A. M. Durbale defends Lebreton's views.

We will try to examine Cyril's views with special care and with particular consideration of Lebreton's proposals. We will keep in mind whether Cyril's view changed when he began to challenge Nestorius. And we will not forget that Cyril was noted even in ancient times for statements that could be misleading; because of such he was accused of favoring Apollinarism and Monophysitism. In fact, prior to the conflict with Nestorius, Cyril even used the notion of inhabitation to designate the relation between the divine and the human in Christ—a typically Nestorian expression.(45)

Finally, it should not be strange if in Cyril we find instances of the seemingly contradictory pairs of assertions noted in earlier writers.

In regard to Lk 2:52, Cyril, like Athanasius, asserts that Christ's humanity advanced and that He took on all our defects:

> If you fully accept the reality of the Word becoming flesh and man...why do you not grant that it also experienced the things fitting for man, without sin? If to grow and mature is proper to the flesh, let Him be said to make progress, as being in it and taking on such passions as are beyond reproach.... Wisdom, in as much as it is wisdom did not make progress, but His humanity made progress in wisdom, gradually gleaming and shining through it [wisdom].(46)

This passage was penned before the outbreak of Nestorianism. In his commentary on Luke, probably written in 430 A.D., after the conflict began, he also wrote: "If then He advanced in wisdom, wisdom did not advance...but human nature advanced in it [wisdom]."(47)

On the other hand, in the very same works Cyril also excludes any real growth in the humanity. In the *Thesaurus*: "Therefore when you hear He advanced in wisdom and grace, do not think there was any advance in wisdom for Him, for the Word of God needs nothing. But because He was wiser...to those who saw (*tois horosi*), He is said to advance; evidently it was the status [*hexis*] of those who then wondered that 'advanced', rather than that His [status] changed."(48) We have translated the Greek *hexis* by status. It is a very broad word, meaning, "being in a certain state...a state of body...state or habit of mind."(49) In other words: the change was *not in Him*, His *hexis* did not change; rather, that of the onlookers did. To make Cyril's statement fit with Lebreton's view we would have to suppose that although Cyril said flatly, without distinction, that there was *no change* in His *hexis*, Cyril really meant there *was a change* in His *hexis*, in His humanity, though not in the divinity. (Really, there was no need to mention the absence of change in the immutable divinity). Cyril gave no hint of this distinction; he just said flatly: His *hexis* did not change—that of the onlookers did.

We find the same statement almost word for word in Cyril's commentary on Luke:

> Therefore, not inasmuch as He is the Word and God is He said to advance, but inasmuch as, always being more to be marveled at, He showed Himself more graced through the things accomplished, to those who saw; or, to speak more precisely, the status [*hexis*] of the wonders in the onlookers' minds was growing rather than [the status—*hexis*] of Him who as God, was perfect as regards grace.... If then He advanced in wisdom, Wisdom did not advance, but human nature had an increase of wisdom.(50)

Almost identical wording also appears in his commentary on John.(51)

The same thought is expressed, with some vehemence, in his

Paschal Letter 17 (Cyril's opening blast against Nestorius): "Do not nonsensically dare to say: Let us apply the words 'to advance...' to the man; for this, I think, is nothing other than to rend the one Christ into two."(52)

All such Biblical expressions were in accord with the divine *oikonomia* or adaptation to human requirements: "The law of nature does not allow that a man have more understanding than the age of His body [warrants].... Since then He had to go along with our natural development.... His body gradually grew. He revealed Himself, and day by day He showed Himself wiser to those who saw and heard Him."(53) And again, in his *Against Nestorius*: "How then was He said to advance? [It happened] when the Word of God, as I think, measured out the manifestation of the divine gifts *which were in Him*, according to the growth and age of His body.... He rebuked even the holy apostles lest they might reveal Him. So, a strange thing, unknown to all, would have been seen...if He, while still an infant, had showed divine wisdom."(54) Cyril's use of the word *oikonomia* will become clearer from a text in the *Thesaurus* on knowing the day, treated below.

When we turn to Mk 13:32 and try to find statements that humanly He did not know, our search is difficult, for almost all statements are so qualified as to imply no ignorance. We can, however, find a text of the sort we seek by taking one out of context, and quoting only half of a sentence (as certain critics love to): "It is necessary...to marvel at His love of man, by which He was impelled to such lowliness that He endured everything human, including ignorance."(55) But here Cyril is presenting the common theme of physical-mystical solidarity in explanation of the redemption: since the humanity of Christ was in solidarity with ours, and since His was in contact with the divinity, that contact as it were spread out and healed our ills. But the sense in which the above statement is to be understood is, of course, to be determined by the whole passage and, indeed, by the whole body of Cyril's thought.

We have already seen that Cyril absolutely excludes growth in wisdom in Jesus, in the common sense of that word. But we need to grasp the full implication of the whole passage from which the half-sentence came:

> If He is the maker of the ages, times, and moments—and this is so—how is He judged by you not to know a certain day and hour? How can He not know that which He Himself made? It is necessary to examine the things said by Him to the disciples; then one can clearly see that He knows the day and hour as God, but *pointing to* His humanity, He *says* He does not know. Now if He explains clearly all whatsoever will happen before that day and hour saying: 'This will be, that will happen, and then the end,' it becomes clear that by knowing what preceded it, He likewise knows the day itself. For after saying these things, He added: 'Then will come the end.' What end? Precisely that last day, which *by way* of *dispensation* (*oikonomikos*) He says he does not know, *preserving again the order proper to humanity*. For it is proper to humanity not to know the future.... if He was not made man, He should say all things as God. But, speaking to His Father, the Savior said: 'Father, the hour has come; glorify your Son.' If then He knew precisely the hour which He said had come, what prevents Him to know also that hour which as man He *says* He does not know because of what is proper to humanity, but which He knows as God? We must avoid inveighing against the Word of God because of this saying, and rashly attributing ignorance to Him; rather it is necessary to marvel at His love of man, by which He was impelled to such lowliness that He endured everything human, including ignorance.

All the italicized words above express limitations; the net result: no ignorance even in His humanity. For Cyril observes that Jesus merely *said* He did not know out of *oikonomia* or adaptation to our condition; then he adds as proof: Jesus did indicate He knew the day by revealing all that would precede it. Jesus uttered those predictions *humanly*; therefore *humanly* He knew them. But, according to Cyril, such knowledge necessarily entailed knowledge of the day. Cyril's use of the word *oikonomia* becomes fully clear in his statement: "Christ acts in *oikonomia*, you see, in saying He does not know [*oikonomei...me eidenai*] the hour; really, He is *not* ignorant."(56) Here the subject of the sentence is not "the Word", but *Christ*—a title never used for the Divinity alone.

Confirmation of the above interpretations may be found in

many places. Shortly before the passage just cited Cyril writes:

> that He might not cause grief to the disciples...He *said* "I do not know," as man; He also had the power of saying this because of having become flesh.... That He said He did not know for the above reason, we know from the following: After the resurrection from the dead, being about to ascend into the heavens, when the disciples asked Him when the end would be and when He would come again, He replied more keenly: It is not *yours* to know the times and moments.... But if He did not know, obviously He should have replied: "I told you I don't know."

Cyril then describes how Yahweh also asked where Adam was and where Abel was. Similar explanations appear in many other places, e.g., in his works: *On Zacharias; On Matthew; Against the Anthropomorphites; Apology against Theodoret of Cyrus; On the true faith to the Augustae,* he wrote (respectively):(57)

> Inasmuch as He is considered as man like us, He *would not* know.... When the disciples wanted to learn things above them, He prudently pretended [*skeptetai*] not to know as man.... According as He is thought of as God, He knows all that the Father [knows]; according as [He is thought of as] man, he does not reject *seeing not to know*, since that is proper to humanity. So, even though He knew all things, He did not blush to *attribute* to Himself the ignorance proper to humanity.... And if He is one and the same, arising from the fact of the true union, and not one and another and divided into parts, it is His *both to know and to SEEM not to know....* Even if humanly He *is said not to know*, he knew divinely.(57)

The passages we have accumulated show clearly that Cyril means not that Jesus really failed to know even humanly, but that He pretended not to know or acted as though He did not know, because that was fitting for humanity, whose weaknesses He had assumed. It was *oikonomia.*

To sum up: Both on Lk 2:52 and Mk 13:32 Cyril presents pairs of statements. On Lk 2:52 there are several that clearly seem to speak of growing humanly; on Mk 13:32, close inspection reveals that Cyril almost always qualified things that at first sight might appear to hold for ignorance. On both texts, Cyril makes clear many times over that He rejects any real growth, any real ignorance, even on the human side. This is especially clear on Lk 2:52 from the distinction made between the status [hexis] of the onlookers and the *hexis* of Jesus Himself; and for Mk 13:32, from the fact that Cyril proves Jesus knew the day because He knew the phenomena preceding it. Now Jesus knew and said these things *humanly*; but *for Cyril* knowledge of these things necessarily entailed knowledge of the day. Hence, for Cyril, Jesus' knowledge of the day was also human.

These facts rule out completely the hypothesis of Lebreton. The evidence reviewed comes from works both before and after the outbreak of Nestorianism.

St. John Chrysostom. In his *Homily on the Prayers of Christ*, Chrysostom explains: "Don't you see how there was no ignorance in the Savior in saying, 'Where have you laid him [Lazarus]?' Certainly there was no ignorance in the Father when saying to Adam, 'Where are you' or to Cain, 'Where is your brother Abel!'"(58) In regard to knowing the day and hour, we find in *Homily 77*, "'About that day and hour no one knows.' By saying 'not the angels' He blocks His audience from wanting to learn what they [the angels] did not know; by saying 'nor the Son' He forestalls not only learning but even the desire to learn.... He Himself knew the Father clearly, as clearly as He knew the Son. Will He not know the day?"(59)

The above texts defend the knowledge of Jesus, but they do not make clear if John refers to His human knowledge. However, in his *De Consubstantiali contra Anomoeos* we find at least a probable answer: "When then you hear Him speaking lowly things, do not think it is in accord with [any] lowness of His nature, but in accord with the weakness of His listeners' understanding."(60) John seems to mean we should not think any weakness of nature in Jesus was the reason for the "lowly words"—rather, it is *oikonomia*.

St. Isidore of Pelusium. In his Epistle 117 we read:

> They say the Lord did not know the day of the consummation. He did not know!—perish the thought. He only refused to explain useless problems. For how could the Maker of the ages, in whom

are all the treasures of wisdom not know the hour and day? One who did not know could not have predicted the signs and fearful events of the last day...it is beneficial [for us] not to know, so that fearing every day to be the last, we may watch and be ready, waiting for it and our Lord.

St. Isidore vehemently rejects any charge of ignorance. And he seems to reject ignorance in the humanity, for he, like Cyril and others, argues that since Jesus told of the signs just before the day, He must know the day. But, Jesus told such things in His humanity, and knew them in His humanity. Hence, the argument would have to mean that in His humanity He also knew the day.

3. The Golden Age: Western Writers

St. Hilary of Poitiers. As a result of his exile in the East, we would expect to find Hilary stressing the same approach as the great Greek Fathers whom we have just studied. Our expectation is realized. In his commentary on Psalm 54:2, we find a general statement: "Jesus speaks at times in the person of man, because as man He was born and suffered and died; at times, however, all His speech is according to God, for from being God, He became man, and from being the Son of God, He became the Son of Man."(62) This suggests *oikonomia* but is not decisive. In his commentary on Matthew 23, "He [Jesus] knew the secrets of thoughts (for God does not fail to see any of the things hidden from men)."(63) Here Hilary attributes all knowledge to Jesus (though he seems to refer to the divine Person).

Of prime importance are his words about the day in *De Trinitate*: "Our Lord Jesus Christ, who in searching hearts...is God, suffers no such infirmity of nature as not to know.... But for Him who knows all, it is sometimes by way of dispensation [same as *oikonomia*] that He *says* He does not know."(64) Here Hilary clearly distinguishes the divine and human aspects: as God, He searches hearts; as man, "He suffers no such infirmity of nature as not to know." So even humanly Jesus did know; He merely *said* He did not know, by way of *oikonomia*. This, of course, is the same as the interpretation given by St. Basil and others.

St. Jerome. In regard to advancing in wisdom, Jerome insists that even as an infant, Jesus possessed divine wisdom. In his commentary on Isaias, Jerome reflects on the prophecy that the Child will eat butter and honey so as to know how to reject evil and choose good. He tells us: "Not that He did this [actually discerned thus as an infant]—rejecting and chosing; but that He *knew how* to.... Through these words *we* should learn that infancy of itself does not prejudge [the question about] divine wisdom [being in Him even then]."(65) We find a clearer statement in his commentary on Jeremias: "The Lord has created a new thing on earth. Without seed from man, without coition and conception, a woman will surround a man in the bosom of her womb; as time passes he will *seem* to make progress in wisdom and age, through crying and infancy; but he will be harbored in the woman's womb as a perfect man for the usual number of months."(66) Progress, for Jerome, is only in manifestation, not in real growth.

Jerome writes more than once about knowing the day. For instance, in his *Tract* on Mark: "If there is one God, how is there different knowledge in the one Godhead? If He is God, how does He not know? For it is said about the Savior Lord: 'All things were made through Him, and without Him was made nothing.' If all things were made through Him, therefore judgment day too.... Can he not know what He has made?"(67)

This text does not clearly indicate whether Jerome attributed knowledge to the humanity. But in his commentary on Matthew, after proving that Jesus did know since He made all that exists and since He knows the Father and since everything belonging to the Father is given to Him, he adds:

> If He does not know the world's final day, he does not know the day before it, and all before that. For He who knows what is second, knows what is first. Therefore, since we have proved that the Son was not ignorant of the day of the consummation, we must explain why He is *said* not to know. The Apostle writes of our Savior, "In him are hidden all treasures of wisdom and knowledge." All treasures are in Him; why then are they hidden? After the resurrection, when asked by the apostles about the day, He answered very clearly: "It is not yours to know." By saying, "It is not yours to know," he shows that He knew....(68)

Jerome employs the argument of many Greek Fathers, that since Jesus knew the signs, He also knew the end. As stated above, the argument is not conclusive, in itself, but it does prove *Jerome thought* that Jesus knew the day humanly. This is confirmed by Jerome's use of the texts from Paul and from Acts cited above.

In a letter to Pope Damasus, Jerome says Jesus as man knew all things: "You ask, why should a just man be left in the dark, and why should be act contrary to his will [referring to Isaac's deception by Jacob]. To this the precise answer is that no *man*, except Him who deigned to assume flesh for our salvation, enjoyed full knowledge and the certainty of all truth."(69) In saying that "no *man* except Him...had full knowledge," Jerome refers to the human knowledge of Jesus.

St. Ambrose. Ambrose shows the tendency common among the Greek writers of using seemingly opposite pairs. In his *De fide ad Gratianum* he seems to affirm human ignorance: "for me not knowing the day of judgment, for us not knowing the day and the hour."(70) Yet a bit farther on in the same work Ambrose speaks again of the humanity of Jesus: "Jesus is wearied from the journey so that He may refresh those who are wearied; He asks to drink, He who is going to give spiritual drink to the thirsty.... He *pretends* not to know [the day of the end] so that He may make those who do not know come to know."(71) More directly on the day and hour, later in the same work: "The Lord, being inclined with very great love for His disciples, prefers to *seem* not to know what He did know, when they asked what He judged not good for them to know. And He prefers to provide for our benefit rather than to show His own power." He then observes that some attribute human ignorance to Jesus and comments: "Let others say these things. I however will return to the above.... I prefer to think that the Son who lived with men and acted as man and assumed human flesh, took on our characteristics, so that because of our ignorance, He *said* He did not know—not that He Himself lacked the information.... There was nothing that the Son of God did not know." Here, clearly, is an instance of feigning for the sake of *oikonomia* and for the benefit of His disciples, a pattern Ambrose may well have taken from Basil, whom he greatly admired.

The objection has been raised that Ambrose shifted his view from that in his *De fide* (dating from 378/9) when writing his *De incarnationis Dominicae sacramento* in 382 A.D.: "How did the Wisdom of God advance? Let the order of the words teach you. It is an advance in age, and an advance in wisdom, human wisdom. Hence the text put the word *age* first, so that you would understand it was said in reference to the humanity. For age pertains not to divinity but to the body. Therefore if He advanced in age as to humanity, He advanced in wisdom as to humanity."(72)

The objection cannot hold, first, because we have met several writers who use such seemingly opposite pairs of statements. Ambrose himself, within the *De fide*, authored seemingly opposite statements (see above, p. 102). Further, in his *Exposition on Luke*, dating from 386-388 A.D., we find a very blunt statement that almost anticipates the formula of Eulogius and Gregory the Great who, as we shall soon see, said Jesus knew *in* His humanity but not *from* His humanity:

> In order not to seem to sadden the disciples if He refused them anything, Jesus says in another place, "About that day and hour no one knows, neither the angels of heaven, nor the Son."(73) Well did He simply say "Son," for the Son of God is also the Son of man, and we ought to think this was said rather according to the Son of man. For He knew the time of the end *not through the nature of man*, but through the nature of God.... He knew the hour too, but He knew it unto Himself; He did not know it for me.(74)

St. Augustine. Augustine too, like so many previous writers, is fond of seemingly opposite pairs. In his *In Ioannem* we find: *"According as He is man*...'Jesus advanced in wisdom and age and grace...'"(75) Similarly in the *Contra Maximinum*: "we read that Jesus advanced in age and wisdom...but *according to the form of man*...."(76)

However, in his *De peccatorum meritis et remissione*, Augustine rules out ignorance, in Jesus, even as man: "In no way could I believe that ignorance could be in that infant in which the

Word was made flesh to dwell among us, nor could I suspect in the little Christ, such weakness of soul as that we see in tiny babes.''(77)

Speaking of knowing the day Augustine asserts:

> Just as God is said to know also when He *causes* someone to know...so also when He is said not to know, it is said either because He does not approve...as it is said, ''I do not know you,'' or it is said because, usefully, He *causes* [others] not to know what is useless to know. So the saying, ''only the Father knows'' is well understood to have been so stated because *He causes the Son to know*; and the saying ''the Son does not know'' was so stated because He causes men not to know; that is, what men would know without profit, they would know uselessly.(78)

Augustine's exegesis may be strained in attributing to Scriptural sayings the notion of eminent causes; nevertheless, it is clear that Augustine insists that Jesus did know the day. He does not specify if Jesus knew humanly. But in a subsequent passage, in the same work, he is much clearer:

> After this life all the veils will be taken away, so that we may see face to face. How much difference there is between the *humanity* which the Wisdom of God bore and through which we are freed, and other men is understood from this: Lazarus was not set free except after coming forth from the tomb; that is, even the reborn soul cannot be free from all sin and ignorance except after the dissolution of the body.... But the linens and handkerchief of Him who did not sin, of Him who was *ignorant of nothing* were indeed found in the tomb; for in the tomb He alone was not weighed down in the flesh, as if any sin were found in Him; but neither was He wound in linens, so that anything might be hidden from Him, or slow Him down from His course.(79)

The passage is an allegory: Lazarus stands for ordinary Christians, who are burdened with ignorance and see God only after burial in a tomb. But the *humanity* of Jesus, insists Augustine, was different—even humanly Jesus saw God before being in the tomb, and was ignorant of nothing. Here Augustine seems clearly to attribute the beatific vision to the human soul of Jesus.

A. M. Durbarle raises an objection because Augustine, farther on in the same work, indulges in yet another allegory. Augustine asks: How can we be inheritors of God, since God cannot die? He answers: "As far as we are concerned, the Father in a certain way dies in a dark manner, not that He dies, but that our imperfect vision of Him is taken away by the perfect vision."(80) He continues: "If pious understanding permits, considering our Lord Jesus Christ not as the Word existing in the beginning with God, but simply as a boy who advanced in age and wisdom...we see,...by whose death, as it were, He possesses the inheritance. For we would not be coheirs with Him, were He not an heir. But if piety does not permit this...let the heir be understood as being His body, which is the Church, of which we are coheirs."

We comment: (1) Augustine is preoccupied here with trying to see how we can be coheirs with Christ. His method is purely allegorical, and that permits free floating speculations, and ample ambiguity; (2) Augustine is doubtful of his own speculation, for he gives alternatives, "if piety does not permit" the thought; (3) He seems not to be aware that this speculation would not fit with the passage about Lazarus. Yet, when one begins with two different starting points, it is possible to reach different conclusions, especially when the procedure is allegorical. Augustine proceeds in this manner also on the important problems of grace.(81)

In spite of objections, the statement which Augustine made Leporius sign (cited below) leaves no doubt that Augustine, and the Council of Carthage with him, considered it erroneous and heretical to hold that Jesus was ignorant even as man.

Leporius was a Pelagian and a Nestorian. When expelled from Gaul, he sought out Augustine, who converted him, and got him to sign the *Libellus emendationis*, which the Council of Carthage accepted in 418 A.D. He could then return to Gaul: "Then [before my conversion] I said...that our Lord Jesus Christ did not know the day, according to man. But now I not only do not presume to say [that], but I even anathematize such a view; it is not permissible to say that the Lord of the prophets was ignorant even according to man...."(82) The Council's acceptance adds further weight to this text.

Vigilius of Thapsus was bishop of Byzacena in Africa, in the fifth century. Of his numerous works there is extant only a dialog against the Arians and a treatise against Eutyches. In the latter we read:

> In order to show the properties of each [nature] in His one self, Jesus spoke and did things pertaining to both, not dividing the words, not separating the attitudes, not distinguishing the deeds, but He Himself, as one, saying and doing what was proper to Himself from each nature and to each nature. And so Christ Himself, the one and the same, is created and not created; has a beginning and lacks a beginning; advances in age and intellect while not receiving any increases of intellect and age...according to [the flesh] He is rightly called the chosen servant, rightly strengthened, rightly filled with wisdom, rightly said to have grown."(83)

Two comments are in order: first, the declaration of Leporius, approved by the Council of Carthage, did not seem to deter Vigilius; (2) second, the practical necessity of combating Monophysitism would seem ample reason to him to write as he did. This consideration, coupled with the fact that so many earlier writers had ruled out ignorance in the humanity of Jesus yet spoke similarly easily explains the case. We need not then, necessarily, conclude that Vigilius actually meant to attribute ignorance to the humanity of Jesus.

4. Later Patristic Period

St. Fulgentius. It is of special importance to observe how Fulgentius uses seemingly opposed pairs of texts, because of his remarkable teaching on Jesus' self-knowledge of His divinity. Occupied with Arian charges, he wrote in his *Ad Trasimundum:* "If there was not true flesh in Christ, what did the Virgin conceive in the womb? And, if a soul or intellect human in nature is believed lacking in Christ, what good or evil is He said not to know as an infant?"(84) Fulgentius is alluding to Is 7:14-16, which he quotes. For purposes of controversy, Fulgentius, like so many others, is willing to seem to attribute ignorance to the humanity of Jesus. Yet, he does not really mean that, for later in the same passage we read: "So the human soul, which was made capable of reason, is *said* not to know good and evil in the infant Christ."

However, much clearer is his celebrated statement in Epistle 14,

> It is very difficult and totally foreign to sound faith to say that Christ did not have full knowledge of His own divinity, with which he is believed to be naturally one Person.(85) And further on: "We can definitely say that the soul of Christ knew its own divinity in the same way as the divinity knows itself; or rather this should be said: it knows *as much as* [*quantum*] it [*the divinity*] knows, but *not in the way* [*non sicut*] it [knows]. For the divnity itself knows itself in such a way that it naturally finds itself to be that which it knows; but the soul knew its own divinity is such a way that it itself still was not the divintiy...that soul has full [*plenam*] knowledge of the Trinity, but nevertheless does not have one nature with the Trinity.(86)

That is, Fulgentius says the soul of Jesus knew the divinity *as fully* [*quantum*] as the divinity knows itself, with the difference, that when God knows Himself, knower and known are both the same God; whereas the soul, as knower, is not God. Now: only a direct vision of God can let a soul know God as fully as God knows Himself. So, at least objectively, the words of Fulgentius imply the beatific vision in Jesus.

Severus of Antioch seems to have had at least some tendency to Monophysitism. According to Cayre, he reduced *physis, hypostatis,* and *prosopon* to person, so that Christ did not *have* a single nature: He *is* a single nature or person.(87) Severus writes in *Philalethes*; "The Word itself which is the wisdom and power of the Father, was made flesh...and in all things...He had what was perfect, and through increase of bodily age gradually showed the divinity imminent in Him in a manner proportionate [to His age]."(88) Hence He always had, in the *one nature*, all knowledge, but only gradually showed that fact.

Stephen of Hierapolis. A clear statement that Jesus humanly knew the day marking the end comes in his work *Against the Agnoites:* "So let no one attribute ignorance either to the divinity of Christ, like the Arians, *or to His humanity*, like the followers of Paul [of Samosata] or Nestorius. For since He is one and the same in person and substance, He has as clear a knowledge of the day and hour as He has of His Father and the lifegiving Spirit, with whom He blesses and makes holy and enlightens every man having come and going to come into the world.''(89)

Pseudo-Leontius. The Greek Patrology attributes the work *De sectis* to Leontius of Byzantium; however it could hardly be by him (as the clash of theology indicates—which we shall see by comparing this text with one by Leontius himself). After reviewing contrary claims then in circulation, with some saying Jesus did not know the day, for He said so and He was like us in all things, while others said He spoke thus only by way of *oikonomia,* our unknown writer adds:

> It is not necessary to investigate subtly about these things; the synod [Chalcedon] did not concern itself about this teaching. But it is to be noted that most of the Fathers, almost all, seem to say Jesus did not know. For if He is said to be like us in all things, and we are ignorant, it is evident that He was ignorant. And, the Scriptures say, ''He advanced in age and wisdom;'' accordingly, it is clear that He learned whatever He did not know.(90)

This testimony, coming from an unknown author, is of no special weight. The fact that Chalcedon did not make a statement on the question merely indicates it had more pressing matters on hand. And the claim that most of the Fathers called Him ignorant hardly stands up in the light of the investigation we are making. Rather, the simplistic statement suggests superficiality and lack of research.

Leontius of Byzantium. From the real Leontius we have a work *Against the Nestorians and Eutychians.* In it are passages which some think teach that Jesus had the beatific vision: ''How will we be imitating God, if we do not sufer with Him who suffered? Did He suffer in some way, but not as we do?.... He was not glorified at all, if He did not receive according to the flesh that which He always possessed according to the spirit.''(91) Jugie wants to make this mean that Jesus always had the beatific vision; ''according to the spirit'' means His human soul, but after His Passion, he received glory in His body also.(92) Galtier objects that flesh and spirit are not to be taken the way St. Paul uses the terms in Romans, and holds that spirit refers to His divinity, and flesh to His entire humanity, body and soul.(93) We consider the passage unclear.

Farther on, Leontius describes how the features of the body of Jesus are the work of the Holy Spirit, but..."as to the sinlessness, the complete holiness, and whole union and fusion with the whole [Word] that assumed; as to the fact that Jesus—is and is called one and Son...—all this was produced by the union of the Word with [our] nature; and inseparable from this union is blessedness, since the union is indissoluble."(94) Here Jugie makes "blessedness" (*makariotes*) mean the beatific vision;(95) Galtier cites texts to establish that "blessedness" stands for the blessedness of divinity itself.(96) Grumel interprets "blessedness" more loosely to refer to the happy state of possessing such gifts, without specifying whether the gifts include the beatific vision or not.(97) The passage remains ambiguous.

Between these two passages, however, another occurs: "Christ's humanity...shared in all the goods of the Word, especially since it had the very source of those goods, the Word; it causes to flow from itself all the things of the Word, thanks to the Word."(98) We are not certain whether the beatific vision is included under the "Goods". However, knowledge of the day and exemption from ignorance should, at least, be included if that humanity "shared in all the goods of the Word."

Eulogius. We are indebted to the *Bibliotheca* of Photius for the thought of Eulogius:

> The saintly Eulogius contends that neither as man, nor, still less, according to the divinity, did the Lord Jesus Christ not know either the tomb of Lazarus or the last day. Neither could the humanity, which coalesces into one person with the unapproachable and substantial wisdom fail to know anything, either present or future nor could what He said be false: "All whatsoever the Father has is mine."(99)

It is abundantly clear that Eulogius denies all ignorance in the humanity of Jesus. Whether or not he means this is as the result of a beatific vision is another consideration. He does speak of that humanity coalescing "into one person with the unapproachable and substantial wisdom."

Photius also reports that Eulogius understood the Fathers as merely employing a tactic against the Arians when they said that humanly Jesus grew, or did not know the day:

> After this he continues, saying that if any of the Fathers admitted ignorance in the Savior on the human side, they did not bring this forth as a dogma, but brought it against the insanity of the Arians, who assigned all human things to the divinity of the only-begotten, so as to present the uncreated Word of God as a creature. They [the Fathers] considered it better policy [*oikonomikoteron*] to ascribe these things to the humanity, than to allow them [the Arians] to drag them into the divinity.(100)

Pope St. Gregory the Great. Gregory was quite pleased with the work of Eulogius and praised him in a letter:

> Just as we call a day joyful—not that the day itself is joyful—but because it makes us joyful, so too the omnipotent Son says He does not know the day, which He *causes to be unknown*—not that He does not know it, but that He does not permit it to be known...this can be understood more subtly: the incarnate only-begotten, made perfect man for us, knew the day and the hour of judgement *in* the nature of humanity, but yet *not from* the nature of humanity.... The matter is quite obvious: whoever is not a Nestorian can by no means be an Agnoite. For he who admits that the Wisdom of God was incarnate, in what way can he say that there was anything that the Wisdom of God did not know.(101)

Observe how in the first part of the passage cited, Gregory repeats the explanation first proposed by Augustine: Jesus knew, but can be said not to know because he causes others not to know; more important, we find here for the first time a new distinction: Jesus knew *in* His humanity, but not *from* His humanity. This seems to mean the same as our modern distinction, in which we ask if a given fact registered on His human consciousness, even if the source of that information was not His human knowledge.

Gregory's final comment, that one is Nestorian if he is Agnoite, remains true, in spite of the change of historical circumstances. For if someone, even apart from our modern framework, claims *He* did not know the day, etc., his statement *necessarily implies* objectively the existence of another person, a human person— because the divine Person could not fail to know all things. Really, many modern writers are guilty of a shocking lapse in scholarship. They know these distinctions, yet they act as though they do not when they persist in saying that *He*, Jesus, did not know.

St. Sophronius writes in his *Epistola Synodica* to Sergius of Constantinople:

> Themistius, that father and...lawless sower of ignorance, babbled about that Christ, our true God, did not know the day of judgment—not knowing what he himself, rejected by God, was saying, nor realizing what he had sounded forth in his stupidity. For if he had not been ignorant of the true meaning of his words, he would not have begotten deadly ignorance; he would not have hotly defended the abomination of ignorance [namely] that Christ did not know—not inasmuch as He was the invisible God but inasmuch as He was truly man—the day of the end and judgement. [Themistius was] spewing out [this view] from a brainless brain.(102)

Sophronius vehemently rejects the opinion that even humanly Jesus did not know.

St. Maximus the Confessor explains the problem very well in his *Quaestiones et dubia 66*,

> If, then, distant things and things beyond human ability were known through illumination by the holy prophets, how could the Son of God not know all things even better—and His humanity would know, not by nature, but by union with the Word. For just as iron, when fired, has all the properties of fire, for it shines and burns, though by nature it is not fire but iron, so also *the humanity* of the Lord, inasmuch as it was united to the Word, *knew all things* and manifested things divinely suitable. But inasmuch as the human nature is [thought of as] not united with the divine, it is *said* not to know.(103)

St. Maximus insists that Jesus knew all things even in His humanity, though not *from* His humanity—the same explanation as given by Pope St. Gregory the Great. It is only if we imagine Christ's humanity as not united with His divinity that He could be said not to know. We note too that Maximus does not explicitly appeal to a beatific vision, but to the transformation arising from the union with the Word.

St. Maximus also repeats the distinction made by St. Gregory

Nazianzus and interprets it in the sense just explained: "Whence the famous God-bearing teacher [Gregory Nazianzus] in his second discourse about the Son, explained these things about ignorance, distinguishing as if by a rule and pattern: 'Is it not clear to all that He knows as God, but *says* He does not know as man, if one separates what appears from what is mentally understood?'"(104)

St. Germanus of Constantinople continues the argument in his *Epistle to the Armenians* 17. "Even though He was sad, ignorant, and showed repugnance to the Passion, all these things happened *to the body* with the consent and decision of the Word living in the flesh and because of His will, for the Word, so far as it pleased Him, conceded to the body to act naturally."(105) Germanus is not really discussing the knowledge of Christ directly; he is speaking of two wills in Christ, and adds that the divine will was always in control. His mention of ignorance in the body ·need not mean anything other than similar statements we have seen in previous writers, many of whom couple such comments with other statements and thereby make clear there was no real ignorance in Christ, only an assumed unawareness stemming from the divinely providential *oikonomia*.

St. John Damascene. In his *De fide orthodoxa*, John attributes all knowledge to Jesus: "The Lord, not being mere man but also God and knowing all things, did not need to resort to consideration or investigation or deliberation."(106) He explicitly attributes knowledge of the future to Christ's humanity:

> It is necessary to know that He took on an ignorant and servile nature. For man's nature is the slave of God who made it; it does not have knowledge of future things. If then, according to Gregory the Theologian, you separate what is seen from what is mentally perceived, the flesh will be *said* to be servile and ignorant; but because of the identity of person and the inseparable unity [of natures], the soul of the Lord was rich in the knowledge of future things and also in divine signs. For just as the flesh of man, according to its proper nature, is not life-giving, and the flesh of the Lord, though united hypostatically to God the Word, was not free of mortality, but became lifegiving because of the hypostatic union with the Word...so also human nature by essence does not possess

knowledge of the future; but the soul of the Lord, because of its union with God the Word Himself, and the identity of person, was rich, as I said, in divine signs and in the knowledge of future things.(107)

On the text that Jesus advanced in wisdom, John comments:

He is said to advance in wisdom and age and grace. On the one hand He did grow in age; but with the increase in age He brought to manifestation the wisdom present within Him.... They who say that He [really] advanced in wisdom and grace...say that the union [with the divinity] did not take place from the very first beginning of the flesh; they do not defend the hypostatic union but, believing foolish-brained Nestorius, they sophistically invent an accidental union and a mere inhabitation—not knowing what they are saying or about what they make affirmations. For if the flesh from the very first beginning was united to God the Word, or rather was in it and had hypostatic identity with it, how could it not be perfectly rich in all wisdom and grace?(108)

St. John Damascene vehemently rejects all ignorance and growth in Jesus. He does not refer to a beatific vision, but speaks of His knowledge as being the inevitable consequence of the hypostatic union and personal identity with the Word.

St. Nicephorus of Constantinople. In his *Antirrheticus* we read:

As God, He knew all things before they happened. Thus once, when He was far away, He as God made clear in advance the death of His friend to the disciples. However, when present, and approaching the tomb, He asked: "Where have you laid Him:"—pointing to the limitation of our nature. Also, Jesus knew their thoughts—what they were ready to ask Him. For *as man He had knowledge of all things because of being united to the Word according to the Person....* And again, He *pretended* not to know the day and the hour...assigning what was proper to what He had assumed.(109)

Obviously Nicephorus was repeating the same teaching as St. John Damascene.

Venerable Bede is not noted for originality, rather for repeating faithfully the traditional doctrine from the Fathers. So it is of special significance to find what we have come to know as "the seemingly contradictory pairs'' in his writings. In his *Exposition on Luke* we find: "The Lord Jesus Christ, in that He was a boy, that is, in that He had put on the habit of human frailty, had to grow and become strong."(110) But focusing upon "wisdom" in his *Homily 12*, Bede shows this really means only gradual manifestation:

> And Jesus, it says, advanced in wisdom, age and grace with God and men...for according to the nature of man He advanced in wisdom, not indeed becoming wiser after a time, He who from the first hour of His conception remained full of the spirit of wisdom, but gradually demonstrating the same wisdom with which He was full to others, as called for by the occasion...not receiving over a period of time what He did not have, but making clear the gift of grace which He possessed.(111)

5. Conclusions from the Patristic Evidence

Before the Golden Age of patristic writing there is no consistency on the matter we are treating. Two writers, under the influence of Greek philosophies, reach opposite conclusions: Clement of Alexandria excludes all ignorance, for Stoic reasons; Origen, following Plato, opts for growth, but holds that before His death Jesus was ignorant on one point only, the day and the hour. Justin, in passing, rules out a particular case of ignorance, but does not speak in general; Irenaeus in passing and in controversy, uses ignorance of the day to confound the pride of the Gnostics.

Early during the Golden Age we find Fathers saying Jesus did not know the day, or that He could grow humanly. These statements appear in order to meets errors of Arians and Apollinarists, and are made mostly within the context of opposing pairs by apologists such as Athanasius, Epiphanius, Basil, Amphilochius, Cyril of Alexandria, Ambrose, Augustine and Hilary (Hilary clearly rejects ignorance in Christ's humanity while his complementary statements are not too clear). Only Eustathius, Gregory of Nyssa, and Vigilius of Thapsus speak of human ignorance outside of the pairs. Of these, Eustathius seems to imply *oikonomia*, while Gregory of Nyssa and Vigilius may not really mean to attribute ignorance (by having only one part of the pair).

These opposing pairs only seem to be contradictory; both judgements are true, with the proper distinctions. With reference to growth in wisdom, many Fathers, beginning with Athanasius, speak of growth in manifestation instead of actual growth. Beginning with Basil, many speak of feigned ignorance of the day, in the framework of divine *oikonomia*.

Others, without using pairs, make clear that Jesus knew the day, and could not grow even humanly, e.g., Gregory of Nazianzus, Isidore of Pelusium, Jerome, Leporius, and the Council of Carthage. A few attribute unlimited knowledge to Him, without making clear if they mean even humanly, e.g., Constantine, Chrysostom, and Eusebius; Eusebius may have in mind the beatific vision when discussing the problem.

After the Golden Age only a few sporadic writers attribute ignorance to Jesus even humanly, e.g., the unknown author of *De sectis*, and perhaps Germanus. Others make fully clear there was no ignorance even humanly, e.g., Fulgentius, Severus, Stephen of Hierapolis, Leontius, Eulogius, Gregory the Great, Sophronius, Maximus, John Damascene, Nicephorus, the Venerable Bede. Fulgentius and Bede retain the use of opposing pairs.

If we set these data against the background of the gradual clarification of revelation, or, what here amounts to the same, if we follow the trajectory of genuine faith, the answer is unmistakable: in the early days there are some bits of confusion and groping, but long before the end of the patristic period the testimony is close to unanimous in favor of rejecting all ignorance in Jesus, even humanly. Patristic tradition certainly votes heavily against ignorance.

We did not say that they spoke of or consciously implied the beatific vision in Jesus. Augustine and Fulgentius do seem to have this in mind; we might perhaps add Leontius of Byzantium and Eusebius of Caesarea. However, it is not at all necessary that they think of or consciously imply that vision in order to exclude all ignorance from the human soul of Jesus. They may simply affirm the *fact* of knowledge, without being able to explain the *how*. Some seem to offer a different kind of explanation, especially John Damascene and Maximus the Confessor who attribute Christ's full knowledge to union with the Word.

NOTES

1 St. Justin Martyr, *Dialog with Trypho* 99 PG 6: 708.
2 St. Irenaeus, *Against Heresies* 2.28.6 PG 7:808-09.
3 *Ibid.* 2.28.8 PG 7:811.
4 Clement of Alexandria, *Pedagogue* 1.6 PG 8:280.
5 *Idem*, *Stromata* 6.9. PG 9:292.
6 Origen, *First Principles* 2.8.4. PG 11:223-24.
7 *Cf.* E. Schulte, *Die Entwicklung der Lehre vom menschlichen Wissen Christi bis zum Beginn der Scholastik*, in *Forschungen zur Christlichen Literatur und Dogmengeshichte*, ed. A. Ehrhard and J.P. Kirsch. XII. Schoeningh, Paderborn, 1914, 21.
8 *Cf.* Phil. 2:7 and Schulte, *op. cit.* 21-22.
9 Origen, *Homily* on Luke 19 (On Lk. 2:52) PG 13:1849.
10 Origen, *On Matthew* 16.55 PG 13:1686.
11 *Ibid. Cf.* J. Lebreton, *Histoire du Dogme de la Trinite*, 9th ed. Beauchesne, Paris, 1927. I. 560-61.
12 Origen, *On Matthew* 16.55 PG 13:1687.
13 *Cf.* G.W.H. Lampe, *A Patristic Greek Lexicon*, Oxford, 1961, 942.
14 Origen, *On Matthew* 10.14. PG 13:865.
15 Eusebius, *Life of Constantine*. 4.55. PG 20.1205-08.
16 Constantine, *Oration to the Assembly of the Saints*, PG 20:1265. On the question of authenticity, *cf.* Johannes Quasten, *Patrology*, Spectrum, Utrecht/Antwerp, 1966, III. 325-26.
17 Eusebius of Caesarea, *Demonstratio Evangelica* 4.13. PG 22:285.
18 Eustathius, *Against the Arians* 6. Fragment in PL 67:795. Cf. Quasten *op. cit.* III.305.
19 Athanasius, *Oration 3 against the Arians* 43. PG 26:413.
20 *Ibid.* 47. PG 26:421-24.
21 *Ibid.* 48. PG 26:425.
22 *Ibid.* 42. PG 26:412.
23 *Ibid.* 52. PG 26:432-33.
24 *Ibid.* 53. PG 26:436. *Cf.* A. Grillmeier, *Christ in Christian Tradition*, tr. J. Bowden, 2nd ed. John Knox Press, Atlanta, 1975. I, 315: "Thus [for Athanasius] Christ's anguish was only 'feigned' and not real anguish; his ignorance was no real ignorance, but only an *ignorantia de jure*, which was proper to the human nature from the start."
25 *Cf.* Quasten, *op. cit.*, III, 71.
26 Athanasius, *Epistle to Serapion* 2.9. PG 26:624.

27 Epiphanius, *Against Heresies*, 77:30. PG 42: 685.
28 *Idem, Ancoratus* 78. PG 43: 165.
29 *Ibid.* 21, PG 43:56.
30 Basil, Epistle 236.2. PG 32:879. An objection might be raised to the argument given above from the fact that some Greek Fathers speak of the Father as the cause (*aitia*) of the Son, while the Latins avoid *causa*. The objection does not hold: (1) The word *aitia* and related words are much broader than Latin *causa*, for they can mean not only *cause* in the Latin or English sense, but also anything that should be mentioned in explaining a thing. But the context here requires that *aitia* would mean strict efficient causality—which is excluded from the divinity even in the Greek Fathers. (2) When the Greeks do speak of the Father as *aitia*, they refer only to the *origin* of the Son, not to anything else. Even then their language is very guarded. *Cf.* Cyril of Alexandria (*in Jn.* 1. PG 73:28), who says that the Son has "in Him the Father who is the beginningless (*anarchon*) beginning of His (the Son's] nature in a certain sense [*hoionei*]." John Chrysostom (*In Jn.* Homil 2 PG 59:33-34) does seem to use the word *aition*, yet he refuses to speak of Father and Son as first and second, and adds we must not think the Son's generation was passive (*patheten*). Rather, He came forth impassively (*to apathos*). John Damascene (*De Fide Orthodoxa* 1.8 PG 94:809) speaks of the Father alone as being *anaition* (without cause). Yet the whole divinity (col. 808) is *apathe* (impassive). Basil himself says somewhat similarly (*Adv. Eunomium* 3.1 PG 29:656) that the Son is "second in order (*taxei*) from the Father since He is from Him, and [second] in position (*axiomati*) since He [the Father]is the principle and cause (*aitia*) on account of being His Father." Basil means substantially the same as do the others; he uses the word *aitia* only in the broad sense, not in the sense of efficient cause; and he confines his statement on cause to *origin*, not extending it to such a thing as the knowledge the Son had. Rather, Basil adds: "but in nature He is no longer second, because there is one divinity in each."
31 *Idem, Epistle* 8:6 PG 32:256.
32 *Idem, Epistle* 8:7 PG 32:256-57.
33 Basil seems to mean sense knowledge.
34 Didymus, *On the Trinity* 3.22 PG 39:920.
35 *Ibid.* PG 39:917.
36 Gregory Nazianzen, *Theological oration* 4.15 (*Oration* 30) PG 36:124.
37 See pp 124-26 above.
38 Gregory Nazianzen, *Oration* 43.38 PG 36:548.
39 Gregory of Nyssa, *Against Eunomius* 6 PG 45:736.
40 *Idem, Against Apollinaris* 24 PG 45:1176.
41 Amphilochius, *Sententiae et Excerpta* 11 PG 39:108.
42 *Ibid.* 8 PG 39:105.

43 Schulte, *op. cit.*, 81, 95-96. *Cf.* J. Mahe, "Cyrille d'Alexandrie" in DTC III, Paris, 1923, 2513 ff.
44 Lebreton, *Op. cit.*, 575-76. *Cf.* A.M. Dubarle, "L'ignorance du Christ chez S. Cyrille d'Alexandrie" in *Ephemerides Theologicae Lovanienses* 16 (1939) 111-20.
45 *Cf.* Quasten, *op. cit.*, III, 137.
46 Cyril of Alexandria, *Thesaurus* 28 PG 75:428;29.
47 *Idem, On Luke* V.52 PG 72:509.
48 *Idem, Thesaurus* 28 PG 75:428.
49 Lampe, *Op. cit.*, 497.
50 Cyril of Alexandria, *On Luke* V.52 PG 72:509.
51 *Idem, On John* 1.14 PG 73:165.
52 *Idem, Paschal Letter* 17 PG 77:780.
53 *Idem, Thesaurus* 28 PG 75:428.
54 *Idem, Against Nestorius* 3.4 PG 76:153.
55 JGM 102. Citing part of *Thesaurus* 22 PG 75:368-69.
56 Cyril of Alexandria, *Thesaurus* 22 75:376-77.
57 *Idem, On Zacharias* 105 PG 72:252; *On Matthew* PG 72:444; *Against the Anthropomorphites* 14 PG 76:1101; *Apology against Theodoret of Cyrus* 4 PG 76:416; *On the true faith to the Augustae* 17 PG 76:1356.
58 John Chrysostom, *Homily* 9.1.2. *On the Prayers of Christ* PG 48:781.
59 *Idem, Homily* 77.1 PG 58:702-03.
60 *Idem, De consubstantiali contra Anomoeos* 7 PG 48:761.
61 Isidore of Pelusium, *Epistle* 117 PG 78:261.
62 Hilary of Poitiers, *On the Psalms* 54.2 PL 9:348.
63 *Idem, On Matthew* 23 PL 9:1044.
64 *Idem, On the Trinity* 9.66 PL 10:333-34. *Cf.* also *ibid.* 9.71-73, 75. PL 10:337-39, 341-42.
65 Jerome, *On Isaias* 3.7.15 PL 24:112-13.
66 *Idem, On Jeremias* 6.31 PL 24:914-15.
67 *Idem, Tract on Mark* 13.32 in *Corpus Christianorum, Series Latina* 76. Brepols, Turnholti, 1958, 496.
68 *Idem, On Matthew* 4.25.36 PL 26:188.
69 *Idem, Epist. 36. ad Damasum* 15 PL 22:459.
70 Ambrose, *De fide ad Gratianum* 2.11 PL 16:604.
71 *Ibid.* 5.4.54 PL 16:687. and *ibid.* 5.18.222,224. PL 16:722,723.
72 *Idem, De incarnationis Dominicae sacramento* 7.72 PL 16:872.
73 *Idem, Expositio in Lucam* 8.34 PL 15:1866.
74 *Cf.* p. 123 above.
75 Augustine, *Tractatus in Ioannem* 82.4 PL 35:184 ƅ
76 *Idem, Contra Maximinum* 2.23 PL 42:802.
77 *Idem, De peccatorum meritis et remissione* 29.48 PL 44:180.
78 *Idem, De diversis quaestionibus LXXXIII.* 60 PL 40:48. As we said above in note 30, the Latin Fathers generally avoid the use of *causa* to

describe the relation of the Father to the Son. Here Augustine has slipped into a loose use of *causa* (parallel to Greek *aitia*) since he is straining to explain seeming ignorance of the day.

79 *Ibid.* 65 PL 40:60.
80 *Ibid.* 75PL 40:87. *Cf.* A.M. Dubarle, "La connaissance humaine du Christ d'apres saint Augustin" in *Ephemerides Theologicae Lovanienses* 18 (1941), 5-25.
81 *Cf.* W.G. Most, *New Answers to Old Questions*, St. Paul, London, 1971, 231-43.
82 Leporius, *Libellus Emendationis* 10 PL 31:1229.
83 Vigilius of Thapsus, *Against Eutyches* 5.7, 12. PL 62:139, 143.
84 Fulgentius, *Ad Trasimundum* 1.8 PL 65:231.
85 *Idem, Epistle* 14.3.26 PL 65:416.
86 *Ibid.* 14:3.31 PL 65:420.
87 F. Cayre, *Manual of Patrology*, tr. H. Howitt, Desclee, Paris, 1940, II, 68.
88 Severus of Antioch, *Philalethes*, ed. A. Sanda, Beryti Phoeniciorum, 1928 27-28. (cited from: B. Xiberta, *Enchiridion de Verbo Incarnato*, Matriti, 1957, 532).
89 Stephen of Hierapolis, *Against the Agnoites.* From the Greek text in: F. Diekamp, *Orientalia Christiana Analecta* 117, Roma, 1938, 156.
90 Pseudo-Leontius, *De sectis* 10.3 PG 86:1261-64.
91 Leontius of Byzantium, *Against the Nestorians and Eutychians* 2 PG 86: 1321.
92 M. Jugie, "La beatitude et la science parfaite de l'ame de Jesus Viateur de'apres Leonce de Byzance...." in *Revue des Sciences Philosophiques et Theologiques.* 1921, 548-59.
93 P. Galtier, "L'enseignement des Peres sur la vision beatifique dans le Christ" in *Recherches de Science Religieuse* 15 (1925) 54-68.
94 Leontius, *op. cit.,* PG 86:1353.
95 Jugie, *art. cit.,* 554-55.
96 Galtier, *art. cit.,* 59.
97 V. Grumel, "Le surnaturel dans l'humanite du Christ viateur d'apres Leonce de Byzance" in *Melanges Mandonnet*, Vrin, Paris, 1930. 2.15-22.
98 Leontius, *op. cit.,* PG 86:1337.
99 Eulogius, *in* Photius, *Bibliotheca* 230. PG 103:1081.
100 *Ibid*, PG 103:1084.
101 Gregory the Great, *Epistula ad Eulogium* DS 474;76.
102 Sophronius, *Epistola Synodica ad Sergium* PG 87:3192.
103 Maximus the Confessor, *Qaeestiones et dubia* 66 PG 90:840.
104 *Idem, Theodori Byzantini Monothelitae Quaestiones cum Maximi Solutionibus* PG 91:221.
105 Germanus of Constantinople, *Epistle to the Armenians* 17 PG 98:144.

106 John Damascene, *De fide orthodoxa* 3.14 PG 94:1044.
107 *Ibid.* 3.21 PG 94:1084-85.
108 *Ibid.* 3.22 PG 94:1085-88.
109 Nicephorus of Constantinople, *Antirrheticus* 1.50 PG 100:328.
110 Venerable Bede, *Exposition on Luke* PL 92:348.
111 *Idem, Homily* 12 PL 94:67.

7. The Magisterium

There is a widespread tendency today to ignore or to minimize Magisterium teaching on all subjects, and of course, on our problem as well. Some in a loose way compare Magisterium teachings in general to poetry.(1) Others speak of them as so historically conditioned that we may see room for important changes.(2) Karl Rahner dismisses many of the statements on the problem we are treating as "marginal and incidental."(3) Avery Dulles asserts that "No generation can formulate the abiding content of the faith 'chemically pure', so as to commit all future generations."(4) Atkins seems to see a vicious circle: the Magisterium tells us to believe the Magisterium; rather he would have "its [the Magisterium's] own self-interpretation...subject to the *theologian's* interpretation."(5)

It is evident that before we take up the Magisterium texts we ought to reflect somewhat on the opinions just mentioned.

First of all, Vatican Council II did insist that the only final interpreter of Scripture and Tradition is the Magisterium: "The task of giving an authentic interpretation of the Word of God, whether in its written form or in the oral form, has been entrusted to the living teaching office of the Church alone. Its authority in this matter is exercised in the name of Jesus Christ."(6) Do we have here a case of what Atkins refers to, viz., a vicious circle? By no means. We *first* validate the general claim of the Church to teach on the basis of the Bible taken as a mere historical document. Not too much is required for this.(7) Some writers prefer to use the historical witnessing of the Church to establish points about Jesus,(8) not, of course, considering the Church as a divinely protected institution, but solely as a human institution extending back to the time of Jesus. Only *after* thus validating the teaching claim of the Church (in either of the two ways) do we find it intellectually possible—and inescapably necessary—to believe the Magisterium.

Furthermore, what Vatican II enunciates is nothing new; rather, it is simply a restatement of what the Church has presupposed from the beginning, i.e., that it has been the witness to Christ and His teaching ever since He Himself told the Apostles (Lk 10:16). "He who hears you hears me."

Vatican II distinguished, as did previous Councils, between defined and infallible truths, and non-defined and non-infallible doctrine. It insisted upon the obligation of giving true internal belief even to non-infallible teachings. The objection has been made that we cannot believe the Church, since it has so often erred in non-defined matters. However, a check of the actual instances proposed reveals only one case in 2000 years is even close to being an erroneous teaching. Actually, only some *theologians* in the Holy Office called Galileo's view heretical. The decision of the Holy Office itself called it only "*suspect* of heresy", and the Pope himself did *not* officially endorse the decision.(10) Other instances that are voiced do not stand up under close examination, e.g., the teaching on usury has not changed. Usury is taking *excessive* interest. Excessive interest rates remain unjust and sinful. Most states still have specific laws against usury. Society determines the precise amount that is *excessive* within its economic structures.

A further objection. Once we admit that there is a chance, even a small chance, of error, no one can be asked to give internal assent. We reply: (1) our assent takes into account that possibility, but does so realisitically, realizing that it is immensely remote; (2) everyday life does and must depend on non-infallible beliefs, e.g., if I eat food from a can, I have no infallible assurance it does not contain deadly botulism—even a laboratory check is not infallible, and of course, cooks do not everlastingly send their kettles of boiling soup to the laboratory. So most persons, including myself, daily risk their lives on non-infallible cooks. Occasionally indeed the undertaker is the court of last resort.

What of the claim that teachings are historically conditioned? In a way they are—revelation took place in concrete historical circumstances. We should, and do, study those circumstances and cultural settings to better understand the meaning as understood at the time the documents were composed: To refuse this type of study would be foolish fundamentalism. On the other hand, to question or discard all past teachings would be equally simplistic. The realistic course is a middle one, namely, to study the actual situation in which a revelation was given.

In making that study, several distinctions, as usual, are needed. First, only that which is *actually the object of judgment* in a given text constitutes the divinely inspired message. We are not called on to do mind reading, or to say that in view of conditions at the time the framers of a text *may* have been thinking of a given point. Of course, as noted, a knowledge of contemporary conditions and of the language employed does help us to see precisely what is actually expressed.

Second, are the forms of expression used in the past beyond all improvement? Vatican II answers, in the *Decree on Ecumenism*: "...if...there have been deficiencies...in the way that Church teaching has been formulated (to be carefully distinguished from the deposit of faith itself), these should be set right at the opportune time."(11) The qualification is obvious.

Obvious too is the fact that God Himself is beyond all human definition, i.e., we can never express His being or wisdom fully in human language. Yet we must not for this reason give up, and say all formulations are so deficient as to be unreliable. For it is precisely *the divine nature itself* that is inexpressible. But when we come, as it were, to derivative truths, these can be expressed and expressed sufficiently well, e.g., the fact that Jesus redeemed us; that He had two natures, divine and human. So we should not fall into nebulous obscurantism; we should carefully distinguish what can and what cannot be adequately expressed in human language.

Even in matters where perfect expression is not possible, *some* true judgments can be made, and made correctly. For this reason Pope Paul VI, in the document *Mysterium fidei*, insists: "The norm...of speaking which the Church...under the protection of the Holy Spirit, has established and confirmed by the authority of the Councils...must be religiously preserved. Let no one at his own whim or under the pretext of new knowledge presume to change it.... For by these formulae...concepts are expressed which are *not tied to one specific form of human civilization, or to one definite period of scientific progress, or to one school of theological thought,* but they present what the human mind...grasps of realities, and they express them in terms that are suitable and accurate.... For this reason, *these formulae are adapted to men of all times and all places.*"(12)

We need to note too that an important and obvious distinction is needed in regard to infallible definitions. Are we asked to consider as infallible both the conclusion (the teaching itself) and the reasons given for it? The Church has never insisted on the latter. Only the teaching itself (the conclusion), is guaranteed; the reasons are not. However, the reasons do have the status of non-infallible teaching.

We proceed, then, to the magisterial evidence:

1. Pope Vigilius

The Agnoites arose in the aftermath of Nestorianism and charged ignorance in the humanity of Jesus. They were quite logical in doing this, for if there were two persons in Jesus, one a merely human person, that human person might not even know about his relation to the divine person. Against such erroneous thinking Pope Vigilius hurled an anathema in his *Constitutum* of May 14, 553 A.D., "If anyone says that the one Jesus Christ, true Son of God and true Son of Man, was ignorant of future things, or of the day of the last judgement, and says He could know only as much as the divinity dwelling in Him as in another made known to Him: let him be anathema."(13)

R. Brown comments: "This error is so tied into the Nestorian theory of two persons or beings in Christ that its condemnation would not really affect the modern non-Nestorian problematic.''(14)

We must, of course, look at the anathema of Pope Vigilius in its historical setting. We must not forget that there was no need to condemn only Nestorianism: a general council had already done that. The Pope intended to add something, a condemnation of the charge of ignorance that had grown out of Nestorianism. And we must recall that the Fathers, as we saw, had studied the question of ignorance *independently of Nestorianism* for several centuries, and a rather general consensus had emerged against admitting any ignorance for any reason.

So, can we realistically suppose, within the actual setting, that Pope Vigilius meant that if a Nestorian charged Jesus with ignorance, he would fall under the anathema, but that if someone else found a different reason for charging ignorance it would be all right?

Yet, because he wrote *and*, not *or*, we cannot strictly prove that intent. For Vigilius joined two ideas grammatically: if a man attributes ignorance to Jesus *and* says Jesus could know only as much as the divinity residing in Him as in another revealed (a Nestorian picture), let him be anathema. Hence, as we said, we cannot strictly *prove* Vigilus meant to condemn charges of ignorance made in another framework. Nevertheless, in view of the long Patristic discussion carried on independently of Nestorianism, it borders on the absurd to suppose he would countenance such charges.

2. Pope St. Gregory the Great

Eulogius, Patriarch of Alexandria, as we noted in chapter 6, strongly attacked those who attributed ignorance to Jesus. Pope Gregory was greatly pleased, and said so in a letter to Eulogius, written probably in August of 600 A.D., ''...*in* the nature of His humanity He knew the day and hour of the judgment, but not however *from* this nature of humanity did He know it.''(15) It is impossible to say what this could mean if it did not say what we today express in different words, namely, that the knowledge of the day registered even *in* the human consciousness of

Jesus—even though it was not *from* any human resource that He knew it.

R. Brown says weakly that Gregory,(16) "tended to interpret Mk 13:32 as an accomodation of God's Son to human speech" and adds, "it is scarcely a *de Fide* pronouncement." Our rebuttal: first, Gregory did not merely *tend* to say Jesus knew even humanly—Gregory quite flatly and insistently said Jesus did know even in His humanity (of course, Gregory thinks Jesus used "accomodation" in the sense of what the Greek Fathers called *oikonoma*). Further, Brown is quite out of order in saying that this is "scarcely" *de fide*, implying that whatever is not *de fide* can be disregarded at will. He forgets the force of non-defined statements, as taught by Vatican II.

Pope St. Gregory also wrote: "The matter however is very evident: whoever is not a Nestorian cannot be an Agnoite. For he who admits that the Wisdom of God is incarnate, in what way can he say that there is anything that the Wisdom of God does not know?"(17) Gregory continues, and mentions that when Jesus asked where Lazarus was buried, He was acting in the same way as the Father had done in Genesis when He said: "Adam, where are you?" or to Cain: "Where is Abel your brother?" The Fathers, as already shown in chapter 6, made the same observation many times over. Brown however reveals a strange lack of perception in commenting that Gregory "would seem to have ruled out even acquired human knowledge"(18) in saying that Jesus knew where Lazarus was. Brown fails to recognize that the very same things can be known via more than one channel. On a TV broadcast I may see the identical event about which I previously had heard on the radio. Or, a closer parallel: I may go and see for myself something I already knew by other means.

Should we say that the teaching of Pope Gregory is so tied to the Nestorian framework that it does not apply outside it? By no means. Gregory does add a comment, in our second citation, on the Nestorian situation. It means that one cannot say *Jesus* did not know unless he holds there was a second person, a human person, in Jesus. For to say a divine Person could be ignorant is most obvious heresy. But Gregory clearly went beyond the

Nestorian framework, as we can see from the distinction he made that Jesus knew the day *in*, but not *from* His humanity. No such distinction is used in discussing Nestorian ideas. Rather, that distinction is at least approximately equivalent to our modern distinction inquiring whether something registered *in* his human mind. In Gregory, that distinction is actually the long sought completion of the Patristic discussion which had gone on for so many centuries largely independently of Nestorianism. Hence, Gregory's remarks are not at all confined to the Nestorian problematic.

3. Decrees of the Holy Office of 1907 and 1918

Only July 3, 1907, the Holy Office, in the Decree *Lamentabili* directed against the Modernists, a document approved by Pope St. Pius X, rejected the following propositions:(19)

> The natural sense of the Gospel texts cannot be reconciled with what our theologians teach about the consciousness and infallible knowledge of Jesus Christ.
>
> A critic cannot assert that the knowledge of Christ was without limit except on the supposition—which historically cannot be conceived, and which is repugnant to moral sense—namely, that Christ as man had the knowledge of God, and nevertheless was unwilling to communicate the knowledge of so many things to the disciples and posterity.
>
> Christ did not always have a consciousness of His messianic dignity.

It is pointed out, and we agree, that it is difficult to determine the precise theological note to be attached to these rejections.(20) Yet we must note that when we read them in context, i.e., in view of previous Magisterium statements, and also of those to follow shortly, they do seem to reject the notion of even human ignorance in Jesus.

On June 5, 1918, the Holy Office issued a Decree, approved by Pope Benedict XV, in which it answered several questions: "Can the following propositions be safely taught? 1. It is not evident that there was in the soul of Christ living among men the knowledge which the blessed who have attained [God] have. 2. Nor can that opinion be called certain which states that the soul of Christ was ignorant of nothing, but that from the beginning He knew in the Word all things, past, present, and future, that is, all things which God knows by the knowledge of vision. 3. The view of certain recent persons about the limited knowledge of the soul of Christ is not to be less accepted in Catholic schools than the view of former [theologians] about [His] universal knowledge.—Response (confimred by the Holy Father on June 6): Negative."(21)

This decree does formulate the problem in the more recent terminology, for it refers to the human soul of Christ. Yet the resolution is that the positions described may not be safely taught.

4. Pius XI: Miserentissimus Redemptor, May 8, 1928

"Now if the soul of Christ [in Gethsemani] was made sorrowful even to death on account of our sins, which were yet to come, but which were foreseen, there is no doubt that He received some consolation from our reparation, likewise foreseen."(22)

It is obvious that Pius XI teaches that the human soul of Jesus in Gethsemani knew both our future sins, and our future reparation.

5. Pius XII: Mystici Corporis, June 29, 1943

But the most loving knowledge of this kind, with which the divine Redeemer pursued us from the first moment of the Incarnation, surpasses the diligent grasp of any human mind; for by that blessed vision which He enjoyed when just received in the womb of the Mother of God, He has all the members of the Mystical Body continuously and perpetually present to Himself, and embraces them with salvific love.... In the manger, on the Cross, in the eternal glory of the Father, Christ has all the members of the Church before Him [conspecta] and joined to Him far more clearly and far more lovingly than a mother has a son of her lap, or than each one knows and loves himself.(23)

Here is a perfectly clear teaching that the human soul of Jesus did enjoy the beatific vision, even from the moment of conception. The particular body of knowledge mentioned here is the knowledge of each member of the Mystical Body—surely, an immense block of information. Of special importance is the fact that this statement was made not within the Nestorian framework, but in a strictly modern framework. By the time *Mystici Corporis* appeared, in 1943, Galtier's book of 1939(24) had already stimulated modern discussion. Within that framework Pius XII spoke strongly and clearly, all in harmony with previous Magisterium teachings and the conclusions of the Fathers.

6. Pius XII, Sempiternus Rex, September 8, 1951

Just a year earlier, in 1950, Pius XII had issued *Humani generis* in which he proscribed a goodly number of errors. In *Sempiternus Rex* he specifically treated the question, then already raging, concerning the consciousness of Jesus: "There are those who...misuse the authority and definition of the Council of Chalcedon.... They so insist on the state and condition of the humanity of Christ that it seems to be considered as a subject, as it were, in itself [*sui iuris*], as if it did not subsist in the person of the Word. But Chalcedon...forbids putting two individuals in Christ so that some 'assumed man,' having full autonomy, is placed with the Word."(25) This document is quite clearly aimed at the loose statements of those theologians who were—and still are—saying, "*He* did not know...." We presume they really mean only to say that a given fact, such as the knowledge of the date of the parousia, did not register on the human consciousness of Jesus, without saying that the Person, a divine Person, the divine *He*, did not know. Pius XII saw the need to rebuke this error—though with little result, for such loose language still abounds today.

It is well known that in an early version of this document the words *"saltem psychologice"* (at least psychologically) were present, but were omitted in the final text. Why? A good reason for omitting the words would have been this: if they were present, someone might think the Pope was forbidding the notion of a *separate human consciousness in Jesus*. Surely, he did not want to forbid that; it would have been false doctrine to forbid it. For the Council of Chalcedon had already taught that there was a real human nature in Jesus. That of course includes a human mind, and a human mind includes a human consciousness. Pius XII, then, wanted to be careful not to even appear to contradict Chalcedon. Did he also, as some claim, mean to leave the door open for saying that many things, including the divine Sonship, did not register on His human consciousness? Definitely not. For the same Pius XII, as we have observed, also taught clearly that the human soul of Jesus enjoyed the beatific vision even from the first moment of His conception.

7. Pius XII, Haurietis aquas, May 15, 1956

In his important encyclical on the theology of the Sacred Heart, Pius XII repeated the teaching of *Mystici Corporis*, with some additions: "It [the Sacred Heart of Jesus] is also a symbol of that most burning love which, infused into His soul, enriches the human will of Christ, and whose activity is illumined and directed by a twofold knowledge, that is, beatific and infused."(26) Here Pius XII reaffirmed the teaching that the human soul of Jesus had the beatific vision. And he added a confirmation of the view of many previous theologians that His soul also enjoyed infused knowledge. Father Bertrand de Margerie, S.J., makes an important comment: "It seems to us that, in contrast to the knowledge of vision and infused knowledge, the infused knowledge of Jesus is the effect of the invisible mission of the Holy Spirit to the Messiah from the first instant of the inhumanation of the Word."(27) And he continues, citing from *Mystici Corporis*: "The Holy Spirit took His delight in dwelling in the soul of the Redeemer as in His well beloved temple; He dwelt in the Christ with such a fulness of graces that one cannot conceive of anything greater."

8. Congregation for the Teaching of the Faith, July 24, 1966

Many theologians had noted the omission of the words "at least psychologically" from the final text of *Sempiternus Rex*, and were using that omission to claim they were free to deny that the divine Sonship, and many other facts, registered on the human consciousness of Jesus. In the context of that situation, the Congregation for the Teaching of the Faith, successor to the Holy Office, spoke quite bluntly:

> It is regrettable that bad news from various places has arrived, of abuses prevailing in interpreting the teaching of the Council, and

> of strange and bold opinions arising here and there which greatly
> disturb the souls of many of the faithful...dogmatic formulae are
> said to be so subject to historical evolution that even their
> objective sense is open to change.... There creeps forth a certain
> Christological humanism in which Christ is reduced to the
> condition of a mere man, who gradually acquired consciousness
> of His divine Sonship.(28)

The Sacred Congregation begins by rejecting the notion that
older formulations are so time-conditioned as to be almost or
entirely useless. In *Mysterium fidei* Paul VI had said the same
even more forcefully the previous year. But the Congregation for
the Teaching of the Faith specifically condemned the idea that the
human consciousness of Jesus only gradually acquired awareness
of His divine Sonship. In so doing, it was reaffirming the teachings
of Pius XII in *Mystici Corporis* and *Haurietis aquas*, which insist
upon the fact that the human soul of Jesus had the beatific vision
from the very first instant of His human conception.

9. Conclusions from the Magisterium

1) We must never say that *He* did not know some things. For
the *He* is a divine Person.

2) The human soul, and so the human consciousness of Jesus,
did enjoy the beatific vision from the first moment of human
conception. That vision made known to Him all the members of His
Mystical Body, of all centuries. It made known also His divine
Sonship. It also made known to Him the day and hour of the
parousia. In itself, the beatific vision contains all knowledge. Yet
any created soul, human or angelic, even the human soul of Jesus,
is finite. Hence, at any given moment, it will not contain infinite
knowledge. So, in itself, that vision could omit a given point such
as the parousaic day and hour. Mk 13:32 tells us that such is the
case with the angels. However, the Magisterium insists that
Jesus, even as man, did know the day and the hour.

3) Since, in the context, Pope Gregory the Great was speaking
of the human knowledge of Jesus, we must take his statement, "Is
there anything that the Wisdom of God does not know?" as
meaning that Jesus, while not having infinite knowledge in His

human soul, yet at all times knew all things as the Word, and that whatever pertained in any way to the matter on hand always registered in His human consciousness.

4) The human soul of Jesus enjoyed infused knowledge.

The doctrinal weight of the above statements was treated in the introductory part of this chapter. These teachings are theologically certain, and, according to Vatican II, require true internal assent.(29)

NOTES

1   Anselm Atkins, "Transcendence and the Expressions of the Magisterium" in *CTSA Proceedings* 23 (1968) 85-95 esp. 92.

2   R.E. Brown, *The Virginal Conception and Bodily Resurrection of Jesus*, Paulist, New York, 1973, 7-14.

3   Karl Rahner, "Dogmatic Reflections on the Knowledge and Self-Consciousness of Christ" in *Theological Investigations*, tr. K.H. Kruger, Helicon, Baltimore, 1966, V. 213-14. The German original has "randhaften beilaufigen" Vol. V, 243. Rahner professes to adhere to the Magisterium on our question (199, 213). See chapter 8 on whether or not he really does.

4   Avery Dulles, "Contemporary Understanding of the Irreformability of Dogma" in *CTSA Proceedings* 25 (1970) 136.

5   Atkins, *art. cit.*, 94 (italics his).

6   Vatican II, Constitution on Divine Revelation #10.

7   *Cf.* Introduction.

8   Avery Dulles, *Apologetics and the Biblical Christ, Woodstock Papers* 6, Newman, Westminster, Maryland, 1963.

9   Vatican II, Constitution on the Church #25.

10 *Cf.* J. Mirus, "Galileo and the Magisterium: A Second Look" in *Faith & Reason* 3.2 (1977) 65-69, and further references there.

11 Vatican II, Decree on Ecumenism #6.

12 Paul VI, *Mysterium fidei*, September 3, 1965. AAS 57 (1965) 758.

13 DS 419.

14 JGM 77, n. 59.

15 DS 475.

16 JGM 77, n. 59 (emphasis added).

17 DS 476.

18 JGM 40-41, n. 4.

19 DS 3432, 3434, 3435.
20 R. Brown, JGM 82, n. 64.
21 DS 3645-47.
22 AAS. 20. 174.
23 DS 3812. K. Rahner, *art. cit.*, 214, n. 13 cites this text (using the old DB number 2289) as an example of a "marginal and incidental" text. Yet the teaching is not incidental and marginal. In that section Pius XII develops the idea that Christ, the Head of the Mystical Body, loved us with infinite knowledge and love before the world began, in His divine nature. To give visible expression to that love, He assumed human nature, and at once, even in the womb of His Mother, He knew and loved each one of us, thanks to the beatific vision. Rahner, as we shall see in chapter 8, wants to make the vision non-beatific, a vague charism that had to grow, and basically the same as the self-knowledge an ordinary person has (in Christ, the self-knowledge would include knowledge of His divine sonship *vaguely*, and so that He had to learn to express it!).

Such a vision is not what the Fathers and Doctors of the Church understand by beatific vision. Nor would so vague an awareness include all the members of His Mystical Body. Pius XII, in the same argument, says Christ had all members of the Church present in a much clearer and more loving manner than that of a mother who clasps her child. Rahner adds, in the same note, "It must always be remembered that the presence of a loved person in consciousness can be conceived in many different ways." He seems to mean a mere *affective* presence—which is not what a *vision* provides, and surely is far less than that of a child being clasped directly by its mother (to which Pius XII compares this presence). Still further, Rahner ignores altogether the teaching of *Haurietis aquas* of Pius XII, which also describes the human knowledge and love of Jesus, and does so as an integral part of the solidly theological discussion of the triple love and triple knowledge of Jesus.

Rahner also argues, in note 10 on p. 203 of the same article, that the word "beatific" can be taken loosely in this text since "...the fact that Jesus was not simply as blessed on earth as the Saints in heaven cannot really be denied." Of course not; but that does not preclude a true beatific vision, for there are various levels of soul, as will be explained in chapter 8. Rahner dismisses these levels as "artificial layer-psychology" (p. 203), in spite of repeated experiences of saints and the resultant findings of mystical theology (see chapter 8).

24 P. Galtier, *L'unite du Christ—Etre, Personne, Conscience*, 3rd ed. Beauchesne, Paris, 1939.
25 DS 3905. The first publication of this Encyclical in *Osservatore Romano* carried the words "saltem psychologice," but the phrase

was omitted in the final, official text of AAS 43 (1951) 638. On the expression, *cf.* P. Galtier, "La conscience humaine du Christ" in *Gregorianum* 32 (1951) 562, n. 68 and K. Rahner, "Current Problems in Christology" in *Theological Investigations*, tr. C. Ernst, Helicon, Baltimore, 1961 I, 159.

26 DS 3924.
27 Bertrand de Margerie, S.J., "De la Science du Christ—Science, prescience et conscience, meme prepascales du Christ Redempteur" in *Espirit et Vie*, 89 (1977) 380 (no. 47).
28 AAS 58 (1966) 659-60.
29 Constitution on the Church #25 (discussed above, pp 135-36).

8. Theological Speculation

A major development in the discussion of Jesus' knowledge came as a result of modern interest in psychology. The discussion was greatly stimulated by P. Galtier in a work entitled *L'unite du Christ, Etre, Personne, Conscience*.(1) In a subsequent publication he modified his opinions somewhat.(2) We have a summary of his views in a 1951 article appearing in the *Gregorianum*: "The key to that psychology seems to me to be found in the Beatific Vision, thanks to which the human nature was able, in a certain sense, to have a consciousness of being united to the divine person, and of making only one substantial being with it. But it does not follow that that consciousness perceived directly and of itself the person to which it belonged."(3) We might loosely compare the difference to the difference between seeing, as on a television screen, the fact of being united to a divine Person, and the direct consciousness of being so united. Galtier argued that we perceive our soul by way of its acts.(4) Since our person and nature are of the one same being, there is no problem. But in Christ the nature that produces the human acts is different from that of the divine Person: hence a difficulty. So he adds that we must recognize in the humanity of Christ "a real psychological autonomy."(5)

Strong reactions followed, especially from the Thomists. The literature is immense.(6) We shall first examine the views of several major thinkers and then propose a solution.

1. Karl Rahner

Rahner's views have been especially influential. He makes a remarkable claim: "There is certainly a nescience which renders the finite person's exercise of freedom possible.... This nescience is, therefore, more perfect for the exercise of freedom than knowledge which would suspend this exercise."(7) He takes note of the teaching of the Church that the soul of Jesus had the beatific vision. He insists that his proposals do not clash with any binding teaching.(8) But he says that it is too easily taken from granted that the vision of God brings bliss, or is beatific. He says there is no reason why "the direct presence to the judging and consuming holiness of the incomprehensible God should necessarily and always have a beatific effect."(9) He holds that Jesus did have a *visio immediata*, but that it was not beatific. He points to "Christ's death-agony and feeling of being forsaken by God"(10) even of a "deadly feeling of being forsaken by God" and asks: "Can one seriously maintain—without applying an artificial layer-psychology—that Jesus enjoyed the beatitude of the blessed,"(11) and says further "...the fact that Jesus was not simply as blessed on earth as the saints in heaven cannot really be denied."(12)

So Rahner proposes a different interpretation of the direct vision of God in Jesus: "...this really existing direct vision of God is nothing other than the original unobjectified consciousness of divine sonship, which is present by the mere fact that there *is* a Hypostatic Union."(13) He compares this to the self-knowledge that an ordinary person has, a knowledge that grows from long experience with himself: "Only in the course of long experience can he [an ordinary man] learn to express to himself what he is and what he indeed he has always already seen in this self-consciousness of his basic condition...so it is also in the case of Christ's consciousness of divine sonship.... We can, therefore, speak without qualms about a spiritual and indeed religious development in Jesus."(14)

There are, however, some problems with Rahner's views. To begin, he thinks that some ignorance is needed for freedom. He asserts: "The objective perception of every individual object right down to the last detail would be the end of freedom."(15) One could counter: What about God Himself? There is no ignorance in Him, there is a knowledge of every object and every detail of every object. Yet He is free, supremely free, the source of our freedom.

Rahner also proposes what may be called a "non-beatific" beatific vision, and observes that a direct presence to God can be not only non-beatific, it can be terrifying if it is the presence of God as Judge, as supreme Holiness. Here Rahner misses two points: (1) The presence of God as Judge, as Holiness, is dreadful only to souls that are not fit, not prepared. Such was not the case with the soul of Christ. (2) Rahner misses the immediacy of the vision (even though he uses the word, saying he proposes a *visio immediata*). The vision of which the Magisterium speaks is most absolutely immediate, and, in a soul that is fit, necessarily produces beatitude. Pope Benedict XII, in his *Benedictus Deus* of December 20, 1336, taught that souls enjoying the beatific vision, "see the divine essence with an intuitive and even face to face vision, *with no creature mediating*, [or] being in the nature of an object seen, but with the divine essence showing itself immediately, without veil, clearly and openly to them, and that seeing [this] they enjoy the same divine essence."(16)

Behind this statement is the obvious fact that no image or creature could show God as He is—for any image or creature is finite. When I see anyone else face to face, I take within me the image of that person. Since the person is finite, an image can let me know that person fully. But as we said, no image, being finite, can show God as he is. Hence, to really know God it is necessary that He join Himself directly to the human intellect, with no intermediary. Such is also the view of St. Thomas Aquinas.(17) This is substantially different from a perception of God as judge, for in that function, He does not join Himself so absolutely directly to the human intellect.

Still further, the kind of vision Rahner proposes hardly should be called a *vision* at all. It is rather just a vague self-knowledge, which Rahner compares to that of an ordinary man. An ordinary man gets to know himself through his actions and experiences. The more of these, the more he can know himself. Hence his self-knowledge can and does grow. Rahner is proposing such a knowledge as an "immediate vision" of the divinity—non-beatific. It could be called a knowledge of the divinity, Rahner thinks, inasmuch as for Jesus to know Himself is to know the divinity of the Word, to which His human soul is united. Such a vague, gradually growing perception hardly matches the description of the beatific vision given by the Magisterium. So, in spite of his protestations that he is not contradicting the Magisterium, Rahner is really doing so in not attributing to Jesus the kind of vision the Magisterium means. Such a vision as Rahner proposes would not really be vision including each member of His Mystical Body; but Pius XII taught it did (cf. Chapter 7).(18)

Rahner also tries to show how the vision was not beatific by pointing to a "deadly feeling of being forsaken by God."(19) Closely allied is his statement, as a result of His sufferings, "Jesus was not simply as blessed on earth as the saints in heaven."(20) First, as to the deadly feeling of being forsaken: here Rahner sounds more like an emotional sermonizer than a theologian. Jesus was simply reciting Psalm 22 when He said, "My God, why have you forsaken me." Psalm 22 was a most suitable prayer because of its remarkable description of His Passion.

Rahner is right, obviously, in saying that Jesus was not as blessed as those in heaven, for His bitter sufferings made a difference. But this fact does not support Rahner's claim that the vision was non-beatific for Jesus, or that a beatific vision would be in Jesus' case, incompatible with suffering. Actually, Rahner knows the key to the problem, but dismisses it, not with scholarly reasoned analysis, but with ridicule when he speaks of "an artificial layer-psychology."(21) The truth is that the beatific vision rules out all suffering in a pure spirit and in a human being with a body transformed after the resurrection. Yet both mystical theology and the experience of many saints give evidence that for a human being with a non-transformed body, even highly pleasurable experiences of direct contact with God in infused contemplation are fully compatible with distress, even with distress of mind. Thus St. Francis de Sales, in his *Treatise on the*

Love of God:

> Alas, Theotimus, that the poor heart is afflicted when, as if abandoned by love, it looks everywhere and does not find it, so it seems. It does not find it in the exterior senses, for they are incapable; nor in the imagination, which is cruelly tormented with various impressions, nor in the intellect, troubled with a thousand obscurities...and strange apprehensions; and although at last it finds it in the peak and supreme region of the spirit, where that divine love resides, nevertheless it does not recognize it, and thinks it is not it, because the greatness of the distress and the darkness prevent feeling its sweetness...it has no strength except to let its will die at the hands of the will of God, imitating sweet Jesus, who, having arrived at the height of the pains of the Cross...and no longer able to resist the extremity of His torments, did as the hart does which is out of breath and pressed by the hounds, yields itself to the hunter, utters its last cries, with tears in its eyes.(22)

Or again:

> It is thus, Theotimus, the soul is sometimes so pressed by interior afflictions that all its faculties and powers are weighed down by privation of all that might give relief and by taking on the impression of all that can cause sadness...having nothing left but the fine supreme point of the spirit, which, attached to the heart and good pleasure of God, says in a very simple resignation: O Eternal Father, may always your will be done, not mine.(23)

St. John of the Cross, a great mystic and subtle mystical theologian, writes in a similar vein: "This is an enkindling of love in the spirit, where, in the midst of these dark afflictions, the soul feels itself to be keenly and acutely wounded in strong divine love, and to have a certain realization and foretaste of God, although it understands nothing definitely, for, as we say, the understanding is in darkness."(24)

It would be easy to fill pages telling of the actual experiences of mystics.(25) Let us cite one passage, from Venerable Sister Barbara: "God has given me to drink the dregs of this most bitter chalice and at the same time communicated a sweetness which must be experienced to be believed. It is sweet and bitter at the same time.... My God has hidden Himself from me and left me in a state of the greatest desolation.... Everywhere there is darkness.''(26)

2. F. E. Crowe

Like Rahner, F. E. Crowe admits that the soul of Jesus had a "direct vision" of God. Rahner specifically calls it non-beatific. Crowe seems to mean the same thing. Rahner admits even religious growth in Jesus; Crowe does so too. But Crowe goes about things quite differently. He thinks that "the efforts made to build a theology of his knowledge of God on his self-consciousness are ill-advised.''(27)

Crowe proposes three "analogies" for the vision of God. He begins with what he calls a Thomist understanding of the vision of God. He says the Thomist doctrine is "transformed by Lonergan into a doctrine of the spontaneously operative notion of being or the pure notion of being: 'The pure notion of being is the detached, disinterested, unrestricted desire to know.'''(28) He thinks this notion of being is present in all our activities of knowing, but is not there consciously as a red light or bell would be, it is, "Not ordinarily adverted to.''(29) This suggests to him a parallel to the vision of God that the soul of Jesus had: "Christ's understanding of the divine mysteries was inexpressible,''(30) like the words St. Paul heard (2 Cor. 12:4). "There had therefore to be a translation from one understanding to the other....'' So, "the vision of God gave him no actual knowledge that was expressible. He had to win this slowly.'' So he had to learn everything,(31) for this "vision" did not include the words *Father*, or *Son*, or *Spirit*, or *Creator*, or *Almighty*, or *Eternal*. It did not supply Jesus with religious ideas at all.(32) And He had to learn to remember the Aramaic equivalents of *Mama* and *Papa*, and so on.

Crowe's second analogy comes from the experience of mystics,(33) who found difficulty in expressing what they learned from their experiences. So also, he says, with the soul of Jesus.

His third analogy rests on, "our own ordinary faith experience...the most fundamental ideas...remain preconceptual...we might think of our inability to say anything appropriate on the great occasions of life—disaster and death, or love and success and triumph."(34)

So the vision gave Jesus only the generic principles, the *"species et genera rerum et rationes earum"* with the result that "the mind of Jesus [had] to operate according to this scissors-action, with the upper blade supplied by his understanding of God and the most general preconceptual ideas that derive from that understanding...and the lower blade supplied by the thousands and thousands of items of data that met his eye and ear and taste and smell and touch during his life on earth."(35) Only by experience, reacting with these vague generalities, would He have any distinct and expressible knowledge.

These analogies are peculiar. In the first, Crowe borrows Lonergan's notion of being as "the detached, disinterested, unrestricted desire to know." But we observe: if *desire* is equated with *being*, then the more desire the more being, and vice versa. But: desire presupposes a *lack*—for we do not desire what we do not lack—so, *the more being, the more lack of being.*

His second analogy in a way blends with the first, for in the first he had spoken of the inexpressible words St. Paul referred to in 2 Cor 12:4. In the second analogy Crowe compares the vision of Jesus to that of the mystics. But again his analogy is far from complete: (1) the mystics did not, as a rule at least, have the beatific vision; they had instead various forms of infused contemplation (which lacks images) or at times sensory or other images. (2) Why were their experinces inexpressible? We must distinguish between the divine essence in itself, and other religious facts. If they in some way contacted the divine essence itself, the divinity *in itself* is inexpressible, or better, is not *fully* expressible in human language. But it is *partly* expressible: hence we do have many defined truths about God in Himself. (3) A large part of the reason the mystics called their experiences inexpressible was not that everything was inexpressible in itself, but that *human language lacks the needed words.* For example, if I say, "red, blue, or green," a man who is not color blind understands, for *we both have had the experience* of these colors. But if I talk of the colors to a colorblind person, there is a lack of common experience. I could tell him the wavelengths of each color, but that would be far from giving him the impression a normal person gets from my words. Similarly, if a person who has had the special experience of infused contemplation talks to one who has not had it—there is almost nothing common in their experience, and so no words suffice. However, if two persons who have both had that experience talk together, they will have a struggle with language, but they will be able to make themselves understood, and to compare notes. For they have had a common experience.

But, further, not everything that is known by any soul in the vision of God is vague and generic. That vision does contain all knowledge. Crowe appeals to a reply given by St. Thomas in *Summa* I.12.8 ad 4, in which Thomas seems to say that souls see only generic things in the vision of God. Unfortunately, Crowe neglects the context. Thomas says souls see all they *desire* to see. They do not desire every last detail in the universe. So they are content with generalities on many things. Yet, in the body of the same article Thomas gives the fundamental principle: "A soul knows the more things, the more perfectly it sees God!"

So there are specific facts in the vision of God. Many of these are readily expressible, because the needed words are found in human language, e.g., the notion of Messiah, Son of God, date of the parousia, and the like.

How many of these things should the human soul of Jesus see? There are two criteria. First, as we saw, Thomas says that the more perfectly a soul sees God, the more it will know. Now the ability to see in that vision is in proportion to grace (or the light of glory). But the soul of Jesus was most full of grace. Hence it was fitted to see more than any other soul ever did or will see in that vision. Further, His mode of contact with the divinity, as it were, is greater than that of any soul—for He is joined even in the unity of one Person (as we shall see more fully presently).

The second criterion is this: any soul ought to see in that vision all that pertains to it, for we can be confident that God will by grace (light of glory) make a soul capable of seeing all that pertains to it. But to Jesus there pertained all that belonged to His mission. And that should include the fullness of truth in religious matters, and who He was, what He was to do.

Crowe's third analogy is feeble indeed. For some persons are far from unable to say anything appropriate on great occasions such as disaster and death, love, success and triumph.

Finally, and very importantly, Crowe like Rahner, has neglected to note that the Magisterium insists that Jesus' soul did see countless distinct things: He knew and loved each one of us from the first instant of His conception. He knew the day of the parousia. Further, the Magisterium does call that vision beatific, a point explictly denied by Rahner and Crowe.

3. Jacques Maritain

Maritain had intended his *Peasant of the Garonne* to be his last book, yet decided to add another, *On the Grace and Humanity of Jesus*.(36) He takes his start from the important text of Luke 2:52 saying that Christ "grew in wisdom, in age, and in grace before God and before men." The Fathers, as we saw in chapter 6, understand this of growth in manifestation, not of growth in actual knowledge and grace. St. Thomas too, speaks in accord with the Fathers.(37) But Maritain says that the Fathers "have but a human authority,"(38) so that if they conflict with St. Luke, they, and St. Thomas too, must be brushed aside. Maritain is certain that, "St. Luke is not thinking of the effects and of the works produced; he is thinking of the *grace* and of the *wisdom* themselves...."(39) But, St. Thomas, "lacked the philosophical instrument of which I have just spoken" which is the notion of a "supraconscious."(40)

Christ's human soul was divided, Maritain thinks, by a "partition"(41) into two realms of consciousnesses, "the divinized supraconscious" and the "crepuscular" consciousness—the latter comparable to the dim light just before dawn, or at sunset.(42) The supraconscious realm has the beatific vision; the crepuscular realm does not: "There was, so to speak, a *partition* between the world of the Beatific Vision and that of the conscious faculties."(43)

Was there intercommunication between the two worlds? Not to any extent: "There was also *a certain incommunicability* between them, which caused that the *content* of the supraconscious heaven of the soul was retained [held back], could not pass into the world of consciousness, of the here-below, except...by mode of general influx, and of comforting and of participated light."(44) Further, "This Paradise *was there* because Christ was *comprehensor* [had beatific vision]. It was *closed* because Christ was *viator* [still on the way to the final goal]."(45) Even the comforting influence was shut off during the Passion, for He was "barred from it by uncrossable barriers; this is why He feels himself abandoned."(46)

This barrier or partition was so great that Maritain can refer to the supraconscious(47) as "a preconscious...of the spirit,"(48) and can even say: "With regard to this 'terrestrial' or 'crepuscular' consciousness the world of the celestial or 'solar' consciousness, the world of the divinized supraconscious was from the point of view of man-*viator* a sort of total 'unconscious', but in a sense entirely different from that in which this word is said of the infraconscious."(49)

How is it that there was such incomunicability? Here we reach the very heart of Maritain's position: "This Vision... is *absolutely simple* (indivisible) and *absolutely inexpressible in any concept, any idea*, even as to the particular things which it makes known. How has one been able sometimes to forget this? As if the Vision was not absolutely indivisible and could be parcelled out! It is precisely for this reason that...absolutely nothing of that which was known by Him in the Vision could directly pass into the sphere of consciousness, be directly known by Him in such a way that He might express it to Himself and express it to others—whether it is a question of His own divinity or of the moment when the Second Coming will take place."(50)

He seems to mean this: When we know in this human life, in which our spiritual intellect has to function together with our physical part, we need concepts, with sensory images. But the beatific vision contains no such things. And it cannot be divided, it is simple and indivisible. Hence the barrier. Hence the need to suppose two realms.

Maritain *seems* to propose a way of getting knowledge into the lower realm. He explains that if one has a thousand dollar bill and stands before a vending machine that takes only quarters, he cannot get orange juice, or anything else, from it. He must first find a moneychanger.(51) But there *seems* to be one: "That which is the case of Christ played the role of money-changer, and enabled Him to know in the sphere of His consciousness, and to express to Himself and to express to others something that He knew already...in His Beatific Vision was His infused science [knowledge]."(52)

Twice we underscored the word *seems* because the solution is not really so helpful as it might appear to be. For Maritain insists that even the infused knowledge of Jesus is divided into the two worlds, or is in "two different states in the heaven of His soul and in the here-below of His soul."(53) The infused knowledge of the upper world is in "a state totally unattainable to the consciousness....[it] was strictly *incommunicable.*"(54)

Hence there had to be a second state of infused knowledge: "It was necessary that this infused science [knowledge] not find itself only in the supraconscious paradise of the soul of Christ; it was necessary that, in proportion as the sphere of the consciousness or of the here-below of the soul of Christ forms itself, His infused science hold sway in this other sphere, where it is subject to the regime *connatural to the human soul* and where...it could *use instrumentally concepts formed under the light of the agent intellect....*"(55)

We note Maritain said in this last quotation that there was a development in the lower sphere "in proportion as the sphere of the consciousness or of the here-below of the soul of Christ forms itself."

Hence Maritain asserts that this awareness of His own divinity, "developed during the childhood of Jesus probably very quickly"(56) and after that "it is absolutely necessary also that it should have grown progressively at the same time as developed His consciousness of Himself, and that the idea of God took better and better shape in His mind."(57)

Unfortunately, Maritain has made a preliminary mistake in his almost fundamentalistic use of Luke 2:52. The Fathers, as we saw in chapter 6, do understand this text of growth only in manifestation and effects, not of actual growth in wisdom and grace. But Maritain dismisses the Fathers as having, "but a human authority."(58) In contrast, Vatican II, as the Church has always done, considers the Fathers as a major part of Tradition, one of the sources of divine revelation,(59) and adds that in interpreting Scripture we must take diligent account of the "living Tradition of the whole Church and the analogy of faith."(60) The analogy of faith bids us understand things in Scripture in the light of how they fit with the entire body of our teachings.

But the most basic error underlying the entire position of Maritain is his insistence that since the beatific vision is simple and indivisible—which is true—that therefore, "absolutely nothing of that which was known by Him in the Vision could be directly known by Him in such a way that He might express it to Himself and express it to others."(61) Maritain fails to note that although such concepts are not formally present in the vision, they can be its effects, caused by it through the action of human faculties. St. Thomas clearly holds this. He uses a comparison: Just as our image-making power can take our concepts or images of a mountain and of gold, and put them together, to get the image or concept of a golden mountain, and just as from an image of a statue we can form the image of him whom the statue represents: "thus [St.] Paul, or anyone else, by seeing God, from the vision itself of the divine essence can form in himself likenesses of the things that are seen in the divine essence. These remained in Paul even after he stopped seeing the essence of God."(62)

Hence St. Thomas, speaking of the beatific knowledge of the human soul of Christ, said that by this vision it knew, "All things that in any way are, or will, or were done or said or thought by anyone, at any time. And so it is to be said that the soul of Christ knew all [actual] things in the Word."(63) St. Thomas continues, adding that His soul did not know all *possibles*—this would be to have infinite knowledge. No created soul, not even His, can contain infinite knowledge.

In regard to Maritain's restriction on Christ's infused knowledge, St. Thomas teaches that the human soul of Christ, by infused knowledge, could know even without the need or use of sensory images.(64)

Maritain calls the notion of the supraconscious a modern one, and says it replaces the older concept of the higher part of the soul.(65) In a note on page 40 he refers us to another work of his, *Creative Intuition in Art and Poetry*. There he distinguishes: "There are two kinds of unconscious, two great domains of psychological activity screened from the grasp of the conscious: the preconscious [same as the supraconscious] of the spirit in its living springs, and the unconscious of blood and flesh, instincts, tendencies, complexes, repressed images and desires, traumatic memories...."(66) The higher of these two is what psychologists commonly call our subconscious—hardly a place for the beatific vision! And there is not really an uncrossable barrier at all between our subconscious and our conscious. As soon as an idea has germinated, as it were, in the subconscious, it literally pops, suddenly, into our consciousness, as a bright thought, in a form we can readily use.

Further, the classic concept, held by St. Thomas and mystical theologians in general(67) of the higher part of the soul does not at all represent an inaccessible region—it is simply a higher realm of operation, which we very much perceive, which gives a peace which nothing can take away even in the midst of deep distress on the lower levels.

Finally, Maritain's picture breaks the unity of Christ, makes Him almost schizoid.

4. Raymond Brown's Objection

Brown has made no substantive contribution to theological speculation on this problem. He seems to have accepted Rahner's view that Jesus had "some sort of intuition or immediate awareness of who he was, but...that the ability to express this in a communicable way had to be acquired gradually."(68) Brown, however, proposes an objection from St. Thomas, which he may have taken from an article by A. Durand.(69) Thomas, as translated by Brown, says: "If there had not been in the soul of Christ some other knowledge besides his divine knowledge, *he* would not have known anything. Divine knowledge cannot be an act of the human soul of Christ; it belongs to another nature.''(70)

First of all, the translation given is inexact. We italicized the pronoun *he*—the Latin would have permitted a rendering of the pronound by *it*, which would refer to the human soul of Christ. St. Thomas clearly meant the latter, for to say *''He* would know nothing: would be heretical, since the *He* is a divine Person. We do not at all suggest Fr. Brown meant heresy; no, it was merely careless language, for Brown seems eager to find reasons that would at least limit the knowledge that registered in the human soul of Jesus.

Brown is fond of saying that texts are ''historically conditioned''. That is true of texts of St. Thomas. If we examine the actual setting, we find that Thomas is referring to and answering an old theory of John of Ripa. Thomas is saying that the human intellect of Jesus could not be *actuated* by an infinite act. That of course is Aristotelian language. It means this: the human intellect of Jesus has a potency (capacity) for knowledge. But that capacity at any one moment is finite, for a human intellect is created and finite. So divine knowledge, which is infinite, could not be the fulfillment (actualization) of that capacity. Brown conveniently omits to note that the same St. Thomas insistently teaches that the human soul of Jesus had the beatific vision, and that from that vision it did register all that God has *actually* done and made, though not all that God *could* do or make (for such is infinite).(71)

5. Toward a Solution

Before advancing a solution to the problems surrounding Christ's consciousness, some preliminary comments are in order on the compatibility between Christ's freedom and meriting on the one hand and His enjoyment of the beatific vision on the other. The New Testament frequently testifies to the providential dispensation that Jesus died as an act of obedience to the Father's will. Hence a problem arises: since His human soul had the beatific vision, was He really free in obeying that will?(72) The Scotists say the beatific vision does not compel souls to love God. Dominicans have proposed either of two solutions. First, there are two acts of love in Jesus, one regulated by the beatific vision, and so necessary; the other, by His infused knowledge, and so free. Others say that the objects loved need to be distinguished, i.e., His human soul could not help loving God; but it might not love all things other than God.

We will not enter into a detailed discussion of these views, since we intend to propose a very different though not necessarily contradictory solution. We do hold that a soul knowing God so directly could not help loving Him, the infinite Good. We agree there is a distinction between loving God Himself and other things. Yet, where there is a command, we think that love of God consists precisely (though not formally) in obedience. In general, love is a desire for the happiness and well-being of another. John 3:16 says God so loved the world that He gave His only-begotten that men might not perish but might have eternal life. In other words, God's love was such that He went that far to bring happiness, eternal happiness, to men. If that was the *effect* of His love, then, clearly, the *cause* of His action was His intense *desire* or *will* for man's eternal beatitude. It should be clear, then, that love is a desire for the well-being and happiness of another.(73)

But this definition needs adjustment, or must be taken analogously when we speak of our love for God. For we, clearly, cannot say to Him: "I hope you are well off and happy and that you get all you need to be so." Yet, Scripture depicts God as pleased when we obey, displeased when we do not. He is pleased for a twofold reason: (1) He loves what is objectively right.(74) It is right that creatures obey their Creator. (2) Even though He cannot receive anything from our obedience, yet He, being generosity, is pleased to be able to *give*. His giving would be in vain if we were not open to receive His gifts. Obedience makes us open. Hence, even though not formally, yet practically, obedience becomes identified with love when we speak of loving God. 2 John 6 says explicitly: "This is love [namely] that we walk according to His commands."

Hence a soul that cannot help loving the God seen directly, cannot refuse His commands.

The proposal that there are two acts of love in Jesus, one

regulated by the beatific vision, and therefore necessary, the other by His infused knowledge, and therefore free—this does not seem viable. As already noted, Rahner was wrong in objecting to what he called "an artificial layer-psychology." For there are many levels of operation within a human being, and so there can be different experiences, ranging from bliss to distress, simultaneously on different levels. Mystical theology and the actual experience of mystics show this is true. But the case of the will of Jesus is not parallel in regard to obedience, for there are many levels in a human being as we said, but only one human will. Having two sources of knowledge does not change the fact that one human will, and one Person too, are affected by both the beatific vision and by infused knowledge. So this solution would fall under Rahner's stricture.

We know for certain that Jesus was free, since He merited for us,(75) and that He had the beatific vision. It is one thing to know the fact, another to explain the how.

We shall attempt a new solution. First, notice that there can be no command in the strict sense, i.e., a command exactly of the same sort as God gives us. For He Himself was God. God cannot, does not command God! So we must understand the word command analogously.

It is best to approach the matter by way of Scripture. Although there are several aspects to the redemption, a most basic, though neglected aspect, is that of covenant. Both the new covenant and the Sinài covenant were *bilateral pacts*.(76) In proposing the Sinai covenant, God is reported to have said (Exod 19:5-6): "If you really obey me and keep my covenant, you will be my own people." In other words, each party was obligated only *conditionally*, and only if the other party carried out its part. Jer 31:31-34 fortells a new covenant which is to be parallel to the old, especially in that both bring into being a favored people, and both do so on condition of obedience, even though in the new, the law is to be written on hearts, not on stone tablets. Vatican II reiterates that Jesus inaugurated the new covenant.(77) So, the command laid upon Jesus was a conditioned command: *If* you wish to acquire a new, favored people in the fullest way, you must do this, must die.

Moreover, redemption, even infinite redemption, was possible in other ways. A finite redemption could have been accepted if the Father had so willed—perhaps just by an Old Testament type sacrifice. But even an infinite redemption would have been possible without death. Jesus could have been born in luxury, not a stable. He could have redeemed the world by simple petition such as, "Father, forgive them," and then He could have ascended without dying. Such a prayer, from an infinite Person, would have had infinite worth. Hence the redemption would have been infinite.

So the Cross would register on Jesus' mind as a good, but not as good in all aspects; for redemption, even infinite redemption, could have been achieved without it. In brief: the command was analogous and conditional: If you want redemption in the fullest possible way—then do this. Such a conditional command does not take away freedom even from one whose will is perfectly united to the will of the Father.

We find a sort of confirmation of this view in Mt 26:53, "Do you think that I cannot appeal to my Father, and he will at once send me more than twelve legions of angels?" If the Father was prepared to do that, the command was definitely conditional. There is probably a similar implication in Is 53:10, "Yet it was the will of the Lord to bruise Him...when [if] he makes himself an offering for sin, he shall see..."

So, with a conditional command that was analogously a command, a command that left room for an alternative mode of redemption, even infinite redemption, there is ample room for freedom.

But the merit of Christ also raises questions about His enjoyment of the beatific vision. We have seen He did have true freedom, even in the presence of the command of the Father. But we can merit only when we are on the way to the beatific vision, not when we have attained it.

We could reply simply that Jesus had a twofold character, in one aspect He was still on the way, in the other, He had already attained the vision.

But again, we prefer a different approach. Merit is not a claim on God in any fundamental or basic sense; no conceivable creature could generate any sort of claim on God. It is only on a *secondary level*, and presupposing a special pact with God, that we can speak of having any sort of claim at all.

We can see the two levels clearly in the old and new covenants. If we ask on the basic level why God gave His favors under the covenant, the answer can only be that He did it out of generosity, the generosity that He *is*. For the observance of the covenant condition had no power of itself to "move" Him, to generate a claim on Him. However, once He freely decided to enter into such a pact, then He was bound. Not that He even then owed anything to a creature formally. But He did owe it to Himself to keep His pledged word—and in practice the effect is the same.

The redemption constituted a new covenant. The claim on the Father is only on the secondary level, even here in the redemption. That claim is produced by obedience within the covenant— essentially, the obedience of Christ; to this, according to the Father's will, the obedience of Mary (on Calvary) and of the membrs of Christ (at Mass) must be joined. Really, the redemption (the death of Jesus) did not *move* the Father to stop being "angry" with us. The Father did not begin to love us again because Jesus came and died. Rather the reverse is true: Jesus came and died because the Father always loved us. So even the death of Jesus worked on the secondary level.

What sort of things can the Father pick as conditions for a claim on the secondary level? We cannot set limits for Him. For us God has limited the scope for merit to the present life. But He can pick whatever conditions He wills. He picked the obedience unto death of His Son as the covenant condition, even though the Son was in one aspect one who already enjoyed the beatific vision. Since the Father willed to establish that sort of condition, that condition generated a claim. That claim was merit.

Understanding these things, we may propose a positive solution. Many authors of heresies have erred precisely because they saw more vividly than most men some one aspect of a truth, and became preoccupied with it to such an extent that they lost balance and damaged the full Christian heritage. Such was the case with Apollinaris. He realized that if one takes two absolutely *complete* beings, and tries to put them together, there will be no unity. It is like trying to mix lead shot and marbles in a bucket: there never will be any unity. So Apollinaris saw that if there were a fully complete divine nature, and a fully complete human nature, the result would be a conglomerate, not a unity. Apollinaris tried to solve the problem by saying that Jesus lacked a human rational soul.

Of course that was an error, and the Church condemned it. Jesus could not lack any of the essential components of humanity and still be true man. So, what could He lack? The answer of the Church was that there is no human person in Jesus. There is only one Person, a divine Person. And so, similarly, His humanity has no *separate* existence; it is hypostatically one with the God-man.

Since Jesus' humanity lacked separate personality and separate existence, it must have had that lack supplied by the second Person of the Trinity, the Word. That is, His humanity had its existence and personality only in the Word.

We leave these conclusions to one side for the moment as we explore more fully the nature of the beatific vision. We already recalled that, according to the teaching of Benedict XII, there is no image or other object between God and the soul in that vision. So, the divinity joins itself directly to the soul, doing, as it were, the work that an image does in any other form of communication. Hence, this direct union of the human soul to the divinity is one requisite for the beatific vision.

There is obviously another requirement: the beatific vision is something immeasurably beyond the natural capacities of a human soul or any conceivable created soul. Therefore, the soul that is to have it must have its capacity or power "elevated", so as to be capable of the vision. That elevation is achieved radically through grace in this present life, and actually in the future life, through the results or consequences of that grace (which is sometimes called the light of glory).

So, clearly, there are two requirements for the beatific vision in an ordinary soul: the elevation of its capacity by grace, and the joining of the divinity to the soul without any intermediary.

Now if we compare the structure, as it were, of Jesus, and these two requirements, we make a fascinating discovery. The first requirement, grace to elevate the powers of the soul, He quite obviously possessed in its fullness. Did He have also the second, the union of His human soul with the divinity, without any intermediary? He not only actually fulfilled that requirement, but could not conceivably have done otherwise. It was inevitable because of His structure or make-up. For the divinity was joined directly, without any intermediary, to His entire humanity—a humanity that lacked separate existence and separate personality. So, since the divinity of the Word was joined to His entire humanity, clearly it was also joined to His human soul *and* to His human intellect. Some theologians have supposed it was only most highly fitting that He have that vision in his human soul. It was indeed fitting. But we must say more; we must say that in view of His structure, He could not conceivably have lacked that vision.

Further, we may say He had something actually beyond the ordinary beatific vision. For when the ordinary soul receives that vision, it is joined with the divinity in such a way that both remain separate persons—God and the human being. But in Jesus, the union is such that there is only one Person, only one existence. There is no separate human existence or separate human person at all.

Here we have the answer to Galtier's worries that Jesus' human soul may have seen the answer (that He was the Son of God) as if displayed on a TV screen, but that He might not have had a *direct* consciousness of it. With a mere beatific vision, if we may coin the expression, that could have been true. But when the vision is beyond the mere beatific because the vision inevitably results from the very structure of Jesus (when there is only one Person, even only one existence), then it becomes evident that no greater directness could be conceived.

We have taken special care to express our theory without using the terminology or framework of any school of philosophy or theology. This is simply the basic truth about the divinity, in non-technical language.

We could, however, express the same theory in the language of

Thomistic Aristotelianism: Within the hypostatic union the humanity of Jesus lacks its own existence, subsistence, and personality. These are supplied by the Word into which it is assumed.

For the beatific vision there are two requisites: (1) the elevation of the obediential potency of the human intellect by grace; (2) the joining of the divinity to that intellect, without any image, in such a way that the divinity performs the function of the intellectual form.

In Jesus these conditions are most fully verified: (1) His humanity is full of grace: (2) His entire humanity, not just His intellect, is joined, without intermediary, to the divinity of the Word so as to form one Person, the humanity lacking its own existence and subsistence. Hence that vision is more than an ordinary beatific vision, and has the greatest conceivable directness. Hence it is not merely something highly fitting and superadded by mere positive decision: it is the inevitable consequence of His very metaphysical structure.

The result is obvious: reason concurs with what the documents of revelation and the Church have taught us, namely, that the human soul and mind of Jesus, from the first instant of its existence, enjoyed the Vision of God. In it Jesus could not help but see His own divinity, and have all knowledge available to Him, as it related to any matter to which He turned His attention. His consciousness was, therefore, fully in keeping with His two natures—human and divine—in one Divine Person.

NOTES

1   P. Galtier, *L'unite du Christ—Etre, Personne, Conscience,* Beauchesne, Paris, 1939.

2   *Idem,* "unite ontologique et Unite psychologique dans le Christ" in *Bulletin de litterature ecclesiastique* (Institut Catholique de Toulouse) 42 (1941) 161-75, 216-32; and, "La conscience humain du Christ a propos de quelques publicationes recentes" in *Gregorianum* 32 (1951) 525-68; and, "Nestorius malcompris, mal traduit" in *Gregorianum* 34 (1953) 427-33; and, "La conscience humain du

Christ. Epilogue" in *Gregorianum* 35 (1954) 225-46.

3 *Ibid.* 540.

4 *Ibid.* 536.

5 *Ibid.* 547.

6 The following treatises are specially to be noted: J. Alfaro, "Cristo glorioso, revelador del Padre: Christus victor mortis" in *Gregorianum* 39 (1958) 222-70. L. Ciappi, "De unitate ontologica ac psychologica personae Christi" in *Angelicum* 29 (1952) 182-89. Crisostomo de Pamplona, "El yo de Cristo y de las divinas personas segun Duns Escoto y Deodat Marie de Basly" in *De doctrina Duns Scoti*, Romae, 1967 IV, 717-37. F.E. Crowe, "Eschaton and Finite Knowledge in the Mind of Jesus," in *The Eschaton: A Community of Love*, ed. Joseph Papin, Villanova Press, 1971, 110-24; and *idem*, "The Mind of Jesus" in *Communio* 1 (1974) 365-84. M. Cuervo, review of Xiberta, "El yo de Jesucristo" in *La Ciencia Tomista* 82 (1955) 105-23. Deodat de Basly, "L'Assumptus Homo. L' emmelement de trois conflits: Pelage, Nestorius, Apollinaire," in *La France Franciscaine* 11 (1928) 285-314; and *idem*, "Scotus docens" in *Suppl. a la France Franciscaine* 17-18 (1934/35) 164; and *idem* "La structure philosophique de Jesus l'Homme-Dieu" in *La France Franciscaine* 20-21, 1937/38. H. Diepen, "La psychologie du Christ selon S. Thomas d'Aquin" in *Revue Thomiste* 50 (1950) 515-62; and *idem*, "Note sur le baslisme et le dogme d' Ephese" in *Revue Thomiste* 51 (1951) 162-69; and *idem*, "L'unique Seigneur Jesus Christ," *ibidem* 53 (1953) 60-75. J. Galot, "La psychologie du Christ" in *Nouvelle Revue Theologique* 90 (1958) 337-58. P. Galtier, *L'unite du Christ, Etre, Personne, Conscience*, 3rd ed. Beauchesne, Paris, 1939; and *idem*, "Unite ontologique et unite psychologique dans le Christ" in *Bulletin de litterature ecclesiastique* (Insitut Catholique de Toulouse) 42 (1941) 161-75, 216-32; and *idem*, "La conscience humain du Christ a propos de quelques publications recentes," in *Gregorianum* 32 (1951) 525-68; and *idem* "Nestorius mal compris, mal traduit" *ibidem* 34(1953) 427-33, and *idem* "La conscience humain du Christi: Epilogue" in *ibid.* 35 (1954) 225-46. R. Garrigou-Lagrange, "L'unique personalite du Christ" in *Angelicum* 29 (1952) 60-75. J. Guillet, *The Consciousness of Jesus*, tr. E. Bonin, Newman, N.Y., 1972. E. Gutwenger, "Das menschliche Wissen des irdischen Christus" in ZKT 76 (1954) 170-86; and *idem*, "The Problem of Christ's Knowledge" in *Concilium* 11, Paulist, N.Y. 1965, 91-105. L. Jammarrone, "L'io psicologico di Cristo secondo la dottrina di G. Duns Scoto" in *Acts of the International Scotist Congress*, Rome, 1968, III, 291-316; and *idem* "La unita psicologica di Cristo secondo S. Bonaventura e il suo valore teologico" in *Misc. Francescana* 74 (1974) 123-60. B. Lonergan, *De constitutione Christi ontologica et*

psychologica, P.U.G. Roma, 1961 and *idem*, "Christ as Subject: a Reply" in *Gregorianum* 40 (1959) 242-70. J. Mouroux, "La conscience du Christ et le temps" in RSR 47 (1950) 321-44. M. J. Nicolas, "Chronique de theologie dogmatique" in *Revue Thomiste* 53 (1953) 421-28. P. Parente "Unita ontologica e psicologica dell 'Uomo-Dio' in *Collectio Urbaniana*, Ser. III. Text ac Docum, 1953, 1-68. and *idem L 'Io did Christo*, Morcelliana, Brescia 2d. ed. 1955. A. Perego, "Il 'lumen gloriae' et l'unita psicologica di Cristo" in *Divus Thomas* (P1) 58 (1955) 90-110; 296-310; and *idem* "Una nuova opinione sull' unita psicologica di Cristo" in *Divinitas* 2 (1958) 409-24. Philippe de la Trinite, "A propos de la conscience cu Christ" Un faux probleme theologique" in *Ephemerides Carmeliticae* 11 (1960) 1-52. K. Rahner, "Dogmatic Reflections on the Self-consciousness of Christ" in *Theological Investigations*, tr. K . H. Kruger, Helicon, Baltimore, 1966, V. 193-215. H. Riedlinger "Geschichtlichkeit und Vollendung des Wissens Jesu" in *Theologische Quartalschrift* 146 (1966) 40-61. E. Schillebeeckx, "Het bewustzijnsleven van Christus" in *Tijdschrift voor Theologie* 1 (1961) 228-51. Piet Schoonenberg, *The Christ*, tr. D. Couling, Herder and Herder, N.Y. 1971, 123-35. F. de P. Sola, "Una nueva explicacion de Yo de Jesucristo" in *Estudios Eccl.* 29 (1955) 443-78. B. M. Xiberta, *El Yo de Jesucristo*, Barcelona, 1954, and *idem*, *Tractatus de Verbo Incarnato*, Barcelona, 1954, and *idem*, *Tractatus de Verbo Incarnato*, Consejo Superior de Investigaciones Cientificas, Matriti, 1954; and *idem*, "In controversiam de conscientia humana Christi animadversiones," in *Euntes docete* 9 (1956) 93-109; and *idem*, "Observaciones al margen de la controversia sobre la conciencia humana de Jesucristo" in *Riv Esp. Teol.* 16 (1956) 215-33.

7   *Art. cit.*, 202.
8   *Ibid.* 199, 213-14.
9   *Ibid*, 203.
10   *Ibid.* 203, 207 ("Todliche Gottverlassenheit").
11   *Ibid.* 203.
12   *Ibid.* 203, n. 10.
13   *Ibid.* 208. (italics his).
14   *Ibid.* 211.
15   *Ibid.* 214.
16   DS 1000.
17   *Summa Theol.* Suppl. 92.1 c. and *Contra Gentiles* 3.52.
18   *Cf.* note 23 on chapter 7.
19   Rahner, *art. cit.*, 207.
20   *Ibid.*, 203, n. 10.
21   *Ibid.*, 203.
22   S. Francois de Sales, *Traitte d l'amour de Dieu* 9.12. *Oeuvres*, Nierat,

Annecy, 1894, V. 148.

23 *Ibid*. 9.3, V, 117.

24 St. John of the Cross *Noche Oscura* 2.11.1. in *Vida y Obras de San Juan de la Cruz*, ed. L. del SS. Sacramento, in *Biblioteca de Autores Cristianos*, Madrid, 1950, 877.

25 *Cf*. A. Poulain, *The Graces of Interior Prayer*, tr. L. L. Smith, Routledge and Kegan Paul, London, 1950, 406, 410; J. G. Arintero, *The Mystical Evolution*, tr. J. Aumann, B. Herder, St. Louis, 1951, II. 184-204, 209, 213, 215-16, 358-59; and St. Francis de Sales, *Spiritual Conferences*, tr. Gasquet and Mackey, Newman, Westminister, Maryland, 1945, 79, 84.

26 Cited from Arintero, *op. cit.*, II. 189, n. 25.

27 F. E. Crowe, "Eschaton and Finite Knowledge in the Mind of Jesus," in: *The Eschaton: A community of Love*, ed. Joseph Papin, Villanova Press, 1971, 110-74. This citation is from 119. *Cf*. also his, "The Mind of Jesus" in *Communio* 1 (1974) 365-84.

28 *Ibid.*, 115-16, citing B. Lonergan, *Insight*, London: Longmans Green, 1957, 352.

29 *Ibid*, 116.

30 *Ibid*, 116.

31 *Ibid*, 117.

32 *Ibid*, 122-23.

33 *Ibid*, 117.

34 *Ibid*, 118.

35 *Ibid*, 121.

36 J. Maritain, *On the Grace and Humanity of Jesus*, tr. Joseph W. Evans, Herder & Herder, New York, 1969.

37 S.T. III.7.12 ad 3.

38 p. 51

39 *ibid*.

40 pp. 50.

41 p. 59

42 p. 56

43 p. 59.

44 *ibid*.

45 p. 61.

46 *ibid*.

47 p. 55.

48 pp. 57-58.

49 See the quote below at note 66.

50 p. 72.

51 pp. 72-73.

52 p. 73.

53 p. 93.

54   p. 94.
55   *ibid.*
56   p. 118.
57   p. 119.
58   p. 51.
59   On Divine Revelation ¶ 9.
60   *Ibid.* ¶12.
61   Maritain, p. 72.
62   ST I.12.9 ad 2, referring to the experience St. Paul reports in 2 Cor 12.2-4, in which Paul says he was taken to the third heaven, and heard "hidden words, which it is not permitted to man to speak." St. Thomas thinks (ST I.12.11 ad 2) that Moses and St. Paul had the beatific vision. By no means would all today agree—there is no necessity to so interpret 2 Cor 12.2-4. It could have been instead a vision in the charismatic category, or a specially high form of infused contemplation. As to Paul's saying he heard words which "it is not permitted to man to speak", there are several possibilities, and no need to take it in support of Maritain's view on p. 72. First it could be that he was literally "not permitted", ordered not to tell. Second, it could be an experience for which existing words do not suffice, when speaking to another who has not had the same experience or a similar one. Thus a person who has experienced infused contemplation does have a clear concept of it, and can talk about it to another who has had the same experience—but can hardly give much of a notion of it to one who has never had it. In any event, St. Thomas obviously thinks St. Paul did have clear concepts from the vision, and retained them after it.
63   ST III. 10.2.c.
64   ST III.11.2.c.
65   *Cf.* pp. 50 and 60, note 15.
66   J. Maritain *Creative Intuition in Art and Poetry*, Pantheon, N.Y. 1953 (3rd printing, with corrections, 1955) p. 91.
67   Cf. St. Thomas ST III.46.8.c. and pp 151-154 above in this chapter.
68   JGM 99-100.
69   A. Durand, "La science du Christ" in *Nouvelle Revue Theologique* 71 (1949) 501.
70   JGM 44. n. 10.
71   *Summa Theol.*, III.10.1, 2. *Cf.* also M. de la Taille, *The Hypostatic Union and Created Actuation by Uncreated Act*, tr. C. Vollert, West Baden College, West Baden Springs, Indiana, 1952, 29-41.
72   *Cf.* I Solano, "De Verbo Incarnato" ##467-74 in *Sacrae Theologiae Summa* III, pp. 194-97, BAC, Matriti, 1953.
73   *Cf.* St. Thomas, *Summa Theol.*, I-II 26.4.c. "To love is to will good to someone."

74 *Cf.* Psalm 11:7.
75 *Cf.* DS 1513, 1529.
76 *Cf.* W. G. Most, "A Biblical Theology of Redemption in a Covenant Framework" in CBQ 29 (1967) 1-19.
77 Constitution on the Church #9.

APPENDIX:

FORM CRITICISM

1. Prejudices and Presuppositions

Our search for the answer to the question of the consciousness of Jesus presupposes the credibility of the Gospels. Their reliability is presented in a positive way, and pertinent objections are answered, in the introduction. However, the greatest challenge to Gospel truth today arises from questionable application of principles proper to form criticism. It is the misuse of form criticism that we must examine—its presuppositions or prejudices along with its immediate bases and its actual techniques.

The credit for the invention of form criticism goes to Hermann Gunkel (1862-1932) who dealt chiefly with the Old Testament. The most important pioneer in applying form criticism to the Gospels was Rudolph Bultmann. Gunkel, however, did not share in most of Bultmann's prejudices which we are about to examine.

First, Bultmann insists that nothing is certain: "Conclusive knowledge is impossible in any science or philosophy."(1) Yet, in spite of such an assertion, Bultmann and his followers are quite certain of a number of things.

They are certain that there are and can be no miralces: "It is impossible to use electric light and wireless...and at the same time to believe in the New Testament world of spirits and miracles."(2) And again, "The miracles of the New Testament have ceased to be miraculous...if we are still left with certain physiological and psychological phenomena which we can only assign to mysterious and enigmatic causes, we are still assigning them to causes, and thus far are trying to make them scientifically intelligible.''(3) In other words: natural science has given a wholly natural explanation for *some* things that might seem marvelous. There are, he admits, some seeming miracles which science admits it cannot presently explain. But, adds Bultmann, he is confident science will some day be able to explain those too.

Our first comment is that this is not science, it is gullibility. Real scientists are not so sanguine and cocksure about such future prospects. Let us mention just a few out of hundreds of scientifically established miracles.

In November 1970, ecclesiastical authorities gave permission for a complete scientific check to be made on a remarkable phenomenon of twelve centuries standing. Around the year 700 A.D., in the church of St. Legonziano in Lanciano, Italy, a priest was celebrating Mass. He was beset with doubts about the Real Presence of Jesus in the host and the chalice. Suddenly most of the host changed to flesh (the center kept the appearance of bread), while the liquid in the chalice changed into five clots of blood. This treasure was guarded successively by the Basilian monks, the Benedictines, and finally by the Conventual Franciscans. In 1713 the Host-Flesh was put into a silver monstrance, and the blood into a crystal cup at the base of the monstrance. These can still be seen in Lanciano.

Four official investigations were made over the centuries by order of Church authorities. The check made in 1970 was most exacting from the viewpoint of science. A team of research scientists was assembled from several universities. A full battery of scientific tests was made. The commission concluded that the flesh was real human flesh—heart muscle. The blood and the flesh, as shown by blood typing, came from the same individual. The proteins in the blood were in normal ratio, as they are in fresh blood; and the other features of the blood chemistry were all normal. Yet, no trace of any preservative or embalming agent was found. Normally, flesh and blood should have started to decompose in a day or two. Yet after so many centuries, there is no decay.

Bultmann thinks all miracles can be explained by natural laws. Why did he not try to suggest what kind of natural laws can change bread and wine into human flesh and blood, and keep it intact for twelve centuries with no preservative? Again, we fear he is not so much scientific as gullible.

Further, in Guadalupe, on the edge of Mexico City, one may see a wondrous, continuing miracle. On Dec. 9, 1531,(5) an Aztec Indian, Juan Diego, claimed to have seen the Virgin Mary. His Bishop, properly, was unconvinced, and demanded proof. On Dec. 12 she appeared again, and Juan, as ordered, asked for a sign. She told him to pick some flowers growing nearby (out of season) and put them into his tilma, a native cloak. He did, picked up the corners of the cloak, and took it all to the Bishop. When Juan opened up the tilma, the flowers fell out. But far more remarkable: on the tilma was a large, full color image of the apparition Juan had seen.

That image has been checked by many scientific tests. It is impossible to determine the process used in putting the colors on the cloak. Clearly, it is not photography, not painting, not any method known to science. Further, a tilma of that sort of material would normally go to pieces in about 25 years. Yet now after four centuries it remains unchanged. Still more; in 1929, while Alfonso Marcue Gonzalez was studying the image, he thought he saw the picture of a man inside the eyes of the image. A commission was appointed in 1951. Dr. Javier Toroello Bueno, an eye specialist, found there was indeed such an image, upside down, in the eyes, which seemed to have depth. In 1956 still another specialist, Dr. Rafael Torija Lavoignet confirmed the discovery.

Now, would Bultmann really expect us to believe there is some natural process that put this image on the tilma, a process known to an ignorant Indian four centuries ago, which our best scientists cannot now decipher? Would he expect us to think the tilma could escape decay, with no preservative, so long after its normal lifespan? Would he ask us to believe some natural process put a picture of Juan Diego (the pictures in the eyes matches an ancient likeness of him) inside the eyes centuries ago?

We could go on and fill an entire volume with meticulously checked cases of cures, such as those at Lourdes.(6) The permanent medical bureau at Lourdes will not even consider a case that conceivably could rest on suggestion. Further, each claim of a cure must be supported by careful medical statements of the condition before the cure and a check made by many doctors after it. Any doctor, atheists included, is welcome at that bureau and may examine cases to his heart's content. One such doctor, Alexis Carrel,(7) came to scoff, stayed to become a Catholic. He lacked the unsupported cocksureness of a Bultmann—who thinks nothing is certain except that science will explain what it admits it canot explain.

To compound the confusion, Bultmann says he will accept as miraculous things that science *can explain*: "A miracle—i.e., an act of God—is not visible or ascertainable...to every other eye than the eye of faith the action of God is hidden."(8) In other words, on an event science can explain, such as a falling leaf, Bultmann would comment "there is certainly no room for an act of God."(9) Nevertheless, for him it could conceal a miracle!

Normal persons, however, think it irrational to believe God has intervened when there is no reason to think He has done so. It is *superstitious* to attribute things to God without proper evidence. It is much like thinking black cats bring bad luck. To hold that is superstition, because, although God could have made things turn out in such a way that bad luck would follow black cats, yet we lack any evidence that He did. In fact, there is good reason to believe He did not. So, when Bultmann wants us to see the hand of God where there is no reason to do so, and where there is reason to exclude it, we must, regretfully, charge him with undiluted superstition.

Yet, (perhaps by a mechanism psychologists call projection) Bultmann avers: "The conception of miracles as ascertainable processess...makes belief in miracles (or rather *superstition*) susceptible to the *justifiable* criticisms of science."(10) In other words, where science cannot explain a marvel and admits it, it would be superstitious to attribute the inexplicable to the intervention of God!

Nevertheless, along with the inherent illogic, there exists a certain inner consistency in Bultmann's wish to consider phenomena miracles when there is no reason to support the belief. For he insists: "The man who wishes to believe in God as his God must realize that he has *nothing* in his hand on which to base his faith. He is suspended in midair and *cannot* demand a proof of the Word which addresses him."(11) So, according to Bultmann, it is wrong—elsewhere he says it is illegitimate and sinful—to seek a rational basis for faith.(12) This, as noted, is consistent with his insistence that there are no miracles that can be recognized as such by rational means, and his desire to accept as miraculous things that science can explain. In other words: there must be no rational basis either for faith or for accepting what Bultmann calls miracles (actually, superstitions).

Bultmann next proudly announces that what St. Paul and Luther did in abolishing good works as a means of salvation,(13) he has matched in abolishing any rational basis for faith.(14) He means his work is parallel: both he and St. Paul have destroyed rational security.

Once he has managed to make faith devoid of rationality, Bultmann is free to show how the Gospels are full of myths. He does not mean mere fairy tales; he means outmoded, ancient ways of expressing things, way that modern sophisticated man cannot and should not accept. Chief among these myths are: original sin, with resultant death; the incarnation of a divine person; the resurrection of Christ; the return of Jesus at the end of time; judgment, followed by an eternal heaven or hell.(15)

How does Bultmann know that these doctrines are myths? Very simple; they do not fit with the *modern world view*: "De-mythologizing takes the modern world-view as a criterion."(16) Modern man is very smart; having seen an electric light bulb and the wireless, he cannot believe in spirits and miracles.(17) Bultmann admits that this "enlightened" modern world view is shifting: "...to be sure, all the results of science are relative and no world-view of yesterday or today or tomorrow is definitive."(18) Yet, he thinks it is better to hold to such an admittedly unstable, unproved hypothesis than to accept the truth of the Gospel miracles and teachings on the spiritual world.

But we still need to discover the kernel of truth, as it were, that lies hidden in the myths. How find it? Very simple, says Bultmann: denude the myth and make the Gospels mean the same as that brand of Existentialism concocted by the modern German Martin Heidegger.(19)

When we do that, we will have to avoid *general* truths, for existentialism contradicts itself whenever it assimilates any general truth. For example: "The affirmation that God is creator cannot be a theoretical statement...in a *general* sense, the affirmation can only be a *personal* confession that *I* understand *myself* to be a creature which owes its existence to God."(20) So, we cannot say that God is the creator of *all*; each one is limited to saying: God is *my* creator.

What does original sin mean when translated into existentialism? There are two kinds of being, they say: *inauthentic being* (such as most things have) and *authentic being*—the kind that a man can have if he makes "the resolve to be a human being, a person who accepts responsibility for his own being."(21) Norman Perrin clarifies that when he says a man has authentic being if he makes a decision in which he "chooses resolutely to accept the certainty of death and the *nothingness of human existence....* he now has no necessity to delude himself about his being-in-the-world.... He comes to know that it is *bounded by death.*"(22) For there is no resurrection, no return of Christ, no judgment at the end, eternal life is what he has here and now. This means we must face a dismal situation. But Perrin adds: "In the resolve to accept this he finds the power to go through with it."(23) (Imagine St. Ignatius of Antioch standing before the lions and thinking that way!). He adds: "Bultmann calls this 'a resolution of despair.'"

So, to make it abundantly clear, the "fall" (original sin) is the lack of such an existential resolve. Everybody must make this resolution because "apart from...the resolve to be a human being...not a single word of Scripture is intelligible as word with an existential relevance."(24) The evangelists, accordingly, are really Heidegger in disguise.

Faith itself is merely this understanding of existence: "It is my definition of faith as an understanding of existence which has evoked the most opposition.''(25) So, continues Bultmann, ''there is nothing mysterious or supernatural about the Christian life,'' since philosophy can discover what it is, as Heidegger has done.(26) And the supernatural does not exist.

What of the redemption? It gives us no inner power or strength; for among the major myths must be listed ''the conception of the intervention of supernatural powers in the inner life of the soul.''(27) Modern man ''finds what the New Testament has to say about the 'Spirit'...and the sacraments utterly strange and incomprehensible.''(28)

What then does the redemption accomplish? It functions as an example: Jesus made the decision to accept the ''nothingness of human existence'' and the fact that our existence is ''bounded by death.'' He thought He would return—but in vain. He will not, no more than we will. Any notion of a resurrection is ''utterly inconceivable.''(29) So let us imitate His decision to die, in vain.

Some scholars have asked: If the redemption gives us nothing, why do we need it? Schubert Ogden, a more thorough-going existentialist than Bultmann, is quite logical in saying that the redemption really accomplished nothing more than a nearby carpenter would by driving a nail into a board.(30) The answer is clear: Bultmann has emptied the redemption of significance.

After wading through this morass of subjectivity, we can understand how right Bultmann is in confessing at one point: ''Naturally enough, our judgment will not be made in terms of objective criteria, but will depend on taste and discrimination.''(31) But a scholar should be free of prejudices or unproved assumptions. It is evident: the Bultmannian form critics have not really demonstrated anything when they propound without proof, or rather, contrary to proof, that there are no miracles—only phenomena more correctly called superstition; when they reject in advance as illegitimate and sinful any rational foundation for faith; when they insist on forcing the first century Semitic Gospels to mean the same as 20th century German existentialism; when they top it all off by conceding explicitly and openly that they are operating ''not in terms of objective criteria'' but depending instead on "taste and discrimination."

Some of the pupils of Bultmann have broken company with him on certain points. Of special importance among them are Ernst Fuchs and Gerhard Ebeling, for their development of the "New Hermeneutic". By this they mean a new theory or process of interpreting the Bible.(32) In general they agree with Bultmann, whose disciples they are. The chief difference is that while Bultmann's theory of demythologizing depends heavily on Heidegger's work, *Being and Time* from 1927, Fuchs and Ebeling are influenced by Heidegger's later ideas on *language*, which appeared in a series of treatises culminating in *Toward Language*, in 1959.

Most persons, including scholars, think of language as a set of signs used to communicate thought and ideas. The New Hermeneutic explicitly rejects this.(33) Fuchs insists it is not true that man has given birth to language: "Rather, man is born out of language."(34) Robinson, a follower of Fuchs and Ebeling, explains: "Man is where the voice of being is heard and given room; man is the loudspeaker for the silent tolling of being. When he fulfills this role, he is truly man."(35) Heidegger himself says that "Man *is* actually this relation of co- 'respond' -ence [to the voice of being] and only this."(36) Still further, according to Fuchs, "...both being and man are directed to language. And to this extent we are related to God."(37) Perhaps the most sweeping claim is this: "Reality is hence not at all simply what is.... Rather the real is only that which can become present as language."(38)

Bultmann, as we saw, had spoken of inauthentic and authentic existence. Fuchs, following the later Heidegger, proposes instead, inauthentic versus authentic language.(39) Everyday language is largely inauthentic, and a means of "unsurped existence."(40) It hides rather than reveals meaning (examples sometimes given are from the language of political promises and advertising). In contrast, authentic language is provocative, i.e., it tends to provoke in the hearer the same *event* that had given rise to it. This calls for decision by man; it is a saving word.(41) It mediates eschatological self-understanding.(42) It frees man from in-authentic language and the fetters of his past and his environment so as to make him stand out, *ex-sist*, open to the possibilities of the future. Thus man is the creature of language inasmuch as he receives authentic self through the living word proclaimed in a sermon.(43)

This saving event of language is called "language event" (*Sprachereignis* or *Wortgeschehen*). Fuchs illustrates language event by saying one does not name a person brother just because of a biological relation. Rather, the person *becomes* a brother by my naming him brother.(44)

Catholicism insists that Scripture is to be interpreted by the Church. Fuchs and Ebeling, making their position line up with both Heidegger's odd thought and classic Lutheranism, insist that Scripture is its own interpreter.(45) Scripture has this in common with authentic language in general: it is not so much that we interpret language. Rather, *the text* interprets us.(46) So: "Indeed it is not man at all who is ex-pressing himself in language. Rather it is language itself that speaks."(47) Even the author of the text being read is put into a low second place: "The basic thing about a text is not what the author intended to express.... Rather, basic is what wills fundamentally to show itself."(48)

What then does the interpreter have to do? Basically, just to remove *obstacles* to understanding, so that the word can speak of itself.(49) Therefore, the New Hermeneutic does not stress getting back to the mentality, culture, and conditions of the time of writing. For, "The short cut of putting myself in the skin of Moses or Paul is popular but no good, for my name is neither Moses nor Paul."(50)

In spite of claiming that the text speaks for itself, Fuchs will still talk of a "hermeneutical principle" which "is that with which the text is confronted to call forth from it what it has to say."(51) That principle is described as our need, which is expressed especially in Rom 7:24, "Who will deliver me from this body of death?" Ebeling, however, says that "The hermeneutical principle is *man as conscience.*"(52) He then apologizes for having to make that clear, since a principle is something that should be obvious of itself.

Let us consider two examples of the actual application of the

New Hermeneutic. Robinson summarizes the work of Fuchs on Jn 1:1, "In the beginning was the word."(53) Fuchs starts by recalling the translation of Faust: "In the beginning was the deed." He then corrects it on the basis of Jn 13:34 ("A new commandment I give to you, that you love one another.") So now we translate: "In the beginning was love." Then, in view of 1 Jn 4:16 ("God is love"), instead of using *love* for *word*, we now use *love* for *God*, thus "In the beginning was the word, and the word was with love, and the word was love." Finally, Fuchs reaches this: "In the beginning was the Yes, and the Yes was love, and love was the Yes." Ebeling, speaking of Jn 1:14, comments: "When Jn 1:14 says that the word became flesh, that surely means...that here word became event in a sense so complete that being and being man became one."(54)

What should we think of the New Hermeneutic? Has it really provided us with a sound, new way to understand Scripture, and has it *proved* its way is correct? Far from it. Instead of trying to understand the mentality and culture of the ancient authors, it says that is "no good" because "my name is neither Moses nor Paul." And it forces Scripture to mean the same in general as Heidegger and Luther. That is hardly objectivity—it is fleeing at full speed away from it. For the same reason it is obvious that the New Hermeneutic has proved nothing against the reliability of Scripture; instead, it has merely shown the unreliability of its own proponents.

Regarding the interpretation of Jn 1:1 by Fuchs may we point out: (1) using Jn 13:34, the new commandment of love, to interpret Jn 1:1 is quite out of place. Jn 1:1 is not speaking of commands to men, but of the Word within the divinity (the Word is said to be with God or in the presence of God). Only in later verses of chapter one does the author speak of the Word coming among men; (2) then Fuchs abandons his own proposal and uses *love* as a substitute for *God*, instead of for *word*. Now it is true that God is love—but there is no hint in Jn 1:1 that the author has that *aspect* of God in mind. On the contrary, a *word* comes more basically from a person's *mind* or *understanding* than from his *will* (in which he loves); (3) the substitution of *Yes* for *word* is still more strained.

As to Ebeling's comment on Jn 1:14—how has he established that *being* and *being man* become one? Or does he mean to equate *being* with *God*, and say God became man? Elsewhere he says that God is not "any separate special Reality."(55) His interpretation is more like reading things into the text than reading out what is there already.

Without intending to make a habit of agreeing with R. Brown, I may say that he does provide a classic comment on the methodology of Fuchs and Ebeling: "Catholic biblical scholars who have had to learn to read Scripture without scholastic glasses are going to be somewhat dubious about substituting another pair of spectacles made in Germany."(56)

NOTES

1   KM 195.
2   KM 5.
3   *Ibid.*
4   A full account of the scientific investigation, with full details and plates, can be found in: Bruno Sammaciccia, *The Eucharistic Miracle of Lanciano, Italy,* tr. A. E. Burakowski. Publ. by F. J. Kuba, C.P., Trumbull, Conn., 1976.
5   *Cf. A Handbook on Guadalupe,* Franciscan Marytown Press, Kenosha, Wis., 1974; *The Dark Virgin* (a documentary anthology) ed. C. Demarest and C. Taylor., Cole Taylor, Inc., Freeport, Maine and N.Y., 1956; Simone Watson, O.S.B., *Cult of Our Lady of Guadalupe, A Historical Study,* The Liturgical Press, Collegeville, Minn., 1964; and Hildebrando Garya, O.S.B., *Madonna of the Americas,* The Liturgical Press, Collegeville, Minn., 1954.
6   Ruth Cranston, *The Miracle of Lourdes,* McGraw-Hill, New York, 1955; Dr. F. de Grandmaison de Bruno, *Twenty Cures at Lourdes Medically Discussed,* tr. H. Bevenotand & L. Izard, Herder, St. Louis, 1912; "The Lourdes Cures:, tr. N. C. Reeves, ed. Peter Flood, O.S.B., in *New Problems in Medical Ethics,* Newman, Westminster, Md. 1953, 171-259.
7   Alexis Carrel, *Man the Unknown,* Harper, New York, 1935; and *idem, The Voyage to Lourdes,* tr. V. Peterson, Harper & Bro., New York, 1950.
8   KM 197.

9   KM 199.
10 KM 199 (italics added).
11 KM 211 (italics added).
12 KM 19.
13 KM 210-11.
14 St. Paul insists over and over that we are not under the Law (e.g., Rom. 3:28; 6:14; Gal. 2:16). Yet he also says that if we do not keep the Law we will not inherit the kingdom (e.g., 1 Cor. 6:9-10; Gal. 5:19-21; Rom. 3:31; 2:13; 2:6). The key is in Rom 6:23, "The *wages* of sin is death, but the unearned gift (*charisma*) of God is eternal life." That is, on the positive side, our good works do not (and can not) earn entrance into the kingdom—that is a gift, unearned, an inheritance from our Father. Yet we can earn to forfeit that gift through the *wages* of sin.
15 KM 8, 39.
16 JCM 35.
17 KM 5.
18 JCM 37.
19 Bultmann follows the early views of Heidegger; the post-Bultmannians follow the later views of Heidegger. For a lucid analysis of Heidegger, see Francis J. Lescoe, *Existentialism With or Without God*, Alba House, N.Y. 1974, 173-263.
20 JCM 69 (italics added).
21 KM 194.
22 N. Perrin, *The Promise of Bultmann* in *The Promise of Theology*, ed. M. Marty, Lippincott, Philadelphia, 1969, 29 (italics added).
23 *Ibid.*
24 KM 194.
25 KM 202.
26 KM 27.
27 JCM 15.
28 KM 6.
29 KM 39.
30 Schubert Ogden, *Christ Without Myth*, Harper and Row, New York, 1961 136. *cf.* 144.
31 HST 47.
32 A good general account, by a scholar who is favorable to the ideas of Fuchs and Ebeling, is found in: James M. Robinson, "Hermeneutic since Barth" in *The New Hermeneutic* in *New Frontiers in Theology* II, ed. by James M. Robinson and John B. Cobb Jr., Harper & Row, New York 1964 (hereafter cited as HSB).
33 HSB 47-48.
34 Fuchs, *Hermeneutik*, 63, cited in *HSB* 50.
35 *HSB* 48.

36 M. Heidegger, *Identitat und Differenz* 22 (italics his). Cited in HSB 47. Heidegger was fascinated by the roots of words, apparently thinking great thinkers enshrined wonderful wisdom in words. A similar notion appears in Plato, *Cratylus*, 389; *Phaedrus* 244.

37 Fuchs, *Zur Frage nach dem historischen Jesus*, 427-29, cited in HSB 55.

38 Fuchs, *Hermeneutik*, 130, cited in HSB 55, n.157.

39 HSB 49.

40 Fuchs, *Hermeneutik* 63, cited in HSB 50.

41 HSB 57.

42 HSB 62.

43 HSB 57, 62.

44 HSB 57. Fuchs here misses a distinction, and so generates confusion: a man may be a brother either (1) biologically by birth, or (2) by attachment, leading to his being *named* brother. Both senses are true.

45 HSB 53, and G. Ebeling, "Word of God and Hermeneutic" in *The New Hermeneutic*, ed. James M. Robinson and John B. Cobb, Jr. in *New Frontiers in Theology* II, Harper and Row, New York, 1964, 79-80, 93 (cited hereafter as WGH).

46 Ebeling, *Theologie und Verkundigung* 14f, cited in HSB 68-69, 52.

47 HSB 46.

48 HSB 46. There is confusion over subject-object. The object of language, they hold, must become the subject—that puts the subject (man) in question: HSB 23-25. This reflects Heidegger's etymologically rooted notion that truth is *a-letheia*—a Greek word meaning "unhiddenness", or being revealing itself, as he thinks. *Cf.* Wm. Barrett, *Irrational Man*, Doubleday, Anchor Books, New York, 1962, 215.

49 WGH 94 seems to enlarge that scope.

50 Manfred Mezger (close friend of Fuchs), "Anleitung zur Predigt" in Z TH K, LVI (1959) 381-87, cited in HSB 59.

51 HSB 53.

52 WGH 110 (italics in original).

53 HSB 60, and 61, note 178.

54 WGH 102.

55 WGH 100, 101.

56 R. Brown, "After Bultmann, What?—An Introduction to the Post-Bultmannians" in CBQ 26 (1964) 30.

2. Immediate Bases

Besides the prejudices reviewed in the last chapter, some prominent form critics have another set of beliefs, more immediately presupposed by form criticism. There are three chief points: (1) the Gospels were put together out of many short units or forms, which circulated before the Gospels were assembled; the Evangelists were not properly authors: they just strung together these units like so many beads; (2) it was the "creative" community that produced these units or forms. The community could be creative since it was not interested in facts. Rather, it was quite willing to create (fake) things as needed to "prove" points. This of course presupposes that there was no effective control by apostles; (3) the Gospels were all too late to be written by eyewitnesses.

We will examine each of these points in detail and conclude with an examination of the arguments which N. Perrin advances in corroboration of their validity.

Form critics hold that the Gospels developed through a three stage process. First, there were the words and acts of Jesus. Like any good speaker He would adapt His presentation to the audience at hand. Second, after His departure, various people would retell things He did or said. They would usually report just one saying or one action at a time. Each of these constituted a unit. The critics, by an odd use of the word, call these units "forms." Third, certain individuals gathered together and put into writing a collection of these units, thus producing the Gospels. They are our evangelists; they were not really authors, rather they just strung the beads on a string.(1)

The fundamental idea that the Gospels developed in these three stages is obviously correct. St. Luke himself in his preface says that many had worked on Gospel accounts before him. However, it is not true that the evangelists were no more than stringers of beads. More recently the critics themselves have admitted that; in what is called redaction criticism, a new group of scholars have (predictably) swung to the opposite extreme of attributing marvelous artistry in a superlative degree to the evangelists: "Today the synoptics are understood to be enormously intricate products containing subtle and ingenious literary patterns and highly developed theological interpretations."(2) N. Perrin, as we shall see later in this chapter, thinks Mk 8:27-32 is so artistic that it must have been "created" by Mark.

We agree that the evangelists are real authors, that they are quite artistic (at times—at other times not) and that they do have a theological framework. We object only to the extremist claims of certain writers. Moreover, certain critics speak of numerous units as stemming initially from the creative community. They give little if any credit to the apostles or to the normative influences for which they were responsible. Rather, they seem to presuppose a headless mob, or more correctly, they logically imply a vast number of headless mobs—one for each, separate Christian community.

Every community was "creative," they say, for nowhere were Christians concerned about facts.(3) They were preoccupied with polemic (as Bultmann(4) says) or with missionary preaching (as Dibelius(5) claims). In its bursting creativity, the primitive community unscrupulously faked accounts to "prove" points. Thus Bultmann teaches that "The Controversy Dialogues as we have them are...creations of the Church."(6) Let us try to visualize this. There are two groups, one within the Church, another also within the Church, or perhaps outside the Church. They are debating with each other. Group A does not really have a genuine saying of Jesus to prove its point, so it makes one up. Group B (if within the Church) composes one to answer Group A. Neither group is concerned about the truth. Truth means little. The only thing that does have meaning is the existential "resolve to be a human being," to "go through with it."(7)

Our comment: the critics themselves surely are creative—they have structured a picture out of their own unsupported fancy, and contrary to the facts as common sense knows them. The Acts of the Apostles, for instance, gives a very different picture of an early Christian community. The position of the apostles was unique, preeminent (Acts 5:13), "None of the rest dared join them (the apostles), but the people held them in high honor" (2:42). "They devoted themselves to the apostles' teaching." We are well aware of how the critics attack the reliability of Acts. It has not yet been demonstrated that Acts was not written by Luke, who, we have shown, was deeply concerned with facts.(8) Attacks on Acts stem from two sources: an a priori conviction that the community was not concerned with facts, and certain alleged contradictions within Acts, all of which can be resolved.(9)

Further, the picture given by Acts is corroborated in the epistles of St. Paul, whose reliability is not in question. St. Paul often claimed authority, e.g., in 2 Cor 13:10, and he set up authorities in his churches at the very beginning of his missionary work, as seen in 1 Thess 5:12. Moreover, the critics' notion which logically presupposes many headless mobs, one for each of the numerous communities scattered all through the Mediterranean world, cannot explain how these many communities, each headless, each independent in faking things, could maintain such harmonious agreement on a multitude of details, facts and doctrines pertaining to the work and words of Jesus.

Finally, as shown in the introduction, the first Christians were supremely concerned with facts;(10) a mere existential resolve "to go through with it" would not have sufficed for persons confronting persecution, discrimination, imprisonment, social ostracism, and even death.

The second basis of form criticism is the critic's assertion that the Gospels are so late that they could not have been written by eyewitnesses, for which two reasons are given. First, says

Bultmann, the Gospels show no sign of the debate, prominent in St. Paul's day, over whether or not Gentile converts were obliged to keep the Mosaic law. He therefore concludes that, by the time the Gospels were written, "It is...already self-evident that the gospel, and the gospel alone apart from the Law, was meant for the heathen."(11) And, although he said, as quoted above,(12) that nothing is certain, he insists this conclusion is part of the "assured results of research."(13)

Two counter-observations: first, Bultmann ignores Mt 5:17-20 where Jesus says:

> Think not that I have come to abolish the law and the prophets; I have come not to abolish them but to fulfill them. For truly I say to you, till heaven and earth pass away, not an iota, not a dot, will pass from the law until all is accomplished. Whoever then relaxes one of the least of these commandments and teaches men so, shall be called least in the kingdom of heaven.

Luke reports the more significant part of this saying (16:17), "It is easier for heaven and earth to pass away, than for one dot of the law to become void." Bultmann simply considers such statements faked-in-debates, to prove points, a neat way to obviate objections!(14)

If we wanted to argue as loosely as does Bultmann we would say: It is clear that Matthew and Luke believe the Law is binding on all: no exception for the Gentiles is mentioned. Therefore, Matthew and Luke must have written *before* the Council of Jerusalem in 49 A.D., at which it was formally promulgated that the Gentiles were not bound. Further, since Bultmann thinks Matthew and Luke used Mark, we must allow a few years before 49 for Mark to write and to be used. So the composition of Matthew and Luke should be dated around 45 A.D., while that of Mark would be around 40 A.D.

We do not seriously propose those dates(15); we merely wish to show that with such loose methods as Bultmann's, one can reach a great variety of erroneous or inconclusive conclusions. The trouble is that Bultmann is working solely with internal evidence, which seldom really proves anything(16); specifically he is here using the *argument from silence*, an internal argument that is even less conclusive.

A telling object lesson on the inconclusiveness of internal evidence concerns the case of the *Dialog on Orators* by the ancient Roman historian Tacitus. Besides that *Dialog* four of his historical works have survived. His style in the historical works is highly distinctive, a style quite evident to anyone who reads the original Latin. It is a style very obviously different from that of the *Dialog* (a computer study made privately by my students confirms this observation). Form critics would probably say the *Dialog* is not by Tacitus, because of literary differences.

The difficulty is further compounded by the fact that a writer from about the same time, Quintilian, wrote a similar work, *On the Causes of the Corruption of Oratory*, which is now lost. Quintilian's style, as known from his extant works, greatly resembles the style of the *Dialog* attributed to Tacitus. So there is a powerful temptation to say that the *Dialog* is not by Tacitus but by Quintilian. Classical scholars, moved by other evidence have nevertheless reached virtual unanimity in attributing the *Dialog* to Tacitus, in spite of the powerful internal evidence. For much less evidence, the form critics would be apt to leap to the opposite conclusion.(17)

Our second comment is this: in contrast to the proffered loose internal arguments, there exists the external witness of an unbroken chain of early writers: for Matthew we have: Papias, Irenaeus, Pantaenus, Clement of Alexandria, Origen, Tertullian, the Monarchian Prolog, Eusebius, St. Jerome, St. Ephrem, St. Epiphanius—all these insist that the Hebrew Matthew was really by an apostle, a companion of Jesus, although the Greek version, which is all we now have, may have been made somewhat later.(18) (It is often argued that our Greek Matthew is not a translation but a new work, because it contains instances of plays on words that are impossible in Hebrew. But that argument proves little, for the translator could have introduced such stylistic niceties. For instance, the Latin translator of Hosea 13:14 introduced a memorable play on words not found in the Hebrew original or in the Septuagint: "Ero mors tua, o mors, morsus tuus ero, inferne.")

We know of course that the testimony of Papias is challenged because Eusebius calls him a man of small intelligence, and says Irenaeus and others copied from him. But we reply that Eusebius made this statement in polemic, to combat Papias' millennium theory, which is erroneous—through many later intelligent writers accepted it. But it is a very different thing, requiring far less intelligence, to report a tradition of who wrote a book, than it is to correctly interpret difficult enigmatic lines in Scripture that could mean a millennium. In the same passage, Eusebius adds: "He [Papias] was also responsible for the fact that many ecclesiastical writers after him, relying on his antiquity, held a like opinion, such as Irenaeus, and whoever else seems to have held like views."(19) Some modern scholars have neglected the context of this sentence, and so have said Eusebius means Papias was the source of later opinions *on the authorship of Matthew*. But the context shows Eusebius refers to *millennium opinions*, actually held by Justin Martyr, Irenaeus and others.

Further, it is from fragments preserved by the same Eusebius(20) that we learn that Irenaeus(21) has data which Papias (at least in Eusebius' quotes from him) lacks, i.e., that Matthew wrote while Peter and Paul were preaching at Rome. And Irenaeus mentions Matthew before he mentions other Evangelists—if Papias knew that point, it does not show in the quotes Eusebius makes from him. So it seems that Irenaeus had sources other than Papias. Still further, Origen, also cited in Eusebius(22), in his commentary on Matthew, says he "learned from tradition about the four Gospels...that the first written was that according to Matthew, once a tax collector, later an apostle of Jesus Christ...." So Origen too seems at least not entirely dependent on Papias.

By no means all scholars are so diffident about Papias: Professor George A. Kennedy, Paddison Professor of Classics at the University of North Carolina, during a session of a Colloquy on the Relationships Among the Gospels, at Trinity University, San Antonio, May 26-29, 1977, in replying to a question about his use of Papias as a credible source answered that "he had studied carefully the second-century evidence for the tradition that Mark's

Gospel reflects directly reminiscences of Peter, and had concluded that he would be thoroughly delighted to find such solid evidence for some other ancient historical tradition...."(23) According to the noted form critic, Reginald Fuller, who was present, "everyone agreed that 'as a result of Kennedy's essay and the subsequent discussion, New Testament scholars have been challenged to take more seriously the external evidence regarding the origin of the Gospels."(24) Professor Kennedy is a Classicist. Classicists once went through an immature period much like that Scripture scholars are now suffering from, but they have outgrown it. Kennedy's judgment would meet with much favor from Classicists.

Even if one might reject the testimony of Papias on Matthew as the author, we have evidence for the authorship of Mark and Luke that is independent of Papias, in the Antimonarchian Prolog, dating from 160-180 A.D., and also from the Muratorian Canon (c.180-190 A.D.), St. Irenaeus, Clement of Alexandria, Origen, Tertullian, Eusebius, and St. Jerome. In fact, all testimonies on Luke are independent of Papias: Papias did not mention Luke. Still further, while someone might write a work and attribute it to a famous personality such as an apostle, it is very unlikely anyone would want to attribute a work to such poorly known persons as Mark, or to Luke—still less known. External witnesses also tell us that Mark learned his facts from the preaching of Peter and association with him, surely a prime eyewitness. Further, the third Gospel was written by a companion of Paul, the apostle who had received the Gospel message directly from Christ on the Damascus road, but who had taken the added precaution (to calm his opponents) of checking his teaching with that of the main eye-witnesses, as he himself tells us in Gal 2:2.

The second reason the critics propose for assigning a late date for the Synoptic Gospels is the fact that they predict the fall of Jerusalem too clearly, especially Luke 21:5ff. But this argument proves nothing except that these critics are following up on their prejudice, namely that there can be no miracles and no such thing as a genuine prophecy of the future. Our study has already shown that retrojection of a prophecy is impossible within the genre of the Synoptics.(25)

It is important to notice too that Matthew, whenever possible, links prophecies to their fulfillment; but he makes no mention of the fulfillment of the prophecy concerning the fall of Jerusalem in 70 A.D. Had he written after 70 A.D., it is hardly likely he could have resisted the opportunity to follow his usual practice and point out how truly the words of Jesus had come to pass. And again, even if the Synoptics were later than the critics think, there would still have been eyewitnesses alive, even persons cured and raised from the dead by Jesus, as we saw from Quadratus, whom we cited in the introduction. These eyewitnesses, realizing their own salvation was at stake, could and would have resisted falsification, had there been any.

Perhaps a new direction has been given to this problem by the appearance of a work of John A. T. Robinson, entitled *Redating the New Testament*. Briefly, the author presents an intriguing case for the composition of *all* the books of the New Testament before the year 70 A.D. The argumentation in favor of early Gospel composition is especially powerful. Other scholarly treatises in favor of an early composition of the Synoptics that have appeared recently are by Dr. William R. Farmer of Southern Methodist University, Dallas, Texas, and Dom Bernard Orchard, O.S.B., of Ealing Abbey in England.(26) One should not forget that not too long ago eminent scholars dated the composition of the Fourth Gospel toward the *end* of the second century until the discovery of the John Rylands papyrus proved the presence of that Gospel in distant Egypt a half century earlier. Ironically indeed, the manuscript found contained the words of Pilate, "What is truth!" (John 18:38).(27)

To round out our treatment of the problem we will focus our attention upon a specific passage from the writings of Norman Perrin. He tells us that the evidence "forces" him to agree with the conclusions of form criticism, chiefly, that neither the community nor the evangelists cared about historical facts, but instead faked freely: "Over and over again, pericopes which have been hitherto accepted as historical reminiscences have been shown (by form criticism) to be something quite different.... We would claim that the gospel materials themselves have forced us to change our mind.... We have been particularly influenced by a consideration of Mark 9:1 and its parallels."(28) So we need to examine Mk 9:1 with great care, to see if it really "forces" anyone.

Mk 9:1 reads, "There are some standing here who will not taste death before they see the Kingdom of God come with power." Mt 16:28 is the same, except that it says they will see "the Son of Man coming in his kingdom." In Lk 9:27 we find substantially the same wording, except that they will see "the kingdom of God."

Perrin understands both Matthew and Mark to refer to the end-time, except that Matthew adds "a characteristic concern for the expectation of the coming of Jesus as Son of man."(29) But Luke, Perrin believes, "completely reformulates the primitive Christian eschatology.... His major concern is the ongoing life and work of the Christian community as it settles down to face, so to speak, the long haul of history."(30) That is, Matthew and Mark both expected the end soon; but Luke had given up and settled down to the long pull. Hence the Gospels must be unreliable.

Exegetically we could consider three possibilities for what these passages refer to: (1) the transfiguration, (2) the coming of the kingdom in power (*dynameis*—miracles) with Pentecost, (3) the parousia.

As to the first option, the transfiguration: all three Synoptics place this saying immediately before their transfiguration account. This is noteworthy, for they do not always agree on sequence. It is at least possible that they meant the saying to refer to the transfiguration, in which some would see the kingdom in power in Jesus transformed. Since this is a reasonable interpretation, Perrin is not really *forced* to regard the passage as historically untrue.

In regard to the second possibility which takes "the kingdom coming in power" to mean the spread of the kingdom by miracles: many exegetes think that the Synoptics do take the kingdom to refer to the church.(31) Stanley, for one thinks Mk 9:1 refers to the coming of the kingdom in the Church after Pentecost with power, i.e., with miracles.(32) St. Paul often speaks in line with this concept, e.g., in 1 Cor 2:4-5 he says that his preaching and the acceptance of the kingdom by the Corinthians did not depend on human wisdom and eloquence, but on "the Spirit and power", i.e., on a number of supportive miracles. (See also Gal 3:5; Rom 15:19 and 2 Cor 12:12.) Further, Paul often makes the kingdom refer to the present Church; for example, in Col 1:13, "He has delivered us from the dominion of darkness, and transferred us to the kingdom of his beloved Son, in whom we have redemption, the forgiveness of sins." (See also 1 Thess 2:12; Col 4:11; Acts 28:31.)

Therefore, the expression of Mark, "the kingdom coming with power" can refer to the establishment of the Church with miracles. Matthew could also mean the same, for as Stanley notes, Matthew at times identifies the kingdom of the Son of Man with the Church.(33) Luke's phrase "the kingdom of God" could refer to the same; his phrase is merely less specific. So again, nothing can *force* someone to reject this second option.

The third option proposes that Matthew and Mark thought the end was near. No proof, however, is offered; we examined the usual attempts at proof in chapter 3. Perrin does give one weak argument: "He [Mt] has also strengthened the reference in the previous verse, changing Mark's '...the Son of man...when he comes....' to '...the Son of man is about to come....'"(34) Perrin thinks "about to come" means the end is viewed as imminent. But the Greek verb *mellei*, though it could mean "he is about to", has other connotations. Easily and very commonly it indicates the ordinary future, "he will come."(35) Perrin has had to strain normal Greek usage to get a reason to "force" himself.

There are, then, three ways to understand Mark 9:1 and its Synoptic parrallels. The first and second ways are truly plausible, and the third as understood by Perrin cannot be corroborated. Hence there is nothing to force Perrin to label the verses as inauthentic; such would follow only if the third view were inescapable.

Perrin adds a few supplementary points. He claims that Luke "subtly alters the tone...[by] the insertion of 'daily' in Luke 9:23."(36) The word "daily" is inserted in the exhortation to take up one's cross and follow Jesus. Does that insertion really make a great and certain difference? Does it *prove* that Matthew and Mark thought the end imminent while Luke did not? Even with a nearby end, one could be urged to imitate Jesus daily, for whatever days might be left. Perrin notes also that Luke omits the words "in power". But if, as we said, those words could refer to the miracles worked in the spread of the kingdom, then to omit the words would not be significant. For we cannot picture Luke denying there were miracles in the spread of the kingdom. Perrin also thinks Mark "created" (faked) the entire incident of the confession of Peter which ends with our verse 9:1. Why? His chief reason seems to be that it is artistically constructed. But what is the structure of the scene? It includes the following: (1) Peter confesses Jesus is the Messiah; (2) Jesus commands silence, and (3) predicts His Passion; (4) Peter reacts and is reproved as a satan;(37) (5) all are urged to take up their cross; (6) some will not die before seeing the kingdom coming in power. One may well ask whether this is so wonderfully artistic a structure that it simply could not have happened in that order. Was it necessary for someone to fake it? It seems the pendulum has swung far, for a few decades ago the critics insisted that the evangelists were not really authors at all; now we find things so elegantly artistic that they must have been faked. Again, Perrin only imagines he is "forced."

Perrin also thinks he finds an argument in this observation: at the start of the scene (Mk 8:27) Jesus is alone with the disciples; later at 8:34, He is speaking to crowds. So, thinks Perrin, here is evidence of "creation". There are at least two ways here of avoiding the need of being "forced". Note first that at the start of the incident Jesus is speaking to the disciples "on the way" to Caesarea Philippi. Naturally, He would arrive there later, and, as usual, a crowd would gather. So we have a plausible explanation. But, secondly, we could also suggest that we might have two scenes here, the second beginning at 8:34. The form critics themselves often divide passages into much smaller units.

Really, we owe a debt of gratitude to Dr. Perrin. For he has shown us his *strongest argument* for rejecting the reliability of the Gospels. Yet, by ordinary analysis, we have found it is defective on many counts and actually proves nothing. If this is the best America's most illustrious form critic can do against the historical credibility of the Gospels, our confidence in their reliability can remain unshaken.

NOTES

1   HST 6.
2   Dan O. Via, Jr. in "Editor's Foreword", v, to Norman Perrin, *What is Redaction Criticism?* Fortress, Philadelphia, 1969. *Cf.* Bultmann in preface to SSG 4.
3   SSG 64.
4   HST 40-41.
5   Martin Dibelius, *From Tradition to Gospel*, tr. B. L. Woolf, Charles Schribner's Sons, New York, (from revised second edition) 13.
6   HST 40, n. 2. *Cf.* also 138, 145-46.
7   N. Perrin, *The Promise of Bultmann* 29, in *The Promise of Theology*, ed. M. Marty, Lippincott, Philadelphia, 1969. *Cf.* KM 194.
8   *Cf* pp 16-20 above.
9   For example: (a) Acts 9:7 says the men who were with Paul heard the voice, while 22:9 says they did not hear it. *Answer:* Greek *akouein* can mean merely to perceive a sound without understanding, or to understand. (b) Acts 9:7 says his companions stood amazed, while 26:14 says they fell to the ground. *Answer:* After falling, it is natural to scramble to one's feet as soon as possible, and then to stand there amazed. (c) In Acts 21:22-24 James tells Paul that pious Jews have heard he departs from the Law, advises him to make the Nazarite vow with others and "Thus all will know that there is nothing in what they have been told about you, but that you yourself live in observance of the law." *Answer:* see note 14 on Appendix: 1. Other objections are equally superficial and soluble.
10 *Cf* pp 15-20 above.
11 SSG 15.
12 KM 195.
13 SSG 17.
14 HST 138, 146.
15 Paul does not really differ with Mt. 5:17. *Cf.* note 14 on Appendix:1.
16 E.g., if a document mentions a recent total eclipse of the sun, that of course permits dating it exactly.
17 *Cf.* F. R. D. Goodyear, *Tacitus*, in *Greece and Rome-new Surveys in the Classics* #4, Clarendon Press, Oxford, 1970, 12-14.
18 For Mark and Luke we have a very similar list. John A. T. Robinson, *Redating the New Testament*, Westminster, Philadelphia, 1976, refreshingly shows a return to external evidence. He shows the flimsy nature of generally accepted evidence on dating. W. R. Farmer, *The Synoptic Problem*, Western North Carolina Press, Dillsboro, North Carolina, 1976 challenges Marcan priority, shows the weak nature of most evidence in discussions of the Synoptic Problem. Similarly, *Matthew, Luke and Mark*, ·by Dom Bernard Orchard, O.S.B.,

Koinonia Press, Manchester, 1977.

19 Eusebius, *Histories*, 3.39.

20 *Ibid*. 5.8.

21 Irenaeus, *Against heresies* 3.1.1.

22 Eusebius 6.25.

23 Cited in Patrick Henry, *New Directions in New Testament Study*, Westminster, Philadelphia, 1979, pp. 33-34.

24 *Ibid*., note 13 on p. 276.

25 *Cf*. p. 27 above. Still another argument says that Matthew could not have been an eyewitness since he uses Mark and Q as sources. We reply: The Two Source Theory is far from proved. On the contrary there is impressive evidence against it. See pp 24-25 above.

26 John A. T. Robinson, *op.cit*. (n.18 above); *The Synoptic Problem* (n.18).

27 *Cf*. W. H. Hatch, *Principal Unical Manuscripts*, University of Chicago, Chicago, 1939.

28 Norman Perrin, *Rediscovering the Teaching of Jesus*, Harper and Row, New York, 1967, 16.

29 *Ibid*. 16-17.

30 *Ibid*. 17.

31 *Cf*. Stanley in JBC II, p. 783, McKenzie, *ibid*. p. 64.

32 *Ibid*.

33 *Ibid*.

34 *Op.cit*. 17.

35 *Cf*. W.F. Arndt, F.W. Gingrich and F.W. Danker, *A Greek-English Lexicon of the New Testament*, 2d ed., University of Chicago Press, Chicago, 1979, 501.

36 *Op. cit*. 17.

37 Luke's version omits this item.

3. Technique

For information on the actual application of form criticism, we will consult Bultmann's *Study of the Synoptic Gospels*. Although it was written some forty years ago (second edition, 1930), the Torch Book Edition of 1962 carries a freshly written preface by Bultmann himself.(1) By this means we know he still accepted what he had written earlier, for the preface is limited to (a) listing new works that appeared in the interval, (b) the admission that now he knows the evangelists were really artistic authors.

The procedure is not at all difficult to understand. Let us first get an overview, and then comment on each step. To facilitate the matter, we will insert numbers: (1) Begin by trying to separate two things: the traditional material which existed before the Gospels were written, from the editorial work of the evangelists. (2) Study how Matthew and Luke worked, using Mark and Q. (Many scholars imagine there must have been a document—Q—which Matthew and Luke used when they did not use Mark, but still agree). (3) Notice that Mark himself worked in a similar way. (4) Therefore, assume that a similar pattern held in the tradition before Mark.(2) (5) Confirm this by noting how the later church worked, especially in the apocrypha. (6) Get added help for the study of tradition by examining the literary forms that were at hand at that time, and by noting that since these forms tended to resist change, editors were at work where there is change. Notice also the life situation in the church that led to the use of each form

(*Sitz-im-Leben*).(7) Add also a study of how primitive literature in general develops. (8) Finally, classify each Gospel passage under one of the major forms and subdivisions. (9) Conclude that (a) the evangelists created the whole setting of the Gospel stories, not knowing times or places,(3) (b) and in many cases without even knowing what the sayings meant—but giving them a definite meaning by the choice of setting in which to report them. (c) As a result, it is clear that the Gospels are not historical.

Step 1

Of course we agree that much of the Gospel story existed as short units. However, there is a vexing problem already in the first step, for it supposes we can draw demarcation lines between the units. But there are no objective criteria for that, and the judgment of the critics is seriously marred by the long list of their prejudices.

To illustrate the problem, let us consider Mark 8:29-33, the confession of Peter. This is one of the most important passages bearing on the question of what Jesus consciously knew.

R. H. Fuller divides the passage into the following units.(4) First, Jesus asks: Who do you apostles say that I am? Peter replies: You are the Messiah. Second, Jesus commands silence on that point. Third, Jesus predicts His Passion and Peter objects. Fourth, Jesus turns on Peter: Get behind me, satan!

The critics leave the first unit as it is, but say the second was invented by the Church and appropriated by Mark in his Messianic secret theme. The third unit, the Passion prediction and Peter's reaction is, they think, also a creation by the Church. So, after eliminating units two and three, we read the real account, they claim: Jesus asks the disicples who they say He is. Peter replies: You are the Messiah. Jesus angrily rejects the title: Get behind me satan! Splendid apologetics for a seventeenth century anti-papist.

Obviously we ought to examine the evidence for eliminating units two and three.

Wilhelm Wrede contended that Jesus never claimed He was the Messiah.(5) Rather, the Church, finding it embarassing that He had never said so, invented the tale that He had really said He was, but insisted on keeping it secret. Wrede has two chief arguments and some lesser ones.

As the first of his arguments, Wrede says that Jesus' command to observe silence after working miracles makes no sense. He proposes as the clearest case the instance after Jesus raised the daughter of Jairus (Mk 5:43): "Here first and foremost the story of Jairus's daughter is very clear...a prohibition by Jesus would be completely without point and...from the historical standpoint it is senseless."(6) for everyone would have to know soon that she was raised. The command therefore must be unhistorical, and, accordingly, faked by the church and incorporated by Mark into his Gospel. Wrede adds that the situation is much the same with other cures: a leper (Mk 1:43-44); a deaf mute (7:36); a blind man (8:23-26), and so on.

Does Wrede's theory hold under analysis? First, he admits that part of the basis for his rejection is that "historical research...does not recognize miracles in the strict sense."(7) Here we have the same gullibly unscientific, unsupported prejudice we found in Bultmann. Second, he says the command to silence makes no sense because no one would keep the secret. There was, however, a real point in the commands. In the case of the daughter of Jairus, if the father would hold off for a short while, Jesus could make an exit. That would be sufficient for His immediate purpose. He wanted to avoid being virtually seized by an emotional crowd and hailed as king Messiah. He knew well that the fickle ardor of the crowd would subside in a few days—recall the Palm Sunday hosannas which changed within the week to "Crucify Him!" In the case of the leper, Mk 1:45 records how Jesus could no longer openly enter cities at that time and place because of the acclaim. In curing the deaf mute, Jesus took him aside, away from the crowd (Mk 7:33).

Thirdly, any good author who writes *fiction* knows enough to avoid the implausible. All admit Mark was an artistic writer. Surely he would know enough to omit fictional, unhistorical incidents if they were implausible. Why not just skip them, if he was merely dealing in fiction? But if, as the case is, he was reporting facts that were true, though strange, he would report things that might *seem* hard to accept. He would report them simply because they were factual. In other words, the very difficulty proper to the account is an argument in favor of the writer reporting historical truth. We might allude to the generally accepted principle of preferring the "more difficult reading" in textual criticism, i.e., if the text of one manuscript is obscure, while the same text in another is clear, that of the former is more likely to be authentic; the assumption is that a copyist might change a difficult reading to an easier one when not able to understand it. But the reverse, changing a clear reading to an obscure one, is hardly likely.

The second argument proposed by Wrede concerns the command to observe silence after the transfiguration (Mk 9:9): "A relatively little-heeded passage provides us with the key to this approach [the Messianic secret]. For me at least it has undoubtedly been the proper starting-point for getting to know this whole series of ideas, and to this extent I regard it as one of the most important sayings written down by Mark. It is the command Jesus gives after the Transfiguration, 9:9...."(8) He notes Jesus told them to keep it secret, "until the Son of man should have risen from the dead." So, Wrede continues, "From this saying it is deduced that the Transfiguration is regarded as a sort of anticipation or preview of the resurrection.... The true meaning...would, however, have been discernible only after the resurrection." He then continues: "If the meaning...was to be discerned only later then it seems more or less harmless if people heard about it earlier." Therefore, according to Wrede, since the prohibition makes little sense, it must be unhistorical.

Wrede has missed a distinction, as he and the critics often do, and in doing so has jumped beyond the evidence. The point of the transfiguration was not just to foretell the resurrection; rather, it revealed *partially* aspects of the true nature of Jesus, and did so in a way that could be understood at once, before the resurrection. Even dull Peter got it for the moment (Mk 9:5): "Let us make three booths." He wanted to stay on permanently in that delightful revelation. People in general would, by this revelation, have found out more than what Jesus wished to reveal of His true nature at that time. After the resurrection there would be ample opportunity to proclaim His glory, and Jesus imposed the obligation to spread the good news. But before the resurrection He did not want His glory known. Hence the prohibition makes excellent sense.(9)

Unit three is rejected because of the form critics' view that the passion predictions are unhistorical. Chiefly three reasons are advanced for this claim, which we will take up in turn. First, the critics argue that the predictions gave detailed knowledge of the passion and resurrection. Yet, these events came as a surprise to the disciples.

We reply: The Gospels record how the disciples were slow to understand, even dull. It is not likely that the community would have regarded them as such unless it were true. Further, it is said that a genius at times will fail to catch on. Teachers, for example, often find that students will not read instructions, printed in large type, at the top of examination forms; instead they will ask for the information already before their very eyes. Even after Jeremiah had proved himself a true prophet in foretelling the disaster that befell Jerusalem, some survivors came to him and asked him to consult the Lord on what they should do; when he gave them the answer, they called him a liar, and did the opposite of what God commanded (Jer 42-43). As already noted, N. Perrin, who was not a dull Galilean fisherman but a university professor, claimed that the evidence "forced" him to consider the Gospel accounts unreliable; actually nothing at all *forced* him. R. Bultmann cites copiously from Scripture to support his claims—most of them are invalid. There are many cases of incredible slowness in the history of the sciences, e.g., when Dr. Ignaz Semmelweis (1817-65) discovered the cause of puerperal fever, men of science forced him into an insane asylum. The trouble was that the discovery of Semmelweis clashed with the existing beliefs of the medical men of his day. So they did not accept the evidence even when experimental proof glared at them. Similarly, the predictions of Jesus that He, the wonderworker and Messiah, should suffer so dreadfully clashed with the mind-set of the disciples. Moreover, the disciples panicked at the time of Christ's arrest, and in panic one forgets everything.

Teilhard de Chardin showed a similar puzzling inability to

grasp things. He painted a glorious picture of the splendid condition of the human race just before the return of Christ at the end. He could not, it seems, fit into that framework some shockingly clear descriptions of the same period found in Scripture, so he ignored, and even contradicted them. For example, in Lk 18:8 Jesus foretold: "When the Son of Man comes, will He find faith on earth?" St. Paul in 2 Thes 2:3 told his people that the end could not come until there had been a great apostasy. Similarly, 2 Tim 3:1-5 warned: "In the last days there will come times of stress. For men will be lovers of self, lovers of money, proud, arrogant, abusive, disobedient to their parents, ungrateful, unholy, inhuman, implacable, slanderers, profligates, fierce, haters of good, treacherous, reckless, swollen with conceit, lovers of pleasure rather than lovers of God, holding the form of religion but denying the power of it." Jesus Himself also warned, in Mt 24:12: "Because wickedness is multiplied, most men's love will grow cold."

Another instance: Galen, a second century Greek physician and authority on anatomy, so dominated the beliefs of later investigators that many times in later centuries discoveries made by dissection that contradicted Galen were disregarded. In fact Fabricius, the anatomy professor of William Harvey (who discovered the circulation of the blood), missed the import of some of his own findings about human veins, since they did not agree with Galen.

There is a specially forceful case of this inability to see things that clash with an established pattern of thought reported by St. Paul in 1 Cor 8-10. In 10:27-29 Paul supposes a Christian goes out to eat, and when seated, another Christian says the meat on the table had been sacrificed to idols. Paul says that in itself it is all right to eat such meat, outside of pagan rituals, but that if there is danger of scandal, one should abstain. But, why does not Paul say instead that they should just tell the worried Christian that he, Paul, says it is all right to eat? Because Paul knows that sort of mentality, and knows that such a person will not be able to grasp that it is all right. So, if he eats, it will be in bad conscience.

Second, the critics argue that the passion prophecies are not found in Q, and consequently must be later. The argument is defective in two ways. First, belief in Q rests on the Two Source Theory; a theory based on a theory makes it a compound—not a proven proposition. In fact current studies are undermining its whole fabric. Second, even if we tentatively accept the theory about Q, the critics' argument is the argument from silence, a flimsy and inconclusive type of argument, especially when we have no tangible and certain means of knowing the precise text of Q. Also, all admit that Matthew and Luke each contain passages wholly independent of hypothetic Q.

Third, our critics also claim that the Passion predictions come from a different set of Son of Man sayings, sayings that have nothing in common with the sayings about the glorious or apocalyptic Son of Man suggested by Dan 7:13. Furthermore, (a) these predictions are structurally integrated by Mark in a way other sayings are not; according to Toedt this shows they are artificial, not historical; (b) the other Son of Man texts refer to the transcendent Son of Man far removed from suffering— accordingly, there was need to add on the Servant of Yahweh and the glorious Son of Man themes, which was done only after the resurrection; (c) in Lk 12:8 Jesus clearly distinguishes between Himself and the future Son of Man.

Our reply? (a) Opinions of scholars as to which Son of Man sayings are authentic vary from book to book, and even within the pages of the same book. Surely, nothing is proved by structural integration or its absence. Without the need of special artistry from Mark, things could have just happened that way, that is, there is no reason why predictions could not have been made at major points in the public life of Jesus.

(b) Nothing proves that Jesus Himself could not have joined the two ideas, Suffering Servant and Son of Man, in His own utterances. Ordinary Jews of His day knew about the atoning power of the death of a just man and its relation to Is 53.(10) And Jesus spoke of His own atonement in language reminiscent of Is 53:11-12, as recorded in Mk 10:45; Mt 20:28.

(c) The claim that Jesus distinguishes, in Lk 12:8, between Himself and the future Son of Man does not stand up. First, Jesus often used "Son of Man" to refer to Himself in His earthly career, such as in Lk 9:58, "Foxes have their holes and the birds of the sky nests, but the Son of Man has nowhere to lay his head." Even more importantly, the critics have failed to explain away certain connections. In Mt 13:36-41, the explanation of the parable of the tares, Jesus makes clear that He Himself is the Son of Man who sows the good seed. Even Toedt admits this though, with no attempt at proof, he dismisses it as editorial work by Matthew.(11) But then in the same passage (Mt 13:41) we find that the eschatological Son of Man who will collect all scandals from His kingdom is the same Jesus, as Toedt admits. Here, then, there is a clear connection, an identification of Jesus as both currently present and as the eschatological Son of Man. Bultmann weakly says(12) that, "most of all it is the absence from the interpretation of a specific point, viz., the exhortation to patience" that shows it is merely the creation of Matthew. Hardly a proof!

In Lk 17:24-25 and 21:8 we find equated the suffering Son of Man and the eschatological Son of Man: "Many will come in my name saying, 'I am he!'...." The "*my* name" clearly refers to Jesus. But He is also the Son of Man who is first to suffer many things. Toedt thinks he has a *decisive* way to break the connection here:

> ...the following fact speaks decisively against his view [Kummel's, who defended the text as reliable early tradition]. Luke 17:24 is taken over form Q. Matt. 24:27, the parallel passage to Luke 17:24, is not followed by a reference to the suffering Son of Man. Since no saying on the suffering Son of Man occur in Q, we may be sure that Luke did not find 17:25 in Q. Luke 17:26f and 17:28f, however, are again taken over from Q. Thus 17:25 appears to be an interpolation into sayings which had been taken over.(13)

Such reasoning depends on an *inference* in relation to Q—and even if the inference were conclusive (which it is not), the very existence of Q is questionable, tied in as it is with the Two Source Theory.

It is evident, then, that there exist no good arguments to prevent us from saying that Lk 9:58 shows that Jesus is the earthly

Son of Man, that Mt 13:36-41 equates the earthly and the eschatological Son of Man, and that Lk 17:24 equates the suffering and the eschatological Son of Man—thus identifying all three phases of the Son of Man's activity with Jesus Himself. We have shown to be weak and unconvincing the arguments that units two and three were "created" (faked) by the Church. There is no reason to say that the incident did not happen as narrated by Mark.

What of the details added in Matthew's account of the same event, i.e., the longer title Peter gave Jesus (Mt 16:16), "the Messiah, the Son of the Living God," and the praise Jesus accorded to Peter and the promise of primacy (Mt 16:17-19)? Matthew was the only synoptic author who would have been present. he could have decided to report fully, whereas Mark, obtaining his information from Peter (as the early external witnesses insist) and secondary sources, opted for what he wrote. Commentators have suggested modesty on the part of Peter, or community slowness in realizing the import of Jesus' words (in line with Peter's recorded slowness, as well as the fact that history indeed shows a gradual development in the Church's appreciation and understanding of this key passage). Also Mark strongly emphasizes the slowness of the Apostles to understand, and so might be less inclined to report Peter's confession (though to say Christ is "Son of God" would not have necessarily meant divinity, as the expression was generally understood then). Interestingly, Professors Albright and Mann, though not Catholic, clearly recognized the grant of real authority to Peter here.(14)

Could the added details in Matthew be retrojected from another scene after Easter? It is not impossible, but neither is there good reason for the claim. On the contrary, the Synoptic genre makes that quite unlikely. Surely the data in Mark cannot be retrojected. If Peter after Easter had merely confessed Jesus to be the Messiah, it would have been ridiculous, for it was then so evident He was immeasurably more.

Step 2

We next turn to an examination of how Matthew and Luke

worked. Bultmann thinks Matthew worked by using Q to fill in scenes from Mark. Here, as constantly, he is presupposing the Two Source Theory is proved. But we have seen it is very flimsy indeed. However, let us examine the first two passages Bultmann uses to prove his point.(15)

First, we are to compare Mt 10:1,7-15 with Mk 6:7-13. He thinks Matthew has taken the scene describing the sending out of the disciples from Mark, and has filled it in with matter from Q. We first notice that the alleged fill-ins are very general in character: heal the sick and preach. The longest is Mt 10:7-8. Are these verses really from Q? If so, there should be no parallel in Mark,(16) but a close parallel in Luke, so close that we would be led to say Matthew and Luke used the common source Q, but Mark did not. In general, Luke 9:1-6 is parallel to Matthew, but if we look for the part that should be close to Mt 10:7-8 we find only the brief verse 2, "Then he sent them out to preach the Kingdom of God and to heal the sick." These words are not so close to Mt 10:7-8 that we would be obliged to say they had a common source. Mt has: "Preach as you go, saying, 'The kingdom of heaven is at hand,' Heal the sick, raise the dead, cleanse lepers, cast out demons. You received without pay, give without pay." This is hardly substantive enough to assure us of an outside common source, Q.

We could also look in chapter 10 of Luke. There Jesus is also described as sending out disciples, but in general that chapter does not parallel closely the passage in Matthew. The lines that would correspond to Mt 10:7-8 (the lines that could be considered as possibly from Q) occur in Lk 10:8, "Whenever you enter a town and they receive you, eat what is set before you." There are no similar words in Matthew. Luke continues: "Heal the sick in it and say to them, 'the kingdom of God has come near to you.'" These words are hardly so close that we would have to say Matthew and Luke used a common source, Q. Some writers have proposed that there is a "variant" in Q here; that, however, defeats the whole argument, namely, the very reason for postulating a Q is the presence of wordings in Matthew and Luke that are so close they must have had a common source other than Mark. If someone thinks Luke really is close enough to make us suppose a common source here, then we reply: there is just as good a reason to say Mk 6:12 is parallel. But then the lines examined could not be from Q, since the very means of determining what is Q is the fact that the matter is lacking in Mark.

We are forced to conclude that Bultmann has failed in his first example to prove that Matthew used Q to fill in scenes from Mark. For the words in question are clearly not from Q.

In the next example, Bultmann thinks Mt 18:1-5 has filled in Mk 9:33-35 from Q. But again, the chief enlargement in Matthew occurs with verses 3-4. These verses are lacking in Luke, who presumably did not find them in Q. The other matter is present in Mark, hence not from Q.

Bultmann further thinks Luke worked by creating new scenes out of typical material; as an example Bultmann suggests the banquet scene in Lk 11:37-54 (compare Mt 15:1-9 and Mk 7:1-9).

Even if Luke did create the scene, we would have no evidence against reliability. But the literary genre of the Synoptics makes it unlikely that he actually did. Further, Matthew and Mark make the Pharisees come from Jerusalem, while Luke speaks of a single Pharisee, privately, at a dinner. The Pharisee makes an attack about the omission of ceremonial washing, a sore spot, one that opponents would regard as a good argument against Jesus; they would be likely to bring it up on more than one occasion. Hence, it is not at all clear that Luke is describing the same incident as Matthew and Mark.

Did Luke draw on Q here? Only at verse 39b do we have matter that could be Q. But the dissimilarities with Matthew are so great that we are far from being obliged to believe it must be Q. For Matthew is sometimes fuller, sometimes less full than Luke. And the sequence of presentation is substantially different, for no discernible reason. To make Matthew parallel to Luke, we would have to move to a different chapter of Matthew (chapter 23), and put the verses in the following order: 25-26, 23, 6-7, 27-28, 4, 29-32, 34-36, 13. Certainly there is no proof here of a common source (even for one who believes in Q), and accordingly Bultmann has offered no proof for his supposition about the way Luke worked.

Bultmann's second example concerns Luke 14:15-24 (cf. Mt 22:1-4; Mark lacks a parallel). But again, the parallels are far from being close enough to require one to see a common source, Q. In Matthew, the parable is about a wedding feast given by a king for his son; in Luke, it is just a dinner, with no mention of a wedding or a king. In Luke, the guests make poor excuses but they do no harm to the messengers. Then the master sends out to get just any guests. But in Matthew, the first group do not make excuses. Then a second set of messengers go, and meet with excuses, insults, death. Not so in Luke. In Matthew the king responds by sending an army to destroy the city, but there is nothing of the sort in Luke. Only after that destruction does the king in Matthew send out for guests, any and all; he finds one without a wedding garment, and throws him out; again, there is no such incident in Luke. Really, what the critics seem to have forgotten is the very obvious fact that Jesus was a traveling speaker. Traveling speakers often re-use material with different audiences, and also, often make variations at different times for various reasons. So the most natural explanation is that Jesus told similar, not identical, parables on several occasions. It is all too often presumed that there was absolutely no repetition in the words and actions of Jesus. What common sense and history take for granted, the critics are often unaware of.

Step 3

Bultmann tells his followers that Mark worked in a way similar to Matthew and Luke.(17) (That is like a house built of cards, since he really never did demonstrate how Matthew and Luke worked.) For the sake of argument, we will look at the first two of his examples from Mark.

He first calls attention to Mark 3:9, a passage in which he asks us to think Jesus entered into a boat to speak. Actually, the Greek text does not make clear whether Jesus did or did not step into the boat. He told them *hina ploiarion proskartere*, which means He directed that a boat *be ready*. We cannot tell if He did or did not actually use it. Things should not remain uncomplicated, so

Bultmann adds: "The motive of Jesus' withdrawing into the boat...is transformed by Mark from 4:1 where it belonged with the traditional material, to 3:9, where it stands in a totally unorganic relation." However, he did not notice that there is an organic reason for the boat, the same one as in 4:1, i.e., the press of the crowds.(18) So again, he has failed to show the working pattern of Mark.

In the second example from Mark (9:36) Bultmann claims that we can easily see "that the motive of Jesus with the children has been carried back from 10:16, where it belongs to the older tradition, to 9:36, where it remains a superfluous touch."(19) A closer look reveals he has done no better this time. In 10:16 Jesus blesses children the apostles wanted to keep away from Him, and uses a child to inculcate the need for humility. In 9:36, after the apostles had wrangled over who was greater, Jesus also used a child to teach the need of a humble childlike attitude. We wonder too how we should suppose Mark to be so dull as not to see that he had "carried back" something that was "superfluous"—while siding with the critics who today consider Mark a superb artist!

Step 4

Quite confident that he has proved how Matthew and Luke worked, and also how Mark worked—though he has failed on both points—Bultmann asks us to *assume* that the unnamed persons who dealt with the Gospel tradition prior to the evangelists worked in the same way.(21) No reply is needed. It is a totally unfounded assumption to suppose that because some persons have worked in one way, others before them have "gone and done likewise."

Step 5

A further quote from Bultmann: "One may...test his skill by studying the manner in which the evangelic material was handed down in the later church, especially in the apocryphal gospels."(22) We are honestly puzzled by Bultmann's claim that the way of working shown in the apocrypha is the same as that in the canonical Gospels! It does not take much study to notice sharp differences, e.g., the apocrypha abound with miracles worked by the infant Jesus or Jesus as a boy. The real Gospels are much more sober. They show Him working no marvel until He was about 30 years old, and then his fellow townspeople were astounded to see how one they had considered very ordinary was so special.

Step 6

Bultmann thinks that the forms of primitive literature are "more or less fixed...[and] have their own laws of style."(23) Where variations appear, an editor has been tinkering. The principle is basically sound. There existed such forms, and their study sheds light. The trouble, however, begins when Bultmann attempts to deal with them practically and concretely. The forms that are most likely to be historical, says he, are the apothegms, i.e., short, important sayings, with a minimum of setting (the setting presently becomes unimportant). These apothegms of Bultmann correspond to the "paradigms" of Dibelius, the other illustrious pioneer critic. Dibelius finds only eight out of eighteen paradigms to be pure in form.(24)

The life situation in the Church (*Sitz-im-Leben*) and the choice of the particular forms interlocked with one another: the situation called for a form, and the form chosen would fit the situation. What more precisely constituted the *Sitz-im-Leben*? Bultmann tells how the controversy dialogues arose "in the apologetic and polemic of the Palestinian Church.... It is quite inappropriate to call these passages paradigms, i.e., examples of preaching as Dibelius does."(25) But Dibelius says the *Sitz-im-Leben* was preaching for missionary purposes. The divergence, then, between these two great pioneers is considerable, and it shows the absence of objectivity, which Bultmann explicitly admitted in regard to the controversy dialogues.(26)

It is illuminating to take a concrete passage and compare the comments on it by our two great critics. For example, Bultmann says that Mark 2:1-12 (cure and forgiveness of a paralytic) is a controversy saying.(27) Dibelius, on the contrary asserts that "such passages cannot be described as disputes."(28) Bultmann says the purpose was to enable the Church to trace its right to forgive sins back to Jesus. Dibelius says the only point is the reality of the forgiveness. Bultmann, oddly, says that verses 5b-10 are a secondary interpolation, for the faith "of the paralytic and his friends, which is demonstrated so clearly in vv. 3f and is verified by Jesus in v.5a disappears in vv.5b-10." The problem is in Bultmann's lack of distinctions. At first, faith appears only in the lame man and his bearers. Later, bystanders (hardly including the scribes) come to faith. There is really no hint that the paralytic, after being cured, could no longer believe.

(In passing it is interesting to note that although many today think that verse 10 is an editorial insertion by Mark, and not part of the words of Jesus, even so, Jesus clearly presents the cure as a proof of forgiveness. Both Bultmann and Dibelius agree. The latter says: "That Jesus should, by the healing, confirm the forgiveness of sins, corresponds to Jewish views of the connection between sin and illness." And Bultmann writes: "It has manifestly arisen from the dispute about the right...to forgive sins, a right which is to be attested by the power to heal miraculously.")

Step 7

Another topic treated by Bultmann concerns the laws operative in the development of popular narratives.(29) Two species are distinguished: (a) the original form presents only short, simple pictures, individual scenes simply described, covering a brief period of time, usually with just two speakers, and with crowds of people serving as backdrop. (b) When the narratives are retold, the "details are subject to the control of fancy and are usually made more explicit and definite."

His first observation, that such narratives are commonly short and simple, with few speakers, is quite correct—provided the story teller is a genius. More often persons who attempt to recount an event will interrupt the sequence with boring, distracting asides, will add needless details, and will all too often leave a hazy picture. A skilled storyteller, ancient or modern, does produce as Bultmann says. But how many such geniuses are in your local community church? Are we to presume an abundance of such in the churches of ancient Syria and Palestine?

As to his second claim, that the accounts when passed on

become longer and have details added by fancy, that too admits elements of fancy. First, Bultmann points to Mark 9:14-29.(30) Here Mark is much longer than the parallel in Lk 9:37-42. Further, Mark 6:32-44 is more detailed than its parallels, Mt 14:13-21 and Lk 9:10-17. Similarly, Mk 5:21-43 is fuller than the parallels in Mt 9:17-26 and Lk 8:40-56. Also, as Buchanan has observed, the Targums which repeat Old Testament passages are not always smoother or more ornate.(31) And, as English teachers have often noticed, students' papers tend to be shorter and less literary than the sources they use!

Are details added by fancy? Leslie R. Keylock studied this matter by examining a large number of parallels.(32) He found that Luke is more precise than Mark 47 times, but less precise 37 times. Matthew is more precise than Mark 58 times, but less precise 54 times. This hardly adds up to a "law" of increasing detail added by fancy.

Step 8

Finally, we are advised to classify each Gospel passage under one of the major forms and their subdivisions.(33) The two chief major forms are the Sayings and the Narratives. Sayings include apothegms and dominical sayings. The apothegms are brief sayings of some importance, and here the background matters little. Apothegms include controversy dialogues, scholastic dialogues (with sincere inquirers), and biographical sayings (apothegms are about the same as the paradigms of Dibelius).

Bultmann proposes that the Gospel apothegms probably originated in Jewish communities, when a counter-question was used to answer a question (a rabbinic trait), or in Greek communities, when we find such patterns as "when he was asked by..." or, "once he observed how..." (similar forms are detected in secular Greek literature).

The use of a counter-question to reply to a question is indeed a special form, though not so unique as to be restricted to the Jewish-Christian church. The forms cited to show Greek origin are much too loose and non-distinctive to prove anything. An example:

> The passage in Luke xvii, 20-21 is formulated in this manner: 'And when he was demanded of the Pharisees when the Kingdom of God should come, he answered them and said, 'The Kingdom of God cometh not with observation....' It may accordingly be concluded that these two accounts [this and Lk. 6:5, in one MS] were first formulated in the Hellenistic Church.(34)

But we fear Bultmann has failed again to notice points to the contrary; the text quoted does indeed have the form some Greek texts have, but that is hardly very distinctive. He should have noted a phrase that really is distinctive: "he answered them and said." Here we have a thoroughly Hebrew idiom. Hence if we wanted to play the game (it would be no more than a guess), we would classify the form of this text as stemming from a Jewish community.

In this connection Bultmann tries at times to distinguish the origin of the narrative framework from that of the saying itself. Thus he points out how the setting in Mk 2:15ff was supplied later: "This is indicated by the wholly unmotivated, and literally impossible, appearance of Pharisaic scribes at a dinner attended by publicans, and further by the remarkable fact that it is the disciples who are questioned and Jesus who replies."(35) Has the learned critic forgotten that banquet places often were open to non-guests?(36) There was also plenty of motivation: the Pharisees were constantly seeking opportunities to attack Jesus. Relative to their questioning the disciples, "Why does your master eat with publicans and sinners?," their query was an obvious dig aimed at Jesus. Naturally, He answered an objection really made against Himself.

Dominical sayings are of lesser moment than apothegms. They include proverbs, which present Jesus as a wisdom teacher; prophetic and apocalyptic sayings, which proclaim the arrival of the kingdom and call to repentance; and laws together with community regulations. Bultmann stresses how many of these derive their meaning only from the immediate context, not from the judgment of Jesus. In regard to the sayings, for instance, about salt and light, he claims that "These examples show that the interpretations of the evangelists are experiments, now and then no doubt quite correct, but at any rate, providing no guarantee of the original meaning."(37) In these passages, however, the problem is not that of meaning. Mt 5:13-15 tells how the disciples must illumine the world and keep it from corruption. If they fail, what else is there? Mk 4:21 brings out the aspect that the disciples are the light of the world—much the same thought, under a different image. Lk 11:33 probably means that Jesus is the light, but He also sends out disciples to be light. Lk 14:34-35 teaches that the disciples must be the salt of the world. Bultmann reminds his readers of how they had to sacrifice all to be so. Quite right: sacrificing all is an aspect of being the salt that preserves the world from corruption. There is one more text about salt, Mk 9:49-50. It is presented in such a way that we cannot be sure of the sense. Nevertheless, there is no proof of any substantial difference in meaning. Even if there were, traveling teachers commonly repeat themselves; and they are apt to vary the implication of their phraseology in adapting it to different crowds and different purposes.(38)

Even if we conceded all of Bultmann's claims about dominical sayings, it would still be true that none of the variations in these sayings is of major import. The facts we need to establish a basis for faith remain firm and reliable.(39)

The second major category of "forms" in the Gospels revolves about narratives; these include miracle stories, historical stories, and legends.

As disciples of Bultmann, many critics regard the miracle stories as formed mostly by the Hellenistic church because of an alleged parallel to pagan-Greek miracle stories. Bultmann himself lists the chief characterisitcs common to both the pagan and the Gospel stories (we have subdivided and grouped them to facilitate comment): a) the grave condition of the patient, with perhaps mention of failures by doctors; the healer imposes hands and utters the healing word; the bystanders cry out in wonder as the one healed shows that he is healed; b) the healing word is often in an unknown tongue; and no one is present, for there is a feeling that the acts of a divinity should not be seen.(40)

Actually group (a) is just a list of practically inescapable generalities. How could one recount the cure without including at least most of these elements? The second group (b) does have some special features. First, the healing word is often in an unknown tongue. That is true of the pagan stories. But in the Gospels foreign words or phrases are seldom used, and when they are, they are not really foreign but Aramaic, the most common language of the land at the time, and they are always translated in the Gospel. Second, Bultmann stresses the absence of witnesses. That may be true in the pagan narrations, but in the Gospels the miracles most often are done in the presence of crowds; at other times at least some witnesses are present.

Bultmann, of course, would fail to notice the really significant points of difference. In the Hellenic stories there are few exorcisms, in the Gospels there are many. In the Greek accounts curious and sometimes indecent details occur; the wonder-workers are usually skilled in medicine or magic, amorous or vengeful, they are highly motivated by money and by the urge to prove their power, contrary to the Gospels. Further, in the Hellenic reports there exists no spiritual significance for the miracles performed, while in the Gospel pattern they are signs of supernatural realities. In the pagan Greek literature, miracles normally happen while the patient is asleep in a temple (incubation), but never so in the Gospels. In the Hellenic stories there is much gibberish and incantation—nothing of the kind in the Gospels.(41) So there are far more differences than there are parallels. Most of the parallels concern points that are inevitable in any account of a cure. Further, even extensive parallels would not *prove* that the Gospel miracles are borrowed from the Greek stories, apart from the fact that many of the latter are later than the Gospels anyway.(42)

The real truth is easy to see: Bultmann, as noted in chapter one, made up his mind in advance that there are and can be no miracles. Naturally, he must try desperately to explain what he meets in the Gospels. So we find him making the profound observation: "I do not think it possible to separate historical stories from legends...."(43) His proof is as good as in instances already treated.

It was necessary for us to review the principles and function of form criticism in order to know what weight it should be given in our examination of the Scriptural evidence on the consciousness of Jesus. We can see that it does make certain contributions to our study; we become more aware of the process by which our Gospel accounts developed. Form criticism shows us that at times we may or even should divide the text into relatively small units, a procedure which may suggest possible solutions to given problems. (For example, in Mk 13:30 we gain a possible answer to a difficulty in chapter three.) In its policy pronouncement on the topic, the Pontifical Biblical Commission details the contributions made by form criticism, while warning of the many underlying prejudices and the abuses that it may occasion.(44)

On the negative side, we have seen that form criticism never strictly *proves* anything whatsoever, since it depends exclusively on *internal evidence*. Such evidence by its very nature is capable of demonstrating points only in very special circumstances, such as if an ancient document reports a total eclipse of the sun that an astronomer centuries later can date.

Sadly, the critics seem quite unaware of the inconclusive nature of internal evidence; are they so busy ignoring the large body of strong, objective, external evidence?(45) Take this admission of Professor Bultmann, for instance: "Naturally enough, our judgement will not be made in terms of objective criteria, but will depend on taste and discrimination."(46)

Are we to depend on his "taste?" Over and over again he has proved that his taste or judgment is extremely poor. He showed it in the long list of prejudices that we reviewed in appendix, chapter 1; he proved it again in the immediate presuppositions or bases of form criticism as we saw in chapter 2 of this appendix; for the most part they do not stand up. He proved it all over again in his presentation of the actual technique of form criticism, which we just reviewed. We scrutinized several of the primary examples he gives to support each step in the process and found he made serious errors at almost every step. Should we now admit that inconclusive, internal evidence, propped up by defective judgment proves his theorizing?

Yet, after such a performance, the critics keep telling us that the burden of proof is on those who accept the Gospels, i.e., we are to presume the biblical account as wrong or unreliable unless we can prove the contrary.(47) We can accept that challenge.

On the negative side, we have already shown how the critics have demonstrated nothing against the Gospels and how they have rendered their own judgments seriously defective and their technique inconclusive. In particular we saw that those powerful arguments, which Perrin says "forced" him to reject the reliability of the Gospels, are worthless.

On the positive side, we pointed out in the introduction to this book how the first Christians and the Gospel writers were supremely concerned with facts, and that out of this life situation (*Sitz-im-Leben*) arose the genre of the Synoptics which intends to report facts as a basis for faith in an easily distinguishable theological framework. We also answered numerous objections that are proposed against this position.

We recall too what many have forgotten, that we do not need to prove a multitude of details to establish the grounds for faith. If, by using the Gospels merely as ancient documents whose genre and reliability has been established, we can be selective, namely, that Jesus claimed to be a messenger from God; that He proved His claim chiefly by miracles worked in such a way that they served as a support for His claim; that He gathered disciples, and an inner circle upon which he enjoined the duty of continuing His teaching; and that He promised providential protection to that Church—if we focus upon these few points (not much more than Bultmann's *Dass*(48)), then we not only may believe, but if we are reasonable, we must believe the teachings of that Church. That Church can then add assurance on many credal tenets, e.g., that Jesus was not only God's messenger, but was God Himself. That Church is able to decide the correct meaning of any point in the words and works of Jesus.

It is necessary, after all, to consider the possibility that many Scripture scholars are going through a period strikingly parallel to that experienced by classical scholars in the early nineteenth century, when the grammatical-critical school (e.g., Hermann, Bekker, Lachmann, Ritschl) cherished a scissors-and-paste textual criticism. For purely subjective reasons or whims, they would move blocks of lines from one place to another, "restoring" the text.(49) Incidentally, they too were influenced by a subjectivistic German philosopher, Emmanual Kant.(50)

But the classicists have now outgrown their folly and today they laugh at it. We pray a similar blessing for so many exegetes who now fall for the excesses of form criticism. In fact, a scholar who does not do so is apt to be labeled a non-scholar.(51) That was part of the reason for a scathing review of Albright's and Mann's commentary on St. Matthew.(52) At the end of the selected bibliography, they were so bold as to add:

> Considering the volume of recent publication in German, or in translation from the German, some surprise may be expressed that so little of it is mentioned here or in the body of the commentary. The fact is that during the past fifty years a steadily increasing proportion of German NT scholarship has been devoted to 'existentialist' and related types of exegesis, *which almost wholly disregard the canons of historical judgment accepted as a matter of course in other historical fields.*(53)

Have the post-Bultmannians done better? As already noted, they have made rather little substantial change except to substitute the later Heidegger for the earlier Heidegger, which is to exchange one unfortunate bias for another.

What of the redaction critics? We venture to say they have more of real value to offer than the form critics. We are thinking, for example, of Lane's commentary on Mark.(54) But even at best, redaction criticism too must labor under the limitations imposed by the fact that it has only internal, and therefore purely subjective, evidence with which to work. G. W. Buchanan gives us a good illustration:

> Whatever his bases, Talbert set out to show that these words were redactional by citing other instances in which he also judged some of the words to be redactional:... *synago* for example, is [according to Talbert] redactional in Matt. 22:34. The reason for judging this to be redactional is not given, but it

happens to occur in Matthew and not in its Marcan parallel. To presume that its absence in Mark makes it redactional in Matthew is circular reasoning. This is especially true of a word that occurs 22 additional times in Matthew, where Talbert could find no signs of redaction.(55)

Finally, the redaction critics tend to attribute too much artistry and ingenuity to the evangelists, in strange, but predictable contrast to the early view of form critics who did not consider them true authors at all.

Even those scholars who oppose the excesses of form criticism and want to defend the reliability of the Gospels are often quite timid and concede too much, without valid reasons, to the critics.(56)

But there are signs of a return to more sane practices. In a volume written to honor the fiftieth birthday of Norman Perrin, one of the contributors, Amos Wilder, dared to say: "There is good reason to think these categories and assumptions [of form criticism and redaction criticism] are being questioned today.... It may be that the tools and focus of observation associated with modern literary method have not been fully suited to what these writings have to say...any too rigorous linking of redactional criticism with form criticism may even handicap the task" of exegesis.(57) Similarly, the noted Protestant form critic, R. H. Fuller, chided R. Brown in his review of Brown's *The Birth of the Messiah*, saying: "It is ironic that just at the time when the limitations of the historical critical method are being discovered in Protestantism, Roman Catholic scholars should be bent on pursuing that method so relentlessly."(58)

Genuine study of the problem by means of multiple literary genres is quite different. Here we have a most valuable and indispensable technique. It provides us with ways of treating problems that baffled scholars for centuries and forced them to fall back on sheer faith that somehow things had to be all right. Ironically, now that we can so easily and solidly defend the inerrancy of Sacred Scripture, many who are well qualified to do so have opted, for no valid reason, in favor of charging multiple errors. The proper use of literary genre as an exegetical technique also helps immensely in avoiding the fantasies of fundamentalism.

The conclusion follows inevitably: neither the form critics nor any similar group have proved any specific point against the truthfulness of the Gospel account. We are well aware that our position may win instant, even unexamined rejection from certain quarters. But we will be happy to be bracketed, though at a distance, with the great W. F. Albright(59) who, in the above citation, chose to disregard those who "almost wholly disregard the canons of historical judgment accepted as a matter of course in other historical fields." For, contrary to the prevailing form critical view, the Gospels remain a thoroughly reliable source for the facts concerning Jesus. We must take into legitimate account the genre and the possibility of some retrojection as well as the increased clarity due to the light of post-Easter understanding. But having made careful provision for these and other factors, we find a thoroughly dependable work, one which deserve the charism of inerrancy as traditionally accorded it by the Catholic Church.

NOTES

1 R. Bultmann and K. Kunds in *Form Criticism*, tr. F.C. Grant, Harper Torchbooks, Harper and Row, New York, 1966: "The Study of the Synoptic Gospels."

2 For the sake of logic and clarity we are inverting the sequence of Bultmann's steps 4 and 5.

3 Bultmann prematurely inserts this conclusion in his step 3.

4 R. H. Fuller, *The Foundations of New Testament Christology*, Charles Scribner's Sons, New York, 1965, 109.

5 W. Wrede, *The Messianic Secret*, tr. J. C. C. Greig, James Clarke Co., Cambridge and London, 1971 (from 3d ed.) esp. 89, 52.

6 *Ibid*. 50-51.

7 *Ibid*. 50.

8 *Ibid*. 67.

9 Wrede's lesser arguments are chiefly these: (1) the demons are said to have known He was Messiah; this is unhistorical p. 50. *Reply*: Wrede rejects *a priori* anything supernatural. (2) There was *public* recognition of Jesus as Messiah even before Peter's confession. *Reply*: They were, except for a few spiritually discerning souls, making reasonable inferences. Jesus did not want to support popular

(erroneous) messianism or occasion emotional demonstrations. (3) Some miracles were done in public, others Jesus tried to keep secret. *Reply*: we do not know the chronological sequence, and other factors too. He may have kept certain activities quiet and changed His method later. (4) The parables, in fact all His doctrine was supposed to be secret; this is ridiculous. *Reply*: Mk. 4:1ff presents Jesus as using parables after the charge He had a devil in 3:22-30. Even with parables, some would get the message (*cf*. Mk. 4:34; and Mt. 11:25—children get it, the educated do not) while the ill-disposed would be hardened in their incredulity.

10   *Cf*. A. Buchler, *Studies in Sin and Atonement in the Rabbinic Literature of the First Century*, Ktav, New York, 1967. J. Jeremias, *New Testament Theology*, tr. John Bowden, Charles Scribner's Sons, New York, 1971, 286-88.

11   H. E. Todt, *The Son of Man in the Synoptic Tradition*, tr. D. M. Barton, Westminster, Philadelphia, 1965, 72.

12   HST 187.

13   Todt 107.

14   W. F. Albright and C. S. Mann, *Matthew*, in *Anchor Bible* 26, Doubleday, Garden City, New York 1971, 195-98, and Peter F. Ellis, *Matthew, His Mind and His Messge*, Liturgical Press, Collegeville, 1974, 126-34.

15   SSG 26-27.

16   Critics sometimes say something found in Q can also be found in Mark, but this holds only where they think (without objective criteria—purely subjectively) the text of Mt. and Lk. is clearly "more original." Such is not the case in the examples presently being examined.

17   SSG 27-28.

18   In regard to the sequence of events in this passage: Mk 3:10 speaks of Jesus healing. The Greek is *etherapeusen*, an aorist. It *could* be rendered by a pluperfect; *cf*. M. Zerwick, *Graecitas Biblica*, ed. 4, Pontifical Biblical Institute, Rome 1960 Art. 290.

19   SSG 27-28.

20   We have here inverted steps 4 and 5 from Bultmann's order, for the sake of logical sequence and clarity.

21   SSG 29-30.

22   *Ibid*.

23   SSG 28, 30.

24   M. Dibelius, *From Tradition to Gospel*, tr. B. L. Woolf, Charles Scribner's Sons, New York, (revised second edition), 43.

25   HST 40-41.

26   HST 47.

27   HST 14-15.

28   Dibelius, *op. cit.*, 66-69.

29   SSG 32, 34-35.

30   SSG 32.

31   G. W. Buchanan, "Has the Griesbach Hypothesis been Falsified?" in JBL 93 (1974) 551.

32   Leslie R. Keylock, "Bultmann's Law of Increasing Distinctness" in *Current Issues in Biblical and Patristic Interpretation*, ed. G. F. Hawthorne, Eerdmans, Grand Rapids, Michigan, 1975, pp. 196-210. *Cf.* also E. P. Sanders, *The Tendencies of the Synoptic Tradition*, Cambridge, 1969.

33   SSG 36-63.

34   SSG 42.

35   SSG 43.

36   *Cf.* Severiano del Paramo, "Evangelio de San Mateo" p. 114, on Mt. 9:11, in *La Sagrada Escritura, Nuevo Testamento* I, Biblioteca de Autores Cristianos, Madrid, 1961.

37   SSG 47.

38   SSG 46-47. Also compares Mt. 5:25-26 with Lk, 12:57-59 and says that "Agree with thine adversary...in the way" is an admonition to reconciliation" while in Luke "they become a parable of warning." But Luke is not in the form of a parable. JBC II, 146 says that in Luke, "The verses contain little more than sound advice." At most, in Mt. there is a general principle, while in Lk. there is perhaps a more specific implication.

39   See pp 33-34 above.

40   SSG 37-39.

41   The above comparisons are made in documented detail in Laurence J. McGinley, "Hellenic Analogies and the Typical Healing Narrative" in *Theological Studies* 4 (1943) 385-419. *Cf.* also TDNT III, 205-13.

42   *Cf.* D. J. McCarthy, *Treaty and Covenant*, in *Analecta Biblica* 21, Pontifical Biblical Institute, Rome, 1963, 58: "...it should be an axiom of form study that similar situations call forth similar responses, and thus formal similarity hardly proves a causal nexus between similar manifestations in different cultures."

43   HST 245.

44   *Instructio de Historica Evangeliorum Veritate*, April 21, 1964, Latin-English text can be seen in CBQ 26 (1964) 299-312.

45   See Appendix: pp 192-194 above.

46   HST 47.

47   *Cf.* N. Perrin, *Rediscovering the Teaching of Jesus*, Harper and Row, New York, 1967, 39.

48   *Cf.* R. Bultmann, *Das Verhaltnis der urchristlichen Christus-botschaft zum historischen Jesus*, Winter, Heidelberg, 1962.

49   An example of this can be easily seen in the Loeb Classical Library

edition of Aratus.

50 It is interesting to note that Aristotelian scholars are taking a second look at the use of internal evidence for dating the works of Aristotle. As Grene shows, on such evidence we could get the following circular order for some of his works: 1. on philosophy; 2. physics II; 3. Metaphysics Alpha; 4. on philosophy. See M. Grene, *A Portrait of Aristotle*, University of Chicago Press, Chicago, 1963, 26.

51 *Cf.* R. E. Brown, *Biblical Reflections on Crises Facing the Church*, Paulist Press, New York, 1975; table on p. 22.

52 In CBQ (Oct. 1972) 481-85.

53 *Op. Cit.* p. cxcviii. (italics mine).

54 W. L. Lane, *Commentary on the Gospel of Mark*, in *New International Commentary on the New Testament*, Eerdmans, Grand Rapids, Michigan, 1974.

55 Art. cit. 553.

56 E.g., G. N. Stanton, *Jesus of Nazareth in New Testament Preaching*, Society for New Testament Studies, Monograph Series 27, Cambridge University Press, London, 1974. C. Leslie Mitton, *Jesus: The Fact Behind the Faith*, Eerdmans, Grand Rapids, Michigan, 1974. On p. 44 Mitton, commenting on Mk. 4:40, cites Mark's report that Jesus said, "Why are you such cowards? Have you no faith even now?", and adds, "Matthew omits the words altogether...." Yet Mt. 8:26 has: "Why are you cowards (Greek *deiloi*, the same word used by Mark), you of little faith (*oligopistoi*)?"

57 Amos Wilder comments on "Norman Perrin, *What is Redaction Criticism*:" in *Christology and a Modern Pilgrimage, A Discussion with Norman Perrin*, ed. Hans Dieter Betz, Society of Biblical Literature, Missoula, Montana, 1974, 91-92.

58 Reginald H. Fuller, review of R. Brown, *The Birth of the Messiah*, in CBQ 40 (1978) 120. Similarly, Paul J. Achtemeier and Gene M. Tucker, in their assessment of "Biblical Studies: The State of the Discipline" (*Council on the Study of Religion Bulletin*, vol. 11, #3, p. 73) write: "...we are at a turning point concerning our fundamental methodologies for interpreting biblical texts. To call the situation a 'crisis' may be a bit too melodramatic, but it is obvious that the historical-critical method...is under fire from many directions. From without, there is new life from the old enemies of critical inquiry.... More decisive, however, for the future of biblical scholarship are the rumblings within the ranks. ...Walter Wink (*The Bible in Human Transformation*) created a minor flap with his assertion that historical biblical criticism is bankrupt.... evidence...can be seen in the numerous publications in biblical studies calling themselves structuralism, literary criticism, rhetorical criticism, linguistic analysis, and even psychoanalytic exegesis, to name just a few." In a

similar way, the Documentary Theory in the Old Testament is meeting with numerous and serious attacks. R. Rendtorff, in "Pentateuchal Studies on the Move" in *Journal for the Study of the Old Testament* 3(1976) 45 wrote: "...there is [sic] clearly signs of great unanimity in the abandoment of the view of the development of the Pentateuch that has been hitherto held...." Bruce Vawter, in *On Genesis*, Doubleday, N.Y. 1977, 16 wrote: "The judgments and reservations of these scholars must certainly be respected, and they do forbid us from pretending to a consensus that no longer exists."

59 Since his death, some of Albright's positions have been attacked, with some success. Yet he remains a great in the field, and his judgment on those who disregard the normal canons of historical judgment will always be valid.

GENERAL INDEX

SCRIPTURE INDEX

ABOUT THE AUTHOR

Rev. William G. Most has taught theology and classics at Loras College in Dubuque, Iowa since 1940. He earned his M.A. in Religious Education (now Theology) and his Ph.D. in Latin and Greek at The Catholic University of America. Born in 1914, Fr. Most completed his seminary studies with the Sulpicians in Washington, D.C. He is the author of ten books and approximately thirty major articles, and holds active membership in seven learned societies. Among his better-known works are *Latin by the Natural Method, New Answers to Old Questions* (on grace), and *Vatican II: Marian Council.* His most recent work is *Covenant and Redemption,* published in Ireland in 1976. Fr. Most is a regular columnist in the *National Catholic Register,* and one of the most respected orthodox Scripture scholars of our time.